D0190600

SLOW WALKS
IN
PARIS

A Visitor's Companion

MICHAEL LEITCH

SLOW WALKS
IN
PARIS

A Visitor's Companion

PERENNIAL LIBRARY

Harper & Row, Publishers, New York
Grand Rapids, Philadelphia, St. Louis, San Francisco
London, Singapore, Sydney, Tokyo, Toronto

First published in Great Britain by Hodder & Stoughton.

First PERENNIAL LIBRARY edition published 1990
Route maps and overall map by Alec Spark.

Library of Congress Cataloging-in-Publication Data
Leitch, Michael.
    Slow walks in Paris : a visitor's companion / Michael Leitch. —
    1st Perennial Library ed.
    p.   cm.
    "First published in Great Britain by Hodder & Stoughton"—T.p.
    verso.
    ISBN 0-06-273175-0
    1. Paris (France)—Description—1975- —Tours.   2. Walking—
    France—Paris—Guide-books.   3. Paris (France)—Maps,
    Tourist.   I. Title.
DC708.L39   1990
914.4'36104839—dc20   89-46103

    92 93 94 MPC 10 9 8 7 6 5 4 3

CONTENTS

What to wear and carry with you; The Geography of Paris; Transport – Métro, buses, taxis; Telephones; Money; Opening Times; Watering Holes; Clothing Sizes; Public Holidays; Toilets; What's On; Paris by Night; Quick Paris; Things in flux.

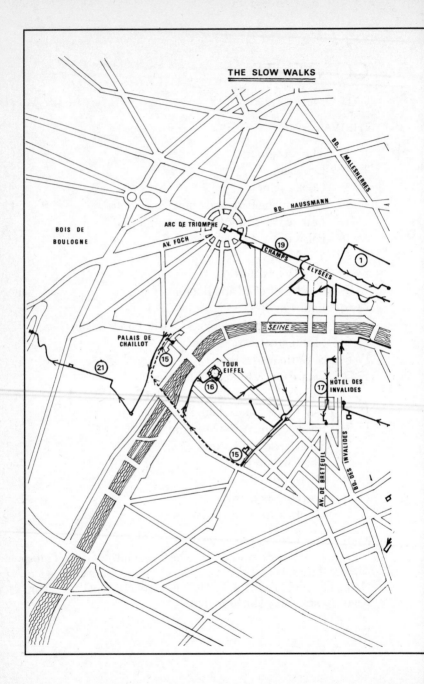

THE SLOW WALKS

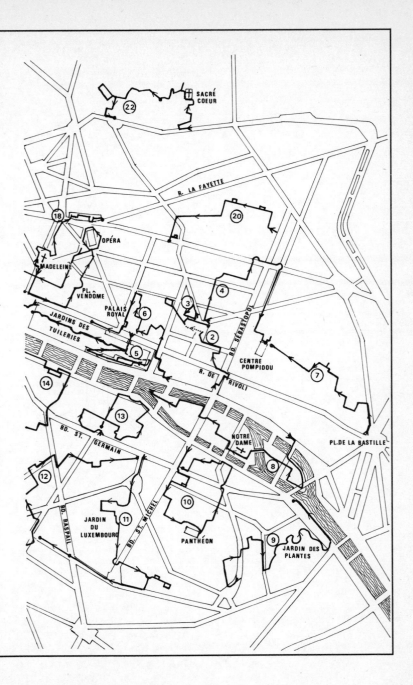

THE WALKS

Each Slow Walk is numbered and listed in order of the *arrondissement* in which it begins. Each opens with a Map and Route guide with street-by-street instructions. The essay which follows is suitable for reading either before you go on the walk, as an expanded briefing, or afterwards as a comparison with how you saw everything.

The following symbols are used, mainly in the Route sections:

👁   Special visit recommended

☂   Suitable for a rainy day

Ⓜ   Métro station

The following abbreviations are used in the Route sections:

Av.   Avenue

Bd   Boulevard

Pl.   Place

Sq.   Square

N, NE, E, etc, to indicate directions

17C   Seventeenth century

All maps are drawn north to south.

WELCOME!

Welcome to *Slow Walks in Paris*. I have set out in these pages to share the tremendous pleasure that Paris has given me since I first went there at the age of ten. Trooping around in a school crocodile, usually at the tail of it, urged on by patient masters, I absorbed sights and smells which have lodged ever since in my memory. Here are one or two samples: hot chocolate in a deep bowl for breakfast, a misty morning at the top of the Eiffel Tower, the pen-knife shop near the Panthéon, gusts of garlic on the Métro, chorus-girl posters in Pigalle, aniseed balls from a slot machine. The usual stuff that schoolboys like, much of it to do with eating.

Since then my picture of the city has grown slightly broader and slightly more detailed, though the method of transport remains the same. We walked then and I walk now. Paris has that special power to stimulate all kinds of people, residents and visitors, to take to the pavements and wander without thought of time from one quarter to the next, developing that mood of unhurried curiosity which is probably the best approach to somewhere as spectacular and diverse, somewhere that lives as well, as this city. Unless you spend years there, you can never hope to see it all; better to explore it one piece at a time. *Slow Walks*, I thought, would be a good way of doing this in print: describing the city through a series of routes that readers could follow in their own time.

Paris is an ideal walking city because it is so compact. Its ring road, the Boulevard Périphérique, encloses an inner city measuring only 10.5 km (6.5 miles) from east to west and 8.7 km (5.4 miles) from north to south, and most of the places a visitor will want to see are gathered inside a much smaller central core.

Where, though, do you begin? For any newcomer, or relative newcomer, the city can seem confusing: fast, noisy, preoccupied with itself, the tall seven-storey buildings a baffle to understanding the nature of the place. Walking in any city is also something of a lottery. If you want to make the most of your time, the constant challenge is to find the most agreeable way of traversing a series of unfamiliar streets to the next objective, whether, as in Paris, it's the Place des Vosges or one of the lesser-known shopping arcades, the Galerie Véro-Dodat or the Passage Verdeau.

To reach Point X, which your street map tells you is two blocks away, do you go along Rue A, then cross Place B to Avenue C? Or would it be more interesting to arrive via Rue D and cut through Galerie E? From where you stand, it's impossible to tell.

In this book I have tried to take care of such choices, and the broader ones of how to round off a morning, or spend an enjoyable day in just one area of the city. There are twenty-two Slow Walks in all, enough to keep most readers busy for at least a fortnight. You don't have to walk all that far on any one outing, but I hope you will end up seeing and doing much more than you may have imagined was possible.

A final point. Although these Slow Walks follow precise routes, it remains one of life's pleasures to become so absorbed with the city that, entranced, you forget where you are and what you are doing. Being tempted into some alley or arcade not part of one of my walks is a joy which I hope you will allow to happen. The only thing is, apart from the temporary panics sometimes associated with being lost (but see 'The Geography of Paris' on page 258), you may find yourself walking further than you intended. And while this book is almost entirely concerned with daytime excursions, I hope you will not spend all your time pounding the pavements to the exclusion of other pleasures. Try, always, to reserve some energy for your evening pursuits, your *noctambulisme*. And good luck.

SLOW WALKS
IN
PARIS
A Visitor's Companion

Walk 1

1er The Ritz Quarter

Paris at its most sumptuous. Potent names in haute couture, jewellery and other de-luxe necessaries maintain strongholds here. Visit the Opera House and the Perfume Museum; window-shop in the Pl. Vendôme and Rue du Faubourg St Honoré; see the residence of the French President and the open-air Stamp Market, and stroll through a half-hidden park beside the Champs Elysées.

Allow 4–5 hours.

Best times Not Sunday or Monday, many ultra-smart shops also closed Saturday.

ROUTE

Begin at Ⓜ Madeleine. Nearest buses 24, 42, 52, 84, 94. Leave Pl. de la Madeleine on S side and walk down Rue Royale to Pl. de la Concorde. Turn left and enter Rue de Rivoli. Walk through arcade and take 4th left into Rue de Castiglione. At Pl. Vendôme, walk through square on right-hand (E) side, past jewellers' shops, and visit base of Column.

Exit on far (N) side of square into Rue de la Paix, walk up to Pl. de l'Opéra and visit the Opera House 👁 ; open 11.00 to 17.00, museum closed Sunday, public holidays and two weeks before Easter. *Admission*. See the foyer, great staircase, museum and auditorium (open when rehearsals not in progress).

Return to entrance, walk anti-clockwise round building, past Café de la Paix to Bd des Capucines and turn right. Take 1st right in Rue

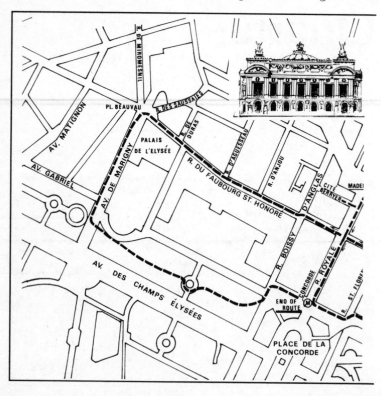

Scribe and at No.9 visit the Perfume Museum (Musée de la Par-
fumerie) 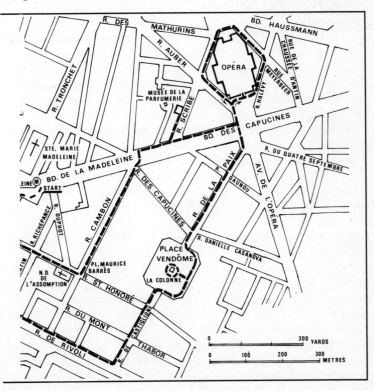; open 09.30 to 17.30, closed Sunday. Return to Bd des
Capucines and turn right.

Continue along boulevard towards Pl. de la Madeleine and take
3rd left into Rue Cambon, passing House of Chanel on right (No.29).
At Pl. Maurice Barrès, turn right into Rue St Honoré. Opposite is the
round 17C Church of Notre-Dame de l'Assomption, now the Polish
Church . Walk on past couture and de-luxe shops, crossing Rue
Royale to Rue du Faubourg St Honoré.

At next corner, kitchenware addicts may enjoy a small diversion,
left into Rue Boissy-d'Anglas, to visit Au Bain Marie at No.12, most
seductive of all Paris's kitchen and tableware shops. Continuing
along Rue du Faubourg St Honoré the parade of haute-couture

boutiques is finally interrupted on left by British Embassy at No. 35. Walk on past Elysée Palace, Paris residence of the French president. At Pl. Beauvau, turn left into Av. de Marigny. On right, by Av. Gabriel, the tented Stamp Market operates on Thursday, Saturday, Sunday.

Turn left at foot of Elysée Palace gardens and walk back along meandering parkland paths to Pl. de la Concorde, passing US Embassy on left. Walk ends here. Nearest refreshments (expensive) in Hôtel Crillon in square; or (more moderate) at Le Peny, 5 Pl. de la Madeleine, which has an excellent view of the square. Nearest Ⓜ Concorde or Madeleine.

Towards the Rue de Rivoli

This is one of our longer walks: in the *patois* of golfers a stiffish par four. Not overwhelmingly long, about 3¼ pavement miles over flat terrain broken only by the staircases of the Opera House and the Perfume Museum; by the finish, though, a Slow Walker may feel he or she has earned proper refreshment, something on the lines, maybe, of a delicious Parisian *hot-dog* – a baguette with toasted cheese and sausage. In the cafés around here they will have the very thing.

We begin in the Place de la Madeleine. Just to stand on one corner of this square gives me a special charge of optimism. It must be the flowers, brimming over in buckets and bins in the market next to the church. The flowers and the plane trees, the sun that warms the morning pavements, the generous cut of the rectangular *place* surrounding the green-roofed temple church. The snap and glamour of boulevard life are almost tangible here, as bold and beckoning as the buttercup-yellow awnings and parasols at the Café Le Peny in the south-west corner.

We look in closer detail at the contents of the Place de la Madeleine in *Walk 18: The Department Stores*. For now, we turn into Rue Royale; in the middle distance the Place de la Concorde stretches away to the river, and on the far bank is the Palais Bourbon where the French Parliament meets. Immediately on the right, through an arch at No. 25 Rue Royale, is the Cité Berryer, a community in miniature of shops and restaurants. On Tuesday and Friday mornings the Poissonnerie Royale and the butchers turn this narrow, open-air passage into a jostling market. Later in the day, a smart clientèle turns up for apéritifs and lunch at Le Moulin du Village or Le Blue Fox Wine Bar, two of the local establishments run by an entrepreneurial Englishman, Stephen Spurrier. Just along the pavement he has a wine merchant's, Les Caves de la Madeleine, and a wine school, L'Académie des Vins.

The Cité Berryer, formerly known as the Marché d'Aguesseau, occupies a special place in the topography of Paris. Behind the streets of the capital lies a random system of *cités, impasses* and covered *passages* and *galeries*, tributaries to the main network which many visitors barely have time to notice, let alone investigate. We will nose our way into several of these in our meandering progress through the city: on other walks we visit the Impasse Berthaud near the Pompidou Centre, the Passage des Panoramas off the Boulevard Montmartre, the Galerie Véro-Dodat next to the Palais Royal which itself contains a pair of high-vaulted arcades in the gardens. These pedestrian byways have a charm quite distinct from the thoroughfares they serve.

In Rue Royale, shop names that breathe four-star living present their windows: china and tableware at Villeroy & Boch (No. 21), cutlery at Christofle (No. 12), crystal at Lalique (No. 11), audacious jewels at Fred (No. 6), currently celebrating fifty years of 'passion' and 'création'. At No. 3 is Maxim's, still a magical name in matters of the stomach, now with its own adjoining florist's and ladies' hat shop.

At No. 8 lived Jacques-Ange Gabriel (1698–1782), architect of the Place de la Concorde which now opens before us, a vast 21-acre expanse which for several hours a day plays host to some of the world's most blood-boiling traffic jams. In *Walk 19: The Champs Elysées* I describe its history and we boldly traverse its central island, viewing the fountains and the obelisk.

Our present route takes us past the Hôtel de la Marine, now the Navy Ministry (*hôtel* means a mansion or public building as well as a resting-place for travellers). Ahead, the Rue de Rivoli funnels into the distance and on the right is the terrace of the Tuileries Gardens. Soon the great arcade begins. It is one of the wonders of modern Paris: begun in 1811 at the instigation of Napoleon I and completed in 1856, its name commemorates a victory over the Austrians in 1797. Away it sweeps, far to the east, block upon block, preserving a marvellous uniformity, five storeys high, the lowest arcaded and the fifth a mansard. If only the purity of concept were matched by purity of occupier. Alas, in the arcade where gas lamps hang from every arch stand shops of a quality that is less than marvellous. It begins well enough at Hilditch & Key, shirtmakers of London and Paris, exuding an agreeable whiff of old St. James's; but then you must file past some gaudy frock shops and one-hour photo joints between the Lanvin men's shop (corner of Rue Cambon) and the liveried workers who totter with rapid steps across the pavement outside the Hotel Intercontinental, weighed down with items of grand luggage.

Two indispensable halts for bookshop browsers lie along this stretch of the Rue de Rivoli: the English-language stores of W.H. Smith (No.248) and the Librairie Galignani (No.224). Both shops cater splendidly for the reading needs of temporary visitors and longer-stay exiles. W.H. Smith currently stock some 8,000 English and American titles in just about every category, and run a subscription service for newspapers and magazines. Alas, the famous old Tea Room was closed in 1989, and in place of muffins and toasted buns they now offer dictionaries and children's books. More profit for them, perhaps, but less fun for us.

Mr G.A. Galignani, founder of 'the oldest foreign bookstore on the Continent', opened in the Rue Vivienne in about 1800. In 1856 the business, now ruled by his half-English sons William and Anthony, moved to the Rue de Rivoli. Meanwhile, Galignani *père* had launched an English-language newspaper, *Galignani's Messenger*, which kept the English colony in touch with home and world events for some eighty years, and the Librairie's reading-room became a favourite resort and meeting-place of tourists and residents. The bookshop continues to flourish. It is particularly strong in art books, and runs an ordering service much valued by lovers of the Anglo-American printed word.

Place Vendôme

Around the corner of Rue de Castiglione lies a first glimpse of the magnificent, if column-heavy, Place Vendôme, named after César de Vendôme, natural son of Henri IV and Gabrielle d'Estées. This finely proportioned square was designed by Jules Hardouin-Mansart (1646–1708), chief architect and city planner to Louis XIV, and was built between 1686 and 1720. It consists of a rectangle measuring 224 × 213 m (245 × 233 yd) with canted corners, flanked by arcaded Classical mansions arranged in a grand symmetrical scheme.

What inevitably seizes the attention is the huge Napoleonic column which stands 44 m (132 ft) high on a central island. Behind its soaring presence lies an extraordinary saga of public passion and political revenge. Before it existed, the focal point of the square was a colossal equestrian statue of Louis XIV by Girardon; in the Revolution this was pulled down and eventually replaced by the present column, raised as a memorial to Napoleon's triumph at Austerlitz (1805). The stone core of the column is clad in a spiralling bronze forged from Russian and Austrian guns taken in the battle. The model for it was Trajan's Column in Rome, and it was originally crowned by Chaudet's statue of Napoleon dressed as Caesar.

For the best part of seventy years the top of the column became a virtual war zone, mirroring the rage and turmoil of post-Revolutionary France. Five times in that period the crowning monument was torn down and four times replaced by another image. On Napoleon's exile in 1814 the Chaudet statue was replaced by one of Henri IV; after the Restoration the Royalists raised a fleur-de-lys, emblem of the Bourbons; in 1833, under the 'bourgeois' King Louis-Philippe, the rehabilitation of Napoleon was marked by the raising of a new statue, the *Petit Caporal* by Seurre which is now at the Invalides; in 1863, down came the Seurre and up went Dumont's copy of the Chaudet original; in 1871 the Commune pulled the whole column down, and finally under the Third Republic it was completely restored.

The numbering of the Place Vendôme begins in the block before the square itself. If you prefer to walk round one side of the square only, there is more to see at ground-floor level on the right-hand or eastern side, so cross the Rue de Castiglione to No. 2 Place Vendôme, occupied by one of four Guerlain boutiques in Paris (perfumes and *les voluptés du bain*), then follow round past Gianmaria Buccellati's sumptuous silver creatures at No. 4 – squashes, shells, serpents, etc. to men's fashion at Giorgio Armani (No. 6) and on to the real business of the Place Vendôme: jewellery.

The displays, judged as examples of the window-dresser's art,

could hardly be called brilliant but then no one seems to be trying very hard, as though they are above competition. To be
faintly generous about it, the very smallness of the merchandise
must raise its own problems: how can you make an interesting
display out of such tiny objects, however much they sparkle? Presumably, too, the paying customers are not influenced one way
or the other by the merchants' insistence on putting a couple of
wristwatches in a tiny frame at the centre of the window and leaving
the rest bare. Here are the shops of Mikimoto (No.8), Chaumet
(No.12, at which address Chopin died in 1849), Aldebert (No.16),
Mauboussin (No.20), Van Cleef & Arpels (Nos 22-24) and Bouche-
ron (No.26). In between are glamorous bags and suitcases at Pascal
Morabito (No.16). On the other side of the square are two Cartier
shops (Nos 7 and 23) and Schiaparelli (No.21), the Ministry of Justice
and, in the north-west corner, the canopies of the illustrious Ritz
Hotel, last word in luxury.

The Ritz is the kind of fabled place people write books about. I on
the other hand have always tended to view it with silent awe. In my
long-ago days as a travel rep. in Paris I don't think our agency ever
reached as high as having a client at the Ritz; if it did, our office man-
ager would almost certainly have kept this great voyager to himself,
leaving the student riff-raff on his staff to deal with the lesser pluto-
crats occupying beds at the Bristol, Grand, Meurice, Plaza Athénée
and so on – all jolly nice places, of course, but lacking the ethereal
zing of the Ritz. Thus one learnt to see a fine distinction between
those hotels where, say, a wealthy widow from Des Moines might lay
her head, and the one place where Coco Chanel, Edward VII and
Marcel Proust rested theirs.

At about the midpoint of the Place Vendôme, walk across to the
base of the column and see at close hand the spiralling bas-reliefs that
glorify Napoleon's German campaigns of 1805–7, and above all,
Austerlitz, his masterpiece.

We move into the Rue de la Paix, less fashionable than it used to
be. Jewellers still operate there, including a large Cartier at Nos 11–
13, but the street has been much penetrated by boring-looking travel
offices. One day last summer, after viewing the minimal-ish window
displays of the Place Vendôme, I looked here for something more
lavish or amusing. At No.15 tobacco experts Alfred Dunhill had

some fine humidifiers, with gauges to indicate temperature and humidity; when after a while none of the needles actually moved, I took myself away to the Place de l'Opéra, a broad deep circus surrounded by prosperous boulevard buildings, the façades decked out with fat advertising signs and bright awnings, on the far side of which stands the most stupendous piece of nineteenth-century eclectic architecture in all Paris.

Opera House

It has been fashionable for some years to deride Charles Garnier's Opera House (1863-75), saying it looks like a Turkish bath and is thoroughly preposterous. It is true that to enjoy it you need a large tolerance for curvaceous gilded ornament and pinky beige marble; in the auditorium, a densely cultivated acreage of maroon plush covers just about everything, and some may find it claustrophobic as well as not to their taste. Soon, however, opera lovers will find themselves facing a painful question which may well start a new wave of enthusiasm for Garnierian floridity. The question is: would you rather watch opera in the company of this showy old diva of a building or in the cold new wonder-block at the Bastille?

Lack of space, strangely, has been the problem at Garnier's Opera House. Although the overall building is enormous, with a stage for 450 artistes, the vestibules, foyers and other 'offices' take up so much room that the auditorium seats fewer than 2,200 people. And that, decreed President Mitterrand, was not enough. Wishing to bring opera to a wider audience, the socialistic leader sanctioned as one of the grand legacies of his rule the building of a huge new opera house in the Place de la Bastille, on the fringes of Eastern Paris, an area hitherto notorious for its resistance to higher forms of culture. It opened to grand acclaim during the Bicentenary junketings of 1989, leaving the old building to concentrate on ballet.

Visits to Garnier's Opera House are self-guided and rather pricey if you cannot get into the auditorium, as you cannot when rehearsals are in progress. Check first with the noticeboard by the *caisse* (ticket desk) before committing your francs. Inside, explore the crepuscular world beneath the candelabra. The Grand Staircase, museum and auditorium are the main places of interest: Chagall's 1964 decorations to the dome are a brilliant addition, the figures hovering above the auditorium; in the museum, wall cabinets display model stage sets and you can see costume designs, portrait busts and – a special delight – sculptured caricatures by Dantan 'Le Jeune' of Paganini, Liszt, Meyerbeer, Rossini and others.

After the interior, take an anti-clockwise stroll around the outside of the building. The pavilion on the east side (Rue Halévy) was built for the greater comfort of subscribers who could be driven directly into the rear courtyard past the ring of lamp-posts with buxom nudes by Carrier-Belleuse. On the west side (Rue Scribe) the Emperor's Pavilion was even grander, designed with a curving ramp so that Napoleon III's carriage could whirl the ruler to within a few paces of the royal box.

Time Out

It may now be lunchtime. One solution is to sit down at the famous Café de la Paix. The interior, another Garnier creation and itself a national monument, is airy and elegant; if you opt for the terrace, avoid the east flank on the Place de l'Opéra, a snarl-up point for traffic where the air is usually filled with exhaust gases. Or seek out one of the neighbourhood cafés or brasseries where local office workers go for a snack lunch or dish of the day; prices are reasonable and you can hope for a brisk and cheerful atmosphere with the odd raucous interlude. The Opéra Paramount in Rue de la Chaussée d'Antin is one such place; another is Le Canari, at the foot of Rue Lafayette, opposite the sports section of Galeries Lafayette.

Just across the road from the Café de la Paix, at 25 Boulevard des Capucines, one of the most charming museums in Paris had its home until June 1988: the Musée Cognacq-Jay, specialising in eighteenth-century paintings and furniture. It was closed down by order of the Mairie and at the time of writing its contents were packed in boxes awaiting removal to their eventual new home in the Marais, the Hôtel Donon at 8 Rue d'Elzévir. Unfortunately the Hôtel first needs' extensive renovation, so it will be at least two years before the Cognacq-Jay collection can be seen again. All being well, I hope to attach it to *Walk 7: The Marais* in a future edition of this book.

Now it is time to exercise our sense of smell. Fragonard's Perfume Museum, occupying an elegant mansion in the Rue Scribe, is really more a commercial for the sampling table and boutique at the end of the tour, but never mind. Go preferably with someone prepared to offer a wrist or two for daubing with essence of lilac, rose, the Fragonard special or some other fragrance selected from a huge array of bottles. They also have soaps, oils and bath salts, beautifully packaged. There is no pressure to buy – just smile and withdraw if you prefer.

In the museum section, among the retorts, stills and other apparatus for extracting essential oils, I was much drawn to the perfume organ, a kind of perfumier's mixing desk. Here the 'organist' or nasal virtuoso sits with a pair of scales in front of a remarkably organ-like piece of furniture and selects from a banked-up display consisting of seven rows of bottles surrounding him or her on three sides. So that's how they do it!

On the north side of the Boulevard des Capucines, a plaque at No. 14 commemorates the first public cinema show, presented by the Lumière brothers in the Salon Indien of the since-departed Grand Café. Further down, at No. 28, is the Olympia music hall, a prestigious venue conquered at various times by some of the glossiest names in French entertainment – Edith Piaf, Yves Montand and, of course, Maurice Chevalier, who with his rakishly tipped boater was a king among the *flâneurs* (strollers) of the Grands Boulevards.

We now turn into the calm of Rue Cambon. On the left, at the back of the Ritz Hotel, signs announce the Espadon Grill, Hemingway Bar and Ritz-Escoffier School; on the right is the gleaming cream-fronted House of Chanel, with blinds to match. Next door is Gianfranco Ferre. Now we are in couture country and soon the great names will reel off at a dizzying rate.

The Polish Church

At the Place Maurice Barrès, prepare to turn right into the Rue St Honoré and then stop. Opposite is the seventeenth-century Church of Notre-Dame de l'Assomption, now the Polish Church. The dome bulks massively over the confines of the tiny square and is best viewed from a suitably distant spot on the far side of the road. Then go inside to visit the spiritual centre of the Polish community. The atmosphere is extraordinary. Perhaps the first surprise after seeing so large a dome is to find that the space beneath it *is* the church: no nave or transepts, no choir or great east window, just a circular room, an altar facing the door. The second surprise comes from its use, for this is unmistakably a political church, the spiritual centre in France for a community of exiles who have fought since the end of the Second World War against implacable regimes in Warsaw and Moscow and now, at last, are seeing some reward. As an organ plays, occasional worshippers come and go; children enter and light candles. Beneath the Solidarity banner on the wall, a plaque in the form of leaves from a book commemorates those Poles who between 1945 and 1982 were assassinated or tortured and killed in the 'state of war' which has plagued their country.

Outside the Polish Church, we adjust to bright daylight and soon revert to our game of happy capitalist window-shopping. The transformation is somehow typical of a visitor's day in Paris: a contrast is sharply felt, then filed with other memories to be thought about later. In the next four hundred yards we come upon an astonishing concentration of famous names in the haute-couture industry, and other luxury trades. On this side of the junction with Rue Royale are Louis Féraud (No.265); a games and toy shop called Au Nain Bleu (No.410), recently doing a strong line in opera dolls in Bakst-style costumes, along with the more conventional armies of model soldiers, and dozens of teddies, doggies, dollies and a couple of twenty-bedroom mansions to keep them in – all beautifully made and finished. For older girls they have wonderful furs at Birger Christensen (No.412), jewels at Fabergé (No.281) and de-luxe stationery and pens at Cassegrain (No.422).

We now cross our earlier path along the Rue Royale and enter the Rue du Faubourg St Honoré. Gucci is at Nos 2 and 27; in between those leather landmarks are fashion heroes and heroines nearly too numerous to mention. Since there is little chance of missing them, I will omit their street numbers in this brief roll-call: Gianni Versace, Lanvin, Karl Lagerfeld, Hermès, Guy Laroche, Ted Lapidus, Balmain, Jean-Claude Jitrois, Torrent, Cardin, Saint Laurent Rive Gauche, Ungaro, Hanae Mori, Sonia Rykiel…Although couturiers are even more renowed than jewellers for not caring overmuch about their window displays, the sheer congestion of big designer names on the fascias of these rather small shops has apparently encouraged them to expose more than one frock at a time, producing a bazaarish atmosphere along the street which at least is colourful and entertaining even if the clothes are not blindingly innovative. But then, as always, another season is just around the corner and what you see in the window is bound to be, *entre nous*, a touch old hat.

At the first turning on the left, cooks and kitchenware enthusiasts will briefly go their own way. At 12 Rue Boissy d'Anglas are the new, quite dazzling premises of Au Bain Marie, formerly in Rue Hérold, near Les Halles. Six black and white banners along the frontage proclaim the self-confidence of this beautifully assembled palace of kitchen- and tableware. To say that they sell glasses, cutlery, gadgets and every kind of plate and vessel does nothing for the mind's eye – you have to see for yourself. My favourite object so far is a large copper pot fashioned in the shape of a rabbit, supplied complete with a carrot of orange cloth. Au Bain Marie has a beautiful linens department and a small bookshop. (In *Walk 3: Cook's Tour* we look at the other famous kitchen shops near Les Halles, where Au Bain Marie was situated before venturing, in autumn 1987, 'up west'.)

Haute couture ends on the south side of the Rue du Faubourg St Honoré at the stone façade of the British Embassy (No. 35). Further along on the same side is the Elysée Palace, residence of the French president. Each Wednesday the Council of Ministers meets here in the Murat Salon, and on that day of the week the road is thick with policemen who may well ask you to cross over and walk past on the far side. It is not easy, on any day, to grab more than a passing glance at the Elysée Palace, an elegant building with a two-storey façade surmounted by a balustrade. It was built in 1718 as the Hôtel d'Evreux and has sheltered many famous residents and visiting heads of state, among them Madame de Pompadour, Napoleon I, the Duke of Wellington, Queen Victoria and Napoleon III, before in 1873 it assumed its present role.

At the far end of the palace wall is Place Beauvau, which acts as a border zone between haute-couture territory and the art galleries that proliferate to the west around Avenue Matignon. We turn left into Avenue de Marigny, exchanging commercial dazzle for a tree-lined drive. On the right, by Avenue Gabriel, is the Stamp Market, a tented souk for enthusiasts with stalls running on either side of a narrow alley towards Avenue Matignon, the polythene side-walls of each canvas-roofed stall hung from top to bottom with stamps.

By the foot of the presidential garden stands a new restaurant in an older building, the Pavillon Elysée. Turn left here and stroll gently back to the Place de la Concorde along winding paths in the little park that almost hides from view between Avenue Gabriel and the Champs Elysées. After the brilliant buzz of the couturier quarter, enjoy the cool dark of the massive chestnut trees, the flower beds and the liberal scattering of benches. Parisians and lovers linger here, so why not you? Maybe a chance will arise for French conversation with one of the many dog-walkers who shuffle past about one a minute, many elderly, some vividly eccentric. Having taken a breather, or not, it only remains to walk past the Espace Pierre Cardin, now a multi-purpose theatre and exhibition centre, on by the US Embassy and the golden façade of the Hôtel Crillon, which shares its mansion with the Automobile Club de France, and your walk is done.

For a marvellous view of the world going home from work try the pretty terrace of Le Peny, 5 Place de la Madeleine; usual café hours.

Bus Ride

After a break, you may have an hour or so to spare. I suggest a bus ride. One of the best routes for sightseeing, No. 24, stops at the foot of Rue Royale (west side). Then, thanks to the one-way system, it keeps to the Right Bank as far as the Ile de la Cité. On the way back it stays on the Left Bank up to the Concorde Bridge, giving you a non-repeating figure-of-eight ride through the centre of Paris.

Take the bus as far as the Pont de Sully, opposite the Ile St Louis. Take the return bus from the other side of the road.

The outward route takes you past the Tuileries Gardens – Louvre – Pont Neuf – Ile de la Cité – Rue St Jacques – Bd St Germain – Place Maubert – Pont de Sully. The inward route takes you along the quayside past the two islands and Notre-Dame – Institut de France – Musée d'Orsay – Pont de la Concorde . . . and back to the starting-point. For information about buses, see page 261.

Walk 2 ☂

1er Les Halles

A tour of the redeveloped market quarter, at its centre the new Forum built on the site of Baltard's 19C pavilions: gardens and gazebos above, the multi-layered shopping mall beneath. Includes old surrounding streets, the Tour St Jacques, Square des Innocents and Church of St Eustache, with a diversion to Pl. des Victoires, an elegant Louis XIV circus recently conquered by new- and medium-wave fashion designers.

Allow 4-5 hours.
Best times Not Sunday, when most shops closed.

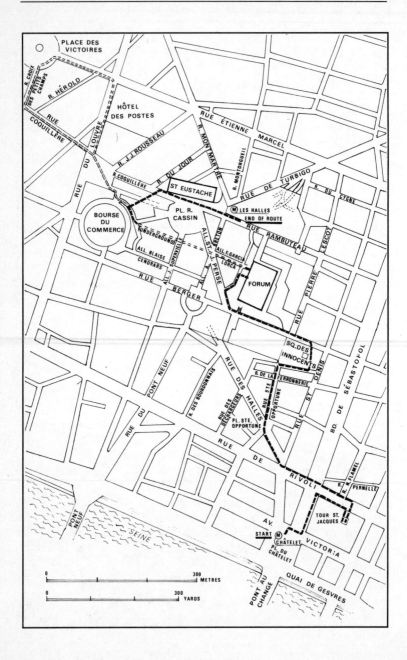

ROUTE

Begin at Ⓜ Châtelet. Nearest buses 21, 38, 69, 72, 85, 96. Exit on Pl. du Châtelet; views all round. Walk N, away from river, crossing Av. Victoria and Bd de Sébastopol to Square and Tower (Tour) of St Jacques ☞.

At top left (NW) corner of square, turn left into Rue de Rivoli, then at next intersection bear right into Rue des Halles. At Pl. Ste Opportune, turn right past VIA (centre for creative furniture design) into Rue Ste Opportune. Walk through paved precinct to Square des Innocents, its historic fountain and trendy (last year, anyway) Café Costes.

Walk across top of square to Forum des Halles, continuing past sunken galleries to central arbour and viewing balcony ☞ . Look around and generally get bearings. Walk down steps to Level -1 of Forum and window-shop round the gallery. Use Point d'Orientation charts to locate places that look especially interesting.

Two museums are on Level -1. The Holography Museum, open 10.30 to 19.00, 13.00 to 19.00 Sunday, Monday and public holidays, and New Grévin Museum, annexe to waxworks on Bd Montmartre (see *Walk 20: Shopping in Paradise*), which shows animated scenes of Paris in 1900s, open 10.30 to 19.30 (ticket desk closes 18.45), 13.00 to 20.00 (desk 19.15) Sunday and public holidays. *Admission to both museums.*

Continue down to Level -2: more shops, cafés both inside and on terrace. Down again to -3 and busy concourse; entrance here to Métro/RER Châtelet-Les-Halles. Look at more shops, go out into piazza. Walk westwards to Pl. Carrée, a large underground space at centre of complex. Walk westwards again to underground Pl. de la Rotonde and take escalator up to Porte du Jour.

Diversion At NW corner of gardens, turn left along Rue Coquillière, take 3rd right into Rue Croix des Petits Champs and visit Pl. des Victoires, where a younger set of fashion designers have installed themselves: Thierry Mugler (No.10), Cacharel pour Hommes (No.5), Kenzo (No.3), etc. At the centre of this royal circus, built in the 1680s to honour Louis XIV, is Bosio's 19C equestrian statue of the monarch. The horse's sprightly position on its rear legs is thanks to a stout iron bar concealed in its plinth-sweeping tail. Return to Les Halles via Rue Etienne Marcel and 2nd right into Rue du Louvre.

Visit the magnificent Church of St Eustache 👁. Walk ends outside church, on edge of gardens. Nearest refreshments all around, but those alongside Forum tend to be noisy and poorish value; a handy exception is La Pointe St Eustache, 1 Rue Montorgueil, a neighbourhood café/brasserie near the east end of the church. Nearest Ⓜ Les Halles, or walk to Châtelet-Les-Halles where Métro authority's own Boutique Chic et Choc sells designer goods bearing Métro-ticket motif; see essay for details.

☂ **Wet Weather Route** Take Métro to Châtelet-Les-Halles. Exit at Pl. Carrée in Forum des Halles, take escalator up to Level -1 and join walk there.

Place du Châtelet

Châtelet is the most frustrating Métro station in Paris. If you know a better candidate, please write in with your nomination and supporting anecdotes. Since the excavations to build the Forum des Halles, the district has acquired an extraordinary number of Métro entrances, some labelled Châtelet, some Châtelet-Les-Halles and some Les Halles. Châtelet, with its cavernous, airport-length corridors, is definitely one of those stations best avoided when changing lines; *Correspondance à Châtelet* would be a good title for one of those three-hour art movies, filmed in a coal mine, where all the characters forget who they are and nothing happens. However, for this walk you do need plain Châtelet station and, on reaching it, the exit to Place du Châtelet.

You emerge on the square's central island to find splendid views in several directions. To the south, the Pont au Change crosses to the Ile de la Cité. On the far side of the bridge, to the left, is the heavy ribbed dome of the Tribunal de Commerce (1860–65) and, further left, the towers and spire of Notre-Dame Cathedral. To the right of the bridge is the best view from any angle of the Conciergerie, the old prison, much of it dating from the fourteenth century; jutting above its roofline is the spire of Ste Chapelle (see *Walk 8: The Two Islands*).

On either side of the Place du Châtelet is a National Theatre. Both were built by Davioud in 1862. On the west side is the old Châtelet Theatre, now the Théâtre Musical de Paris (TMP) which specialises in ballet and classical concerts; on the east side is the old Sarah Bernhardt Theatre, now the Théâtre de la Ville which puts on plays, concerts and dance shows (see *Pariscope* for what's on).

In the middle of the square is the Fontaine du Palmier (Palm Fountain) , built in 1808 as a memorial to Napoleon's victories. Water spurts in a hoselike trajectory from four pipes and in a more vomitory way from the mouths of four sphinxes added in 1858. Above the fountain rises a thinnish column banded with battle names in gold capitals, surmounted by a winged gold statue of Fame. Most Napoleonic memorials utterly dominate their surroundings – think of the Vendôme Column or the Arc de Triomphe – but this one is surprisingly modest, even rather weedy compared with the others. At least it is mercifully in scale with the rest of the tree-fringed square, whose mild exterior cloaks a grim past.

They used to torture people here. A grand barbican or fortress known as the Royal Châtelet guarded the bridge and served as the headquarters of the Provost of Paris. It was here that prisoners were tried, tortured in horrific manner and imprisoned; those sentenced to die were usually taken a hundred metres east to the Place de Grève (now the Place de l'Hôtel de Ville) for public execution. Another gibbet stood at Les Halles.

The Châtelet was built in the twelfth century, then enlarged in several phases before its demolition in 1802; a plaque on the right-hand side of the nearby Chambre des Notaires (Guild of Notaries) shows how the fortress looked in its final version.

St Jacques Tower

We now cross the Avenue Victoria, where the all-night buses start from, and steer to the right of the Notaries' building towards the Tour St Jacques. This is the Butchers' Tower, 52 m (172 ft. high), the only surviving element of the Church of St Jacques la Boucherie, built in 1505–25. The parish church of the Butchers' Guild, it was destroyed in the Revolution but the tower was saved and is one of the finest examples in Paris of the Flamboyant Gothic style. The statues on top of the tower are of St Jacques and three animals symbolising the Evangelists – the eagle of St John, the bull of St Luke and the lion of St Mark. These statues are copies, dating from 1854 when the tower was restored by Ballu; the battered originals stand, rather groggily like a group of bewildered winos, in the gardens of the Cluny Museum (see *Walk 10: Latin Quarter*).

At the foot of the tower, a statue of the philosopher-scientist Blaise Pascal (1623–62) commemorates the experiments into the weight of air which he carried out there in the 1640s. The statue is nowadays a favourite target for defacing with moronscript; this may be cleaned off on the day you are there, but it is characteristic of morons to strike repeatedly in the same place and you may be unlucky. The tower maintains its scientific tradition by serving today as a meteorological station.

Square des Innocents

Our next destination is the Square des Innocents. A few strides along the Rue des Halles we come first to the Place Ste Opportune, head-quarters and showroom of VIA, a body which promotes innovation in furniture design. They have established their own mark of approval, the VIA label, and plan to open a permanent exhibition, 'Habiter', at the Parc de la Villette, the new science park in the north-east of Paris. In their 'designer-earnestness' they somehow typify the new breed of trader in the streets around the old market.

From the Rue Ste Opportune a paved walk leads across the Rue de la Ferronnerie and through an arch to the Square and Fontaine des Innocents. The restored version of Pierre Lescot's beautiful Renais-sance fountain (1548) stands at the centre, a soft flow of water rippling down its steps. When first built it had only three sides and was backed up to a wall at the corner of Rue aux Fers (now Rue Berger) and Rue St Denis. In about 1788 it was remade by Payet, who added a fourth side, the one facing south; the original bas-reliefs by Jean Goujon are in the Louvre (*Walk 5*).

In this peaceful setting it is almost incredible to think that the Square des Innocents was the site of an infamous, evil-smelling cemetery and charnel-house – 'one of the most filthy and nasty places I ever was in,' wrote William Cole, the English clergyman and travel-ler, recording a visit there in November 1765. The detailed descrip-tion in his *Journal* should be read with all the windows open. Twenty years after Cole reeled back at the stench from rows of badly-jointed coffins, the Cemetery of the Holy Innocents was closed and the remains transferred to the Catacombs on the Left Bank; the square became a market and the fountain its centrepiece.

On the north side of the square the neat terrace of the Café Costes is an essential calling-place for the smart young of every nation and there is much posing and dressing to shock or amuse. Walk across to the corner and enter the new gardens of Les Halles. Stroll through to the central arbour and viewing platform and there survey it all.

Forum des Halles

For eight centuries there were markets on this site, a vast rectangle running from the circular Bourse du Commerce in the west, formerly the corn exchange, to the far side of the sunken Forum in the east. Before it began specialising in food during the sixteenth century it was a mixed market and traders grouped themselves in streets named after their wares: Rue de la Lingerie (linens), Rue de la Tonnellerie (coopers), Rue des Fourreurs (furriers), Rue de la Grande et Petite Friperie (second-hand clothes), etc. It was *the* focus of working-class life in the city: riots began there, people were hanged and beheaded there. Pandemonium was its natural pace of life, and this had altered little by the time Victor Baltard's market halls were built in 1857–68, ten huge pavilions of brick, cast-iron and glass, installed to accommodate the alimentary demands of a much-enlarged capital. Even these pavilions were not big enough to hold all the immense cargo of fruit, vegetables, meat, poultry, fish and dairy products arriving nightly at the wholesalers in the market proper, and scores of small retailers set up in business around the market, selling from shops, carts and baskets.

This barely controlled furore continued until 1969 when the wholesalers moved to a modern market at Rungis in the suburbs near Orly airport. All but one of the pavilions were demolished by 1974 (the survivor going to a site in Nogent-sur-Marne) and a gigantic hole was excavated in preparation for the total redevelopment of what Zola had called *le ventre de Paris* (the belly of Paris). Then, while the rest of Paris got stuck into an immense controversy over the future of *le trou* (the hole), builders installed new railway lines and a station for the RER suburban express service, along with underground roads and car parks. Finally, after a series of top-level political rows, the present scheme was started and gradually the layers of the new Forum were assembled; while still very incomplete, the complex was inaugurated in 1979.

Looking out from our gazebo in the gardens, what has survived, what is new? The Bourse du Commerce (the commodities exchange) is still there, and the Church of St Eustache now rises more magnificently over the scene than it can have done for centuries. Obviously, much of the peripheral building is not original, for instance the Novotel and the blocks lining the Rue Rambuteau. In the north-east corner is a splendid example of the French severed house, exhibiting several storeys of blank side-wall where, presumably, its neighbour used to be. Then the eye swivels round to face the plantiform conservatory architecture of the underground Forum and its attendant arts pavilions.

It looks so blank and bland it could only be a shopping mall, this series of stacked glass tunnels that you can't see into from outside. Ah well, plunge inside and see what it offers; it can't be that bad, they say it's the biggest pedestrian concourse in Europe . . .

In fact it isn't bad at all, for a shopping mall, and there are other attractions too. But first, the layout. The Forum is on four underground levels: -1 is the first you reach from the gardens, -2 is the next one down, then -3 and -4 which houses the Métro/RER station.

Here on Level -1, also pompously known as the Grand Balcon de la Place des Verreries, is the Holography Museum. This is both instructive and fun, charting the progress of holograms since Dennis Gabor discovered the holographic principle in 1947. In 1960 the introduction of lasers gave holograms all kinds of practical applications: in museums, for instance, where a hologram can be substituted for a rare or fragile piece. Each hologram, so far as I could see, makes its own focal demands on the viewer. Thus you find yourself bobbing your head from side to side while your feet dink backwards and forwards as you try to trap each image in focus. You must look like a kind of Hulot in Wonderland, you think, then you notice other visitors doing exactly the same, and stop thinking about it.

Around the galleries, direction boards (*points d'orientation*) light up on demand to show you where shops, etc, are situated. There are some two hundred shops in all and several big high street and fashion names have taken units, as well as a good sprinkling of attractive specialists. On Level -1, for instance, are Daniel Hechter (men's and women's), Dorothée *bis*, Brummel (the Au Printemps men's shop) and Hédiard of the Place de la Madeleine, a very de-luxe food store; next to its delicatessen Hédiard have a coffee shop where you can eat a delicious pastry chosen from the shelf. An interesting specialist is the boutique of the Musée de la Presse, selling reproductions of pages from newspapers and magazines.

This level contains another museum, the Belle Epoque annexe of the Musée Grévin, the famous old waxworks on the Boulevard Montmartre. This Nouveau Musée Grévin offers a rather rigidly over-guided tour through twenty animated tableaux recreating the spirit of the years at the turn of the century. Here you can see scenes of how Montmartre and the boulevards looked in those days, Pasteur in his laboratory, a submarine by Jules Verne and a fascinating predecessor of the cinema, Emile Reynaud's Optical Theatre.

On the next level down, -2, are Le Musée, selling reproductions of objects in the Louvre, ivory animals at Vina, a large branch of Habitat, and Dubernet's excellent delicatessen. Here is a good choice of lunch-stops: outside on the terrace at La Chope des Halles, or inside at La Tonnelle des Halles or next door at Dubernet.

Most shopping malls are bestrewn with average novelty and gift shops. A cut above the usual run are La Boutique du Sommeil, which stocks just about everything to do with sleeping (and going to the bathroom first) and its pretty neighbours La Liste de Mariage and La Gadgeterie. In one corner on -2 is the entrance to a big branch of FNAC, selling cameras, film and stereo equipment on this floor, then down an internal escalator to its extensive bookshop, record store, video club, auditorium and booking office for shows and concerts.

On the concourse at Level -3, the shoppers and strollers are at large in greater numbers, streaming up from the station on the level beneath and returning to it. Go out into the piazza, the Place Basse, where students bask in the afternoon sun and quietly enjoy the puzzlement of visitors goggling at a strange statue in pink marble called *Pyègemalion*. Personally I think it is pretty daft, though if you seek an explanation I can offer the following limpid piece of artspeak from a well-known tourist guide:

'. . . next to a unicorn, the Buddha-like figure of the Dream-keeper presenting her twin lunar and solar faces watches over the young girl asleep created by Pygmalion. The latter is depicted stilled for eternity in his fruitless quest while his desire is exemplified by a pig-headed man devouring the snake of temptation.'

An exit leads to the Place Carrée, a large underground space at the centre of the *trou* of Les Halles. In this part of the complex, and around the western end at the Place de la Rotonde is a collection of larger establishments which are not shops: they include a concert hall, cinemas, a gymnasium and a swimming pool. Escalators lead up to the Auditorium des Halles (concerts and cultural events, see leaflets at desk and *Pariscope* for details). Nearby are the Discothèque, an impressively large record library, and the Vidéothèque. This is a new ambitious project where, for the modest price of a day ticket, you can choose and view on a private monitor cassettes dealing with aspects of Paris from 1896 to the present. The collection of 2,500 cassettes is drawn from films, news clips, television documentaries and advertisements; two other rooms run continuous shows of prepared programmes, mixing shorts and full-length feature movies (see *Pariscope* for details).

At Level -3 walk through to the Place de la Rotonde, an underground circus at the western end of Les Halles. Here are the six cinemas of the Forum Horizon, a gymnasium and a swimming pool – swimmers visible through a glass wall at the shallow end. The indefatigable *Pariscope* publishes a list of swimming pools in central Paris; this one is open at various times every day, with late nights to 22.00 on Tuesday, Thursday, Friday. Take the escalator up to ground level and emerge on the edge of the gardens at the Porte du Jour. Away to the east the pipes of the Pompidou Centre crown the horizon.

So ends our visit to the new Les Halles. On reflection it seems that the supporters of Le Forum and the revitalised streets around it have got what they wanted and are more or less content. Apologists for the government and city planners who built it could also claim that the Forum has repaid a debt. In recent years many Parisians have been dislodged from their homes by building projects such as the two on the Beaubourg plateau, Les Halles and the Pompidou Centre. Now the planners can say that by building these shopping and cultural centres they have achieved an important objective: the creation of somewhere decent for the next generation to amuse and educate themselves.

Those against say the new projects have merely encouraged the spawning of a rootless, trivial-minded, video-gawping class of *Beaubourgeoisie* whose goals and ideals are sorrowfully mediocre. The antis demand something better for their children; all roads do not, and should not, lead to the Forum.

Changes of this kind are happening in other European cities; Londoners may well think of Covent Garden. Paris, though, seems to be a special case. The very compact nature of the inner city heightens the drama. In those tightly packed neighbourhoods, where jobs and attitudes can differ radically from street to street, cultural change on the model of Les Halles is seen by its victims as a monstrous personal upheaval. When natives or long-term residents of somewhere central like the Beaubourg plateau are forced by lack of space and soaring rents to relocate to one of those crashingly dull suburbs beyond the Boulevard Périphérique, the gap between the quality of life they must leave and the one they must join is, for many, worse than depressing to contemplate.

Church of St Eustache

It is extraordinary to find such a large church pressed so hard by the surrounding streets. The rose window in the north transept seems almost forced sideways by the line of the narrow Impasse St Eustache, and flying buttresses rear over the Rue du Jour, the narrow street where in 1793 market traders threw up barricades of fruit and vegetable carts to protect their priest from maddened Revolutionaries.

This imposing church, the 'soul' of the market quarter, took more than a century to build. Begun in 1532, its progress was continually held up by financial shortfalls and religious wars; when completed in 1640 it emerged as a rare blend of Gothic structure and Renaissance decoration. The least successful part is the west front, commissioned after the original façade subsided and had to be pulled down; the replacement, a thin imitation of St Sulpice (*Walk 12*), has never been completed.

Inside, the columns of the nave climb to a dizzying height,

surmounted by Flamboyant vaulting. Look for the fine stained glass in the choir, and the great organ. St Eustache has a long musical tradition: here Berlioz and Liszt directed performances of their work, and in recent years the Chanteurs de St Eustache, formed in 1945, have won international acclaim. The treasures of the church include the tomb of Colbert, benefactor of St Eustache, and an early Rubens, *The Pilgrims at Emmaus*. The connections with the market were maintained to the last: in the fourth chapel on the north side is a suitably polychrome sculpture by Raymond Mason called *The Departure of the Fruit and Vegetables from the Heart of Paris, 28 February 1969*.

Our walk ends on the worn steps of St Eustache. In the middle of the saucer-shaped Place René Cassin nearby is a new (1986) sculpture, a curiously sympathetic colossal head resting on the ground with a hand cupped to one ear. It is called *Ecoute* ('Listen') and is by Henri de Miller. While contemplating its strange charm, you may be wondering what to do next, in which case I have several suggestions. I have already mentioned, in the Route section, the diversion to Place des Victoires. Another idea is to take the brief *Cook's Tour (Walk 3)* which begins at Ⓜ Les Halles a few steps away. Or, if you are not totally fed up with shopping, try the Boutique Chic et Choc, the Métro's own boutique selling china, playing cards, key rings, umbrellas, notepads, T-shirts, etc, printed with the Métro device. It will cost you a ticket to get to the shop which is in the Salle de Correspondances of Châtelet-les-Halles station, so make this something you do on the way to your next destination. Easiest way to it is from the Place Carrée at Level -3 of the Forum.

Walk 3

1er Cook's Tour

A small pilgrimage to the north of Les Halles for devotees of kitchenware – those copper pans, pots, dishes and other items of fine ironmongery at which French manufacturers excel. Includes some of the best-known specialists in Paris.
Allow 1 hour, more if buying.
Best times Not Sunday; usual opening hours for kitchen shops are Monday to Saturday, 08.30 to 18.30, closed Sunday; some may close for lunch and/or Saturday afternoon.

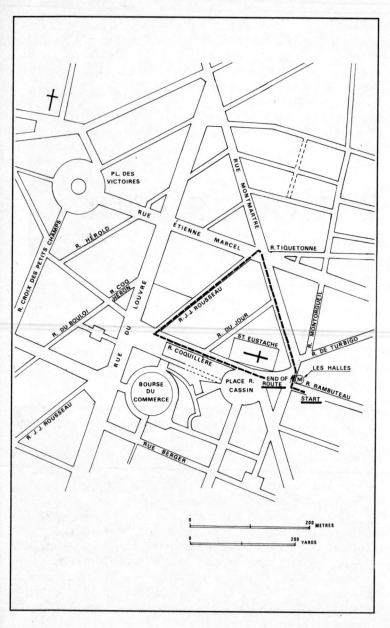

ROUTE

Begin at Ⓜ Les Halles. Nearest buses 29, 38, 47, 67, 74, 85. In Rue Rambuteau, turn right and 1st right by eastern end of Church of St Eustache. Fork left into Rue Montmartre. In this street are MORA (No.13), La Corpo (No.19) and, opposite, Bovida (No.36). On the corner at the intersection with Rue Etienne Marcel is A. Simon, with its annexe in the passage across Rue Montmartre (No.48).

Facing left (west) along Rue Etienne Marcel, turn left into Rue J.-J. Rousseau. At far end, on corner of Rue Coquillière, is E. Dehillerin. Continue back towards Church of St Eustache. For good measure try 9–11 Rue du Jour (1st turning left), a delightful sewing and knitting shop called La Droguerie.

Walk ends outside Church of St Eustache. Nearest refreshments at Guyomard, facing church in Rue du Jour. More substantial fare at plump brasseries overlooking Les Halles – Au Pied de Cochon and l'Alsace aux Halles. Nearest Ⓜ Les Halles.

Like its neighbour, Rue Montorgueil, the Rue Montmartre is very much in the business of juicy poultry, mouthwatering fish and all the artful cuts of the butcher's trade. We, though, are here to look at where the raw materials of lunch and supper go next, i.e. into the pot and on to the table.

The kitchen shops around here are culinary arsenals, supplying the chefs of Paris with their formidable *batteries de cuisine*, those quasi-military parades of pots and pans which you may just glimpse through a swinging door linking restaurant and kitchen, or spy through a barred window in some modest street adjoining a great hotel. In rooms beyond, a secret legion labours in an operatic turmoil of bellowed orders and clanging copper saucepans and, as you stand watching, gouts of steam may suddenly burst through gratings in the pavement and curl round your feet.

Emissaries from that mysterious world are the primary customers at the kitchen shops of Les Halles, though the individual or private chef is by no means ignored. In fact, there could hardly be a better place than this to pursue your quest for that stout iron pan that will be a friend for life, or a classic jelly mould, or the ideal knife.

First call is MORA, its windows stacked with equipment – a powerful-looking duck press, copper containers by the score, coffee-makers and moulds in nests. Upstairs they have tableware, toasters, jugs and cutlery. At the back, downstairs, are hundreds of knives and kitchen implements. Do not be put off by a sign saying 'Vente Exclusive aux Professionnels'; you don't really have to be in the trade to buy. MORA, by the way, is a family name; the capital letters they use, resembling initials, have no special meaning.

On the same side of the street is La Corpo, specialists in cutlery. Their recent summer window had a brilliant display of things for outdoor parties: parasols, flares, drinking straws with windmills, masks and decorations. At the back of the shop were the staple items of cutlery, glass, tableware and gadgets.

Cross the street to Bovida. A little more stolid; a shop that depends on selling to professionals who know it well. Around the corner in Rue Etienne Marcel they also have a small boutique supplying equipment for restaurants.

Over the crossroads stands A. Simon's vast store, selling much the same range as the others, though displayed with the public much more in mind. A huge choice of white earthenware, glass and cutlery awaits all polished and sparkling for your inspection. Two orders of price here: 'Hors Taxe' (without tax) for professionals; others pay the basic price plus 18.6% VAT (TVA). The shop continues along Rue Montmartre and they have an annexe across the road at the end of the passage (No. 48).

Turn down Rue J.-J. Rousseau, where the poet, one of the 'fathers of the Revolution', lived from 1770–78 on the top floor of a building now replaced by Nos 52–54. Here the promeneur solitaire was visited by Bernardin de Saint-Pierre, the naturalist and author of the novel Paul et Virginie. He found Rousseau at work in a frock coat and blue cap. While he copied a piece of music (long his chief source of income) his wife Thérèse sat near him sewing, a canary sang in its cage and sparrows flew down to take bread from window-sills crowded with flower pots and window-boxes. The small apartment, just a few steps from the teeming market of Les Halles, seems to have made a perfect urban retreat for Rousseau to work in the last years of his life.

On the corner with Rue Coquillière, a little dusty but very committed, is the emporium of E. Dehillerin, one of the biggest names in the kitchenware trade. In the window is a prize item not for sale, a splendid brass and copper cockerel standing on a ball. Admire their enormous stock: anything from a simple wooden spoon to a copper kettle, a pair of nutcrackers or some grape scissors. The atmosphere is resolutely practical, like a country ironmonger's where, behind the counter, every nail, screw and washer devised by man has its place in a tiny labelled box somewhere on the wall.

Our final shop is not in line with the others. But, while here, anyone with an interest in dressmaking would want to take a look inside La Droguerie in Rue du Jour, with its tempting collection of wool, ribbons, buttons and everything to do with needlework.

That is our Cook's Tour completed. It is not all-embracing – you will find other kitchenware shops in plenty of other districts – but in these streets close to the old market you will see just about the best that is available. Of the others, in *Walk 1: The Ritz Quarter* we look at the splendid Au Bain Marie, now in Rue Boissy-d'Anglas, 8e. Another favourite with Parisians is the enormous Bazar de l'Hôtel de Ville, known generally by its initials (pronounced 'Bay-Ache-Vay') and located at 52 Rue de Rivoli, 4e, Ⓜ Hôtel de Ville; kitchenware is on the 3rd floor.

Walk 4

1er Old working Paris and Pompidou Centre

Traditional industries in the old working city: food, clothes, love for sale, fine arts. Includes Rue Montorgueil street market, the garment district, Horloge (Clock) quarter and Pompidou Centre. Many picturesque streets and passageways.

Allow 2–3 hours, extra for Pompidou Centre (which may detain you for the rest of the day).

Best times Not Tuesday, when Pompidou Centre closed; other days it opens 12.00 to 22.00 (10.00 Saturday and Sunday); street market best in morning.

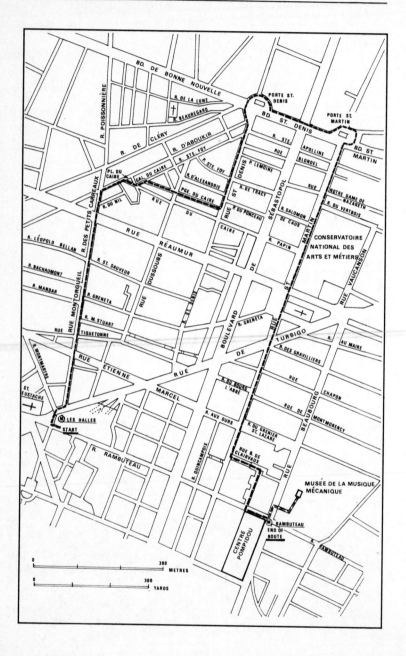

ROUTE

Begin at ⓜ Les Halles. Nearest buses 29, 38, 47, 67, 74, 85. In Rue Rambuteau, turn right and 1st right by eastern end of Church of St Eustache. Fork right into Rue Montorgueil. Follow street market to end in Rue des Petits Carreaux.

Cross Rue Réaumur and take 2nd right into Rue d'Aboukir and walk to Place du Caire. Here at the heart of the ragtrade district, walk across the square and into the Passage du Caire (entrance in building with 'Egyptian' heads on the wall). Inside, bear right and follow the arcaded passage past garment shops all the way to the Rue St Denis.

Turn left past row of hookers to the Bds Bonne Nouvelle/St Denis. Walk round behind the arch (Porte St Denis) and continue E along Bd St Denis to second arch (Porte St Martin). Pass behind this arch, cross boulevard just before Théâtre de la Renaissance and walk S down Rue St Martin.

Keep straight on for several blocks, passing Conservatoire National des Arts et Métiers and crossing Rue Réaumur, Rue de Turbigo and Rue du Grenier St Lazare. Turn left into Rue Bernard de Clairvaux, indicated by a brown sign to 'Horloge à Automate', i.e. the Defender of Time clock mounted on wall facing café Le Salon de l'Horloge. Clock comes to life every hour on the hour; see essay for details. ☞

Continue to next corner, turn right into Rue Brantôme and walk up to Pompidou Centre ☞. Main entrance is along W side of sloping piazza. At Welcome desk, collect brochure explaining where things are, tariffs and special events for the week. In general, best way round Centre is to enter external tube escalator and go straight to 5th floor observation platform for views of Paris. Restaurant/cafeteria. Then go down by escalator (not always open) or lift to 4th floor and enter upper storey of Modern Art Museum (Musée National d'Art Moderne). *Admission (free Sunday 10.00 to 14.00).* Return to 2nd floor (BPI information library) and ground floor (bookshop, cinema in Salle Garance, etc).

On S side of Centre is a large pond with jolly animated water-spouting creations by Jean Tinguely and Niki de St Phalle. Walk ends here. Nearest refreshments in square, or try Pacific Palisades at 51 Rue Quincampoix. Nearest ⓜ Rambuteau.

Diversion After locating Pompidou Centre, visit the intriguing Musée de la Musique Mécanique, open only on Saturday, Sunday and holidays, 14.00 to 19.00. *Admission*. The museum has a large and delightful collection of street organs, musical boxes, gramophones, automatic pianos, etc, restored and in working order. Hear two birds sing the *Marseillaise*; a mechanical banjo recital; a German piano-organ-cymbals combo which crashes through the *Lambeth Walk* and other music-hall numbers. To get there, follow Rue Beaubourg N past Ⓜ Rambuteau and take 1st right into Impasse Berthaud; museum is at far end, past dog-leg.

Montorgueil market

This is raw Paris; a narrow street market that breathes the coarse spirit of Les Halles as it was before the market removed to Rungis in the southern suburbs and the huge hole in the ground was turned into a commercial palm court (see *Walk 2: Les Halles*). It is a considerable relief, on each return visit, to find the Rue Montorgueil so unchanged; not quite so many food stalls on the street as before, but raucous, alive and stoutly unboutiquified, though one or two have crept in.

In the Musée d'Orsay (*Walk 14: Quai d'Orsay to Rodin Museum*) is a painting by Claude Monet which depicts Rue Montorgueil *en fête*. The date is precise: 30 June 1878, a national holiday. Tricolors fly from the narrow seven-storey buildings and the street buzzes with stick figures swaying and darting in every direction. The view is very like what we now see before us at the Pointe Montorgueil, literally the top or peak of the street, with the Church of St Eustache on our left.

The Pointe Montorgueil is also the name of the first big butcher's shop we come to: *Viande – Triperie – Volailles* are their trade (meat, offal, poultry), the front counter loaded with great pyramids of pork. All the cuts and joints are lined up alongside tongues, trotters, bunches of pig's heads and sausages hung in nets, hooked up in loops and dangling in bunches like bananas.

Across the street they have *real* bananas, from Martinique, and a fat selection of tropical roots: *malangas, dachines, ignames* (yams). Nearby is a shop which specialises in poultry. Rue Montorgueil is a wonderful place for brushing up your menu-reading. Just look at something and name the dish. Here, for instance, the labels offer *aile de dinde, blanquette, cuisse de dinde, poule, aile de poulet, poulet à rôtir, pintade, lapin, coq au vin, caille.* Next door is more pork and other cuts of meat: *queue de porc, échine de porc, pied de veau, bavette, flanchet de bœuf, gîte-gîte, macreuse, gigot d'agneau, cuisse de poulet, côte de chèvre, entrecôte, cervelle d'agneau.**

At the intersection with Rue Etienne Marcel is a sumptuously verdant self-service flower shop, where pots and stands overflow into the parking spaces on the road. In the next part of Rue Montorgueil the food sellers yield ground to hardware shops with the necessaries of life: a broom, a bucket, a pair of espadrilles. On the left, from No. 49 to No. 53, is a line of bakers-cum-pâtissiers: Le Fournil de Pierre, Pâtisserie Stohrer (established in 1730), and the Boulangerie next door which sells rolls and pastries from a stall on the road. Opposite, in a stunning display of fish at Poissonnerie Pilote, the eye is irresistibly drawn to a gigantic, feebly writhing mound of live and recently departed lobsters, their pincers taped; those with any steam left in them twitch and scrape their last minutes away. At the back of the shop a large and pouting, red-lipped blonde bestrides the *caisse*: a kind of Head Mermaid, she fans her salmon-pink cheeks with a fistful of bills to fend off the toasting rays of the freezer motors. Then there are the fish themselves, wondrously bright and gleaming, lined up in overlapping rows: *truites, homards, maquereaux, huîtres, moules, merlan, dorade rose, colin, bar, rouget barbet.***

The garment district

The market begins to peter out where Rue Montorgueil runs into its continuation, the Rue des Petits Carreaux, though officially it continues as far as the tall openwork gateway which spans the road with its legend 'MARCHÉ MONTORGUEIL'. Now we are at Rue Réaumur. On the right are the offices of *France-Soir*, the newspaper

* Poultry: turkey wing, blanquette (veal for serving in white sauce), turkey drumstick, boiling fowl, chicken wing, chicken for roasting, guinea-fowl, rabbit, coq (for serving *au vin*), quail. Meat: pig's tail, chine of pork, calf's foot, tip of sirloin, flank of beef, shin of beef, shoulder of beef, leg of lamb, chicken drumstick, side of goat, entrecôte steak, lamb's brains.
**Trout, lobster, mackerel, oysters, mussels, whiting, red sea bream, hake, bass, red mullet.

which reckons to keep several fingers on the pulse, heartbeat and belly of Paris. On the near side of the road by the ticketholder-only entrance to Sentier Métro station, is a small arena for *pétanque*, two tracks wide, which during normal office hours I have never seen unoccupied.

Our way lies straight ahead, up the hill and into the Rue d'Aboukir. At any moment a harassed ragtrader may suddenly trot across your path pushing a rack of gaudy dresses from van to shop or vice versa. Garment districts everywhere seem to require a shabby, even sleazy exterior as a badge of their sweated existence, and the triangular Place du Caire, just round the corner, makes a suitably drab centrepiece.

In the Middle Ages this was an infamous quarter. Just down the nearby Rue de Damiette lay the Cour des Miracles, a sanctuary for thieves and cut-throats. Every evening the 'blind' beggars of Paris and their maimed and paralysed colleagues returned to this courtyard and there 'miraculously' recovered the use of their limbs and defective organs. Victor Hugo described the nightly roisterings of these gangs of desperate men ' in *Notre-Dame de Paris* (1831). Understandably, the forces of law were not keen to venture down the leprous alleys and passageways leading to the Cour des Miracles, and the villains enjoyed a lasting immunity in their stronghold.

But that is all in the past, we must tell ourselves as we cross the Place du Caire and plunge into the tunnel beyond: the Passage du Caire, helpfully indicated by three 'Egyptian' heads with cabbage ears on the wall above the entrance. These pseudo-Pharaohs were installed during a wave of enthusiasm that followed Napoleon's victories in Egypt in 1798; various street names in the quarter followed the same fashion. In the early 1900s the Rue and Place du Caire were the centre of the flower and plumage trades; today, the wholesale shops here sell clothes for the ready-to-wear industry, and mannequins and chrome racks to hang or put them on when they reach the retailer's window. Stroll through the Passage and enjoy the bazaar-like spectacle. No prices are on view, except for bulk supplies.

Porte St Denis

At the end of the Passage, turn left into Rue St Denis and head for the splendiferous Gate on the boulevard, the Porte St Denis. This stretch of pavement also marks one end of the Rue St Denis vice district, and at almost every hour of the day, except sometimes between sun-up and breakfast, you can expect to pass a line of brown-limbed hookers, leaning on walls in the way they do and exposing large cleavages from doorways. One or two of them are quite gorgeous, surprisingly so you may think, for girls working the street (though some may not be girls). It is the also-rans, the doughy majority, overweight and blank-faced under the influence of heaven knows what, who more comprehensibly affirm the unloveliness of their trade.

The Porte St Denis is a memorial on the Roman scale to Louis XIV, the 'LUDOVICO MAGNO' engraved on it in four places in giant lettering, and celebrates his victories on the Rhine. Designed by Blondel and built in 1672, it is 23m (75 ft) high and carved with weighty pyramids, trophies, allegorical figures and scenes showing the crossing of the Rhine and the fall of Maastricht. The reliefs were designed by Girardon and carved by the Anguier brothers.

Walk round to the rear of the Gate and continue a few paces down the Rue du Faubourg St Denis, then turn to face the way you came. This was how travellers from the north first saw central Paris in the old coaching days before the railways were built. In *The Paris Sketch Book* (1840) W.M. Thackeray describes how his coach carried him first down the Faubourg St Denis and then to the Gate.

'Passing, then, *round* the gate, and not under it (after the general custom in respect of triumphal arches), you cross the boulevard, which gives a glimpse of trees and sunshine, and gleaming white buildings; then, dashing down the Rue de Bourbon Villeneuve (now the Rue d'Aboukir), a dirty street, which seems interminable, and the Rue St Eustache, the conductor gives a last blast on his horn, and the great vehicle clatters into the courtyard, where its journey is destined to conclude.'

We now walk east, crossing the Boulevard de Strasbourg – the great pavilion of the Gare de l'Est in the distance – and walk up to a second memorial gate, the Porte St Martin. Smaller and possibly even sootier than the Porte St Denis, it is 17m (55 ft) high and was designed by Bullet and built in 1674 to celebrate the capture of Besançon and other victories by Generals Turenne and Condé. The sculptures are by Le Hongre, Le Gros, Marsy and Desjardins.

Continue a few yards east, then turn south across the boulevard by the Théâtre de la Renaissance, where Sarah Bernhardt reigned from 1893 to 1899, and enter the Rue St Martin. This is one of the oldest streets in Paris: with the Rue St Jacques on the Left Bank it formed part of the old Roman road which crossed Gaul from north to south. The Rue St Martin leads us to the Conservatoire National des Arts et Métiers, a technical institute established in 1794 by the Revolutionary Convention, where today congresses are held on such themes as 'The Psychology of Work' and 'Taking Risks at Work'. On the right of the front courtyard, the *cour d'honneur*, is the fine thirteenth-century Refectory by Pierre de Montreuil, formerly part of the Benedictine Abbey of St Martin des Champs and now the library of the Conservatoire. The Revolutionary Convention also founded the Musée National des Techniques (National Technical Museum) in the next-door building; open Tuesday to Saturday 13.00 to 17.30, Sunday 10.00 to 17.15, closed Monday and holidays. The collection is due to be transferred to the Centre des Sciences et Techniques at La Villette.

Clock quarter

Keeping to the Rue St Martin, we pass the Church of St Nicolas des Champs, cross the Rue de Turbigo and the next main intersection with Rue du Grenier St Lazare. Then, just past the Russian restaurant, Anna Karenina, look for the sign 'Horloge à Automate' and turn left into the Rue Bernard de Clairvaux.

The Defender of Time clock is immediately ahead, mounted on the wall, a one-ton fantasy in brass designed by Jacques Monestier and completed in 1979. At each hour of the day between 09.00 and 22.00 the clock comes to life. Three knocks announce the show: a bronze drum sounds the hour and the central figure, the sword-bearing Defender of Time, is attacked by one of three animals on the rock where he guards the Ball of Time. These beasts, the crab, the dragon and the bird, respectively symbolise the sea, the earth and the heavens. Best of all, at 12.00, 18.00 and 22.00, all three animals threaten our hero and he puts the lot to the sword.

If you can gear your timing to arrive shortly before, say, noon, the spectacle is enjoyable, though brief. Quite a crowd gathers on the pavement and the best place to watch is from the terrace of the café opposite, Le Salon de l'Horloge. By this time you may in any case feel you have earned a drink-stop. This café also has free, seated loos; with the price of a pee now risen to F2.00 in some establishments, you have to think of these things.

In the house next to the Defender of Time clock there used to be an exhibition of animated tableaux, La Magie des Automates, but it has been closed since 1987. Continue to the next corner, turn right into the Rue Brantôme and walk up to the Pompidou Centre. Its full title is the Centre National d'Art et de Culture Georges Pompidou, or CNAC in its abbreviated form; sometimes, too, the name is shortened in French to Centre Georges Pompidou and sometimes, less obviously, to Beaubourg, in line with the Parisian preference for calling things by the place they are at, in this instance the site of the old village of Beaubourg.

Pompidou Centre

How to describe this Old Blue Steamer? Think of it, perhaps, as a warehouse, cunningly designed to enclose a gigantic floorspace with lifts, escalators, ventilation shafts and other services strapped on to its outer frame of steel and glass. Its functions, too, are as diverse as the sprawl of coloured pipes and tubes that enwrap it, and confusing to any visitor who does not regard it, first and foremost, as the home of the National Museum of Modern Art. Even this function needs to be qualified: Modern here means from 1905 to the present day, in other words this museum carries on where the even newer Musée d'Orsay (*Walk 14*) ends its coverage, broadly the period from 1850 to the early years of this century.

The Centre was conceived in 1969 as a multi-purpose cultural complex and is named after the man who pushed the plan through, Georges Pompidou (1911–74), then President of France. Had he not done so, we could now be looking at a public library, which was the original idea when the Beaubourg site came up for redevelopment. Undoubtedly, it would not have looked like this.

The architects were Richard Rogers and Renzo Piano, a Briton and an Italian. Their inside-out skeletal building, completed in 1977, is 166m (544 ft) long, 60m (197 ft) wide and 42m (138 ft) high, and contains a total exhibition space of 19,000m^2 (204,514 sq.ft). When it was going up, and for a year or so after its completion, film crews and commentators from all over the world flew to it like bugs to a bonfire, wrestling to find adequate pseudonyms for what is really a shed. 'Totally futuristic in conception' is still the verdict of one tourist guide. With the advantages of hindsight it is difficult to see what they were on about. The Pompidou Centre has aged alarmingly in the dozen years since its inauguration, and nowadays I can't see anyone being 'shocked' by it, as people claimed they were. Personally, I like it as a building even if it does seem out of date, a beached relic of the first Hi-Tech era; even if, what is more, it is weathering at a dangerous rate, apparently powerless against the diseases to which this generation of architecture is particularly prone: grime, graffiti, peeling paintwork, etc. If Old Blue Steamer she be, they should look after the old girl better than they do.

On the west side of the Centre is a large sloping piazza which operates as an open-air platform for street theatricals – mimes, acrobats, jugglers, fire-eaters, violinists – in short, a predictable range of fringe performers. More organised shows, up to a complete circus, appear there from time to time.

Inside the building, the atmosphere is relaxed but in a calm way, very different from the holiday-camp jollity of the piazza. Expect a crowd, especially on the external escalator which caterpillars across and up the west façade. The Centre now attracts upwards of eight million visitors a year, which makes it, in sheer-volume terms, the most popular building in Europe.

Not everyone, of course, wants to visit the Modern Art Museum and relatively few make use of the facilities on the other floors. At the *Accueil* (information desk) you can pick up a free brochure which summarises all the activities of the Centre and has news of special events for the week; it also contains a useful cross-section diagram to help you find your way around the place. The long opening hours of the Centre – 12.00 to 22.00 on weekdays, and from 10.00 at weekends – allow time for a programme of lectures, films, concerts and shows for children that is both extensive and splendidly varied. To take better advantage of it all, consider buying a day-ticket (*laissez-passer un jour*).

The principal departments of the Centre are listed below. Refer to the visitors' brochure for details of performances, lectures, etc.

Musée National d'Art Moderne (National Museum of Modern Art)   On 3rd and 4th floors, entrance on 4th. *Admission.* Huge collection of paintings, drawings and sculptures from 1905 to the present. Works by Matisse, Picasso, Braque, Léger, Kandinsky, Klee, Rouault, Brancusi, Chagall, Miró, Dubuffet, Ernst, Balthus, Giacometti, Pollock, Bacon and many representatives of the latest -isms. Special exhibitions held on 3rd floor, reached by internal escalator. On the south mezzanine are the Galeries Contemporaines, displaying works by younger artists.

Centre de Création Industrielle (CCI) (Industrial Design Centre) Ground floor and north mezzanine. Examines society in terms of buildings, signs, visual ideas, covering fields of architecture, design, communications, etc.

Bibliothèque Publique d'Information (BPI) (Public Information Library)   Entrance on 2nd floor. Free access to very large collection of books, slides, records, videos.

Institut de Recherche et de Coordination Acoustique/Musique (IRCAM) (Institute for Acoustic and Musical Research)   Below ground at 31 Rue St Merri. Director Pierre Boulez. Research studios for study of sounds and music (not for general public). Organises concerts, studios and seminars (see brochure).

Visual Arts   Cinema (Salle Garance), theatre and dance (Grande Salle), video shows in various rooms (see brochure).

Atelier des Enfants (Children's Workshop)   Ground floor. For ages 5–12. Temporary exhibitions and animation workshops with practical sessions using film, photography, theatre, dance, etc (see brochure).

In the Route section at the beginning of this walk I suggested an all-purpose tour of the Centre, beginning at the foot of the tube escalator and rising directly to the 5th floor. The views of Paris grow more dramatic as the Piazza Beaubourg slips away. At the top, from the observation platform, the view to the south is rich in architectural landmarks rising from a sprawl of higgledy-piggledy mansards – that essential feature which still, thank goodness, makes up the core of any worthwhile Parisian roofscape. From left to right or east to west are Notre-Dame Cathedral, the Church of St Merri in the foreground, just behind it the Tour St Jacques with its eccentric topping of statuary, then round to the Eiffel Tower and the black battlements of La Défense.

Having visited the Museum of Modern Art, and made your way down to the ground floor (*rez-de-chaussée*), wander through the hall, stepping round the rucksacks which accumulate there, and visit the large and well-stocked bookshop. On the way, you may notice what looks like the bristle section of an enormous upside-down hairbrush. It is yellow and white and suspended from the ceiling just outside the entrance to the CCI information centre. I might never have noticed it without the innocent guidance of a German student who was lying on the floor underneath it, pointing his camera upwards into the belly of the brush. It is, in fact, a sculpture by the Venezuelan artist Soto, an exercise in 'space perception' called *Volume Virtuel*, conceived in 1987 and, so we are led to believe, on view in the front hall *en permanence*. This phrase, I have found, tends to mean 'a bit longer than temporarily' rather than 'for ever', but I hope Soto's thing will still be there when you next visit the Pompidou Centre.

Outside in the square to the south is one of the great joys of the whole *surface pompidolienne*: the pond in the Place Igor Stravinsky where athletic fountains spurt jets of water in every direction. The black pieces are by Jean Tinguely, the bold stripey ones by Niki de St Phalle, and jointly they form *L'Hommage à Stravinsky*. Mesmerising. Well worth the price of a seat on one of the nearby café terraces. What better way to be entertained at the end of a Slow Walk?

Walk 5 ☂

1ᵉʳ Louvre Palace and Tuileries Gardens

A brief guide to the treasures of the Louvre Museum, concentrating on the new Pyramid, the medieval fortress of Philippe Auguste, the Classical sculpture galleries and the various national schools of painting, 14–19C. Continues through Tuileries Gardens to Place de la Concorde.
Allow 3–4 hours.
Best times Not Tuesday or public holidays, when museum closed; permanent collections open 09.00 to 18.00, Wednesday open until 21.45, Monday some sections (on rotating basis) open until 21.45.

ROUTE

Begin at Ⓜ Palais Royal. Nearest buses 21, 24, 27, 67, 69, 72, 74, 76, 81, 85. Walk S through Passage Richelieu and enter museum at Pyramid. *Admission.* Descend to Napoleon Reception Hall and buy ticket. Head E towards Sully pavilion, go up escalator and follow signs 'Sully Louvre Médiéval'. Continue to crypt containing restored fortress of Philippe Auguste (c.1200). Walk round two sides of outer wall and penetrate to circular keep (*donjon*) at centre. Walk round and retrace steps to entrance to keep.

Turn right up steps to sphinx, turn right and go up more stairs to Classical galleries. *Vénus de Milo* is directly ahead. Continue to large *Torso of Man.* Go up stairs at far end and join stairs leading up to *Winged Victory of Samothrace.* Go left past statue and right into Galerie

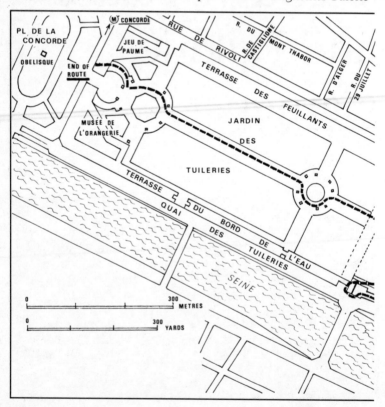

d'Apollon and Crown Jewels.

Return to *Winged Victory* and go up stairs ahead to European paintings. Turn left to Dutch masters and continue past Rembrandts to end. This brings you to Grande Galerie overlooking river. Turn right to French 18C (Watteau, Boucher, Fragonard). Turn right into *Mona Lisa* room (works by Leonardo, Raphael, Titian, Veronese, etc.).

Return to Grande Galerie and turn right to French 18–19C (Greuze, Ingres, Géricault). To right are small rooms temporarily crowded with French masters from Boucher to Corot. Ahead in Grande Galerie are Italian Primitives and Quattrocento. At end is mixed gallery of 17C (Van Dyck, Rubens) leading to Salle Rubens

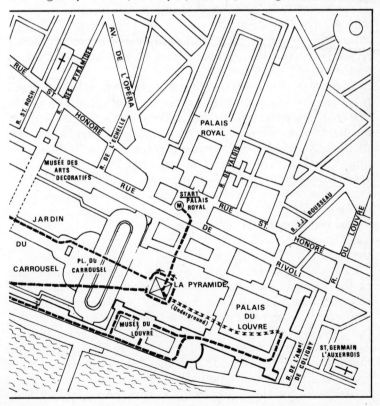

and his Marie de Médicis series. At far end, continue to Italian 17–18C, then Bestegui Collection and Spanish 15–19C. Take staircase down to Romantic Sculpture and exit through Porte Jaujard.

Turn right towards Pyramid for refreshment or walk directly to Carrousel Arch (Arc de Triomphe du Carrousel) and continue to Tuileries Gardens. Walk past ponds to end at Pl. de la Concorde. On left is Musée de l'Orangerie (Monet's waterlilies); on right is Jeu de Paume (closed for renovation). Walk ends here. Tea recommended at Angelina, 226 Rue de Rivoli; open 10.00 to 19.00, closed in August, Nearest Ⓜ Concorde.

The Museum: A Provisional Tour

The great upheavals at the Louvre are well advanced, though expected to continue until 1995 when restoration of the old galleries should be completed. In the meantime the grand design can be seen and provisional judgments made.

To previous visitors who have yet to see the Pyramid, the changes may seem vast and unsettling: an experience rather like returning to one's old school to find that a new and revolutionary head has dug a great pit in the hallowed front yard, shuffled all the old familiar rooms and divided a homogeneous community into three rival houses (Richelieu, Sully and Denon) and three sets of colours (blue for ground floor, red for 1st floor and yellow for 2nd floor). Baffling, indeed, to a newcomer are these vertical *and* horizontal distinctions. Never mind, we will take them slowly and in our stride.

The first thing to get right is your Métro stop. Ⓜ Louvre is no longer the place. Replicas of Old Egypt still adorn the platforms, but the correct stop is now Palais Royal.

From the island in Place du Palais Royal, walk through the arcade of the Richelieu wing. Formerly occupied by the Ministry of Finance, these blocks are to become part of the museum and the two courtyards on either side of the arcade, covered with glass roofs, will be used to display French sculpture from the permanent collection. These and other works around the Carrousel Arch should be finished in 1993, to coincide with the 200th anniversary of the founding of the museum (another bicentenary!).

Emerge in the Cour Napoléon, its heart pierced by I.M. Pei's controversial Pyramid, opened in March 1989. This is the principal entrance to the museum. Step inside and walk down an elegant spiralling stairway to the Napoleon Reception Hall, dressed in soothing creamy stone. Look upward into the walls of the Pyramid.

Perhaps it is not so thrilling after all, seen from this angle. Unsightly even, a cat's cradle of thickish stainless steel frames, solid rod cables and nodular fastenings. At worst, it serves its function adequately – to admit deep light into the massive underground hall which now unites all the surrounding blocks.

This hall is in fact more important than the Pyramid. For the first time in its history the museum extends, or will extend, to all parts of the Louvre Palace. Huge new spaces have been made available to equip the long-out-of-date museum with better reserve areas for works of art not on display, better rooms for temporary exhibitions, an auditorium, modern restaurants, a central reception hall, and improved office and service areas.

Now to find a way through it. The hall is the focal point, and from it passageways lead in four main directions, corresponding to the sides of the Pyramid above. To the north is the sector now labelled Richelieu, which will contain the sculpture courts; to left and right of the north stairway are, respectively, a cafeteria and restaurant and a 420-seater auditorium. To the east is Sully, the passage leading to the medieval crypt beneath the Cour Carrée and the galleries for Antiquities, Objets d'art and French paintings (14th to 17th century). To the south is Denon, currently the main pavilion for European paintings and sculpture. To the west the Louvre-Carrousel passage will become a shopping mall connecting with a new underground bus and car park. To the south-west, a fifth avenue leads to the new bookshop.

At the circular information desk in the hall, pick up a free orientation guide, buy an entrance ticket at one of the ticket booths and head east up the escalator to Sully. Our first destination is signposted 'Sully Louvre Médiéval', the twelfth-century fortress built by King Philippe Auguste and recently excavated beneath the floor of the Cour Carrée, the Louvre's easternmost courtyard.

The original fortress was quadrangular in shape, flanked by towers and surrounded by moats. We penetrate the gloom of the crypt and walk along the line of the old east moat, past floodlit stone towers that once formed the gates to the city of Paris. Around the corner, a passage leads into the core of the structure, the great circular keep or *donjon*. Its top and those of the towers were demolished long ago when the fortress, after being extended by Charles V (1338–80) into a palace, was abandoned and finally replaced by the Renaissance wings of the Cour Carrée.

The archaeological programme of 1983–84 which uncovered these fascinating remains was something of a happy bonus. Had there not been a Grand Louvre plan to revitalise the museum, it is more than likely that the medieval fortress would have been left, ignored, beneath the cobblestones.

Back at the entrance to the keep, we head into the museum proper. Past the twelve-ton granite sphinx from Tanis in Lower Egypt (1900 BC) and upstairs to the *Vénus de Milo*. And there she is, in her familiar setting in the brown marble gallery now classified on plans of the museum as Sully Blue 8 (that is, Sully pavilion, ground floor, room 8).

The *Vénus de Milo* was found in fragments on the Greek island of Melos, brought to Paris in 1832 and restored in the Louvre. Dated to the second century BC, she is the world's most famous ancient statue. The calm dignity of the face and the easy gracefulness of the stance have compelled millions to come and admire her classical perfection. During the museum's opening times she gives a perpetual photo-call to the crowds massing at her front, and enervating employment to the guard who shouts 'No flash, pas de flash!' every few seconds and dashes into the sea of anoraks to remonstrate with those who ignore him. The scene here is a reminder that the Louvre is different from other museums. *Everyone* goes to the Louvre, almost by command, just as they go to the Eiffel Tower and the Champs Elysées. It is almost always crowded, and the best course for any visitor is to make an early start, which means being there at opening time.

Continue through the Classical sculpture galleries, passing from Sully pavilion into Denon. On the left, beyond the massive *Torso of Man* (c. 480-470 BC) is the *Dame d'Auxerre*, her right hand crossed over her breasts – one of the earliest known Greek sculptures (7th century BC).

At the far end go up the stairs, then turn and face upwards to another of the Louvre's most celebrated landmarks, the *Winged Victory of Samothrace* (3rd century BC) which dominates the stairhead with spread wings and a forward-thrusting torso. The statue was discovered in 1863 and probably commemorates a naval victory by the fleet of Rhodes.

Behind the *Winged Victory* is the gilded Galerie d'Apollon, a dusty treasure house of *objets d'art:* fine glass and plate, a chess set made of quartz and rock crystal, the ornamental sword of the Grand Master of the Order of Malta, and an abundance of royal jewels. Biggest of the crowns is the openwork plum pudding of 1722 which Louis XV wore for his coronation (alas, the glittering stones are copies). Tread back along the creaking parquet to the *Winged Victory* and then, in line with her jutting torso, go upstairs to see the European paintings.

Now chaos takes over. Where once it was possible to trace a more or less chronological path from the Middle Ages to the nineteenth century, the current alterations have left us with a strange jumble. Already gone are the early French paintings (14th–17th centuries), removed to the second floor of the Sully pavilion (Yellow 1–4). Reluctantly, and chiefly for navigational reasons, I have omitted them from our tour; you may care to return to them later.

What is now happening in these galleries is part of a revolutionary process that will change the way all the paintings are shown. In place of the former loose chronological pattern we are to be given national schools, each in its own separate block: the French, the Dutch, Italian, German, Spanish, etc. To their credit, the authorities do not claim that the present interim layout is anything other than inconvenient, involving such strange hops in time as those between Géricault and Cimabue via Boucher and Corot. We, however, must make the best of it.

We begin, therefore, with a choice. Ahead, in Denon Red 2, is a selection of French nineteenth-century paintings – Ingres, Delacroix, Chassériau and others. To the left, in Denon Red 4, are Dutch masters of the seventeenth century. If you opt for the latter, you will find splendid portraits and scenes by Frans Hals, landscapes by Van Goyen, and a large assembly of Rembrandts. Among the many self-portraits is the celebrated picture of the artist in old age (1660) and the sparkling painting of *Bethsheba au Bain* (1654). Continue past bright interiors by Pieter de Hooch and domestic scenes by Gerard

Dou and the Van Mieris family.

This route brings you to the Grande Galerie by the river, and a group of French eighteenth-century works. The clown figure of Watteau's *Gilles* faces the same artist's delicate *Pilgrimage to the Isle of Scythera*. Turn right to a feast of Bouchers – *Marriage of Psyche and Eros* and *Diana Resting after her Bath* – and the cool greys of Perronneau's *Madame de Sorquainville*. Then portraits by Fragonard, his impressionistic *Beggar's Dream* and stormily erotic *Le Verrou* – the lovers struggle while the man slips home the bolt on the door.

Turn right to the *Mona Lisa* room. It is, of course, much more than a shrine to the world's most famous painting, but the small armoured glass box on the wall is the magnet which draws the daily multitudes. Wait patiently for your turn while guides jabber in Italian and Japanese, dismantling the magic smile. To the right of the *Mona Lisa* is Andrea del Sarto's *Holy Family*, and to the left are three small masterpieces: Raphael's *St George* and *St Michael* flanking Perugino's *Apollo and Marsyas*. Next to them are more wonderful pictures by Leonardo da Vinci: the joyous celebration of *The Virgin, the Child and St Anne*, *The Virgin of the Rocks*, *St John the Baptist* and the portrait of *La Belle Ferronnière*.

For now this room is uncomfortably overfilled with Italian masters waiting for a more spacious permanent home. On the far wall an exhibition has been made of the restoration of Veronese's *Marriage at Cana*. Facing the *Mona Lisa* is a double bank of Titians: *François I of France*, *Portrait of a Man*, *Man with a Glove* and *The Pilgrims at Emmaus*.

Return to the Grande Galerie and turn right to the glorious works of Ingres: *La Baigneuse* and, on the facing wall, the lute-playing central figure of *Le Bain Turc*. Move on to the fluid Romanticism of Géricault. Now comes another emphatic parting of the ways. On the right is a trio of small galleries crammed with French paintings in transit to their next resting-place in the Sully pavilion: works by Boucher, Fragonard, Watteau, Chardin, Ingres, Delacroix, Géricault, and the landscapes of Corot and Théodore Rousseau.

In the Grande Galerie the way forward leads to Italian Primitives and the Quattrocento: works by Cimabue, Veneziano, Fra Lippo Lippi, Sassetta, Uccello, then Bellini's fine *Portrait of a Man*, Mantegna's *Calvary* and *St Sebastian*, and three superb paintings by Botticelli: *Virgin and Child and Angels*, *Portrait of a Young Man* and

Madonna of the Guides of Faenza. Here too are Piero di Cosimo's *St John the Baptist as a Child*, Raphael's *Angel* and a group of works by Fra Angelico.

On to a mixed gallery of seventeenth-century painters which acts as a vestibule to the Galerie Médicis, in which twenty large paintings by Rubens illustrate the life of Marie de Médicis. Continue to Italian painters of the eighteenth century, including Francesco Guardi's ten views of Venice (c.1770). Then comes the Bestegui Collection, donated to the Louvre in 1942 and exhibited as a whole, thereby uniting Fragonard, Sir Thomas Lawrence, Rubens, Van Dyck and Ingres. Wired off from these but shown in the same room is Goya's fascinating *Marquesa de la Solana*.

The Goya is a prelude to the small but excellent collection of Spanish paintings in the Pavillon de Flore. Here are El Greco's *Christ on the Cross* (c.1580), portraits by Goya and works by Ribera, Murillo and Velazquez. This is the westernmost wing of the museum, and the quality of the paintings – never mind their disposition, at least for now – has remained compelling to the very end.

We make our way downstairs, walk briefly through Romantic Sculpture and exit through the Porte Jaujard. If a break seems called for, stroll back towards the Pyramid and try the cafeteria or the Grand Louvre restaurant. (Keep your admission ticket for entry to the cafeteria.)

From Palace to Museum

The Grand Louvre project took shape in 1983 when President Mitterrand commissioned the Chinese-American architect Ieoh Ming Pei to devise a scheme to enlarge and improve the museum facilities at the Louvre. I.M. Pei, best known for his remarkable East Building at the National Gallery in Washington D.C., decided that the space beneath the Cour Napoléon must become the new centre of the museum with passageways radiating to the riverside blocks, the cour Carrée to the east, and the wing to the north then occupied by the Ministry of Finance.

The architect saw his plan as a way of opening up the palace's hitherto closed façades, particularly those on the north side which have always presented a forbidding 'cliff' to the Rue de Rivoli and the

Place du Palais Royal. For him a pyramid was the only possible way of lighting up the deep interior of the new reception hall. Other possibilities were considered but soon rejected. In the architect's words: 'A simple *plateau d'eau* [a kind of roof of water] would have given neither light nor space below ground. A flat glass covering would have been dirty in five days; it would have been like an aquarium...' Choosing a pyramidal shape had nothing to do with either the Egyptians or Napleon. Rather, it was seen as the best shape for the desired *émergence* above the underground areas, a thrusting-out from one environment into another. It was also an efficient, structurally stable shape, requiring a minimum of support.

So there we have it. A glass pyramid 21.6 m (71 ft) high, surrounded by triangular water gardens and three dwarf pyramids. There are some who think – and I am one of them – that the surface of the Cour Napoléon, dating from the 1850s, should have been left alone; that the Pyramid is disruptive and harmful to the immediate environment, and that this kind of flamboyant architecture may be fine in a new development such as La Défense, but not in the middle of the Palais du Louvre.

Nevertheless, I think the public will soon come to accept or put up with the Pyramid, if a trifle sourly in some cases. There are, of course, those who genuinely like it, and many more who profess to like it, not wishing to be thought backward. As a subject for debate it is not in the same class as the Eiffel Tower (born 1889) which in its early days had French intellectuals rummaging long and hard in those cellars where they store their ripest, most poetic insults.

No, the Pyramid is not big enough for that. I doubt it will go away, however, particularly after all the worldwide publicity it has attracted. I resolve in future to treat it as an unfortunate blip in the honourable history of the palace, and to remind myself that it is, after all, only an entrance, a way in to an institution far greater than itself.

The origins of the palace go back to the fortress of King Philippe Auguste, which we have visited. Charles V expanded the fort into a dwelling-place, and this building was later abandoned by the Valois kings during the Hundred Years' War (1337–1453). In 1546 François I commissioned Pierre Lescot to build a new royal palace on the same site, and the present buildings were added over the next three hundred years.

The western half of the complex began under Catherine de Médicis with the Galerie du Bord de l'Eau or Grande Galerie, and was extended by Henri IV. Napoleon added the Galerie du Nord, and the buildings to the north and south of the new Pyramid were designed from 1852 in the reign of Napoleon III.

The Louvre did not exist as a museum before the Revolution, though by then the royal collection included several thousand paintings distributed among various places. On 10 August 1793 the Revolutionary Convention opened the Grande Galerie to the public and now the collection includes some three hundred thousand works of art.

To see everything is impossible short of getting a job there. Even to see everything that can be put on view would take a very long time and require walking many miles. Up till now visitors have usually accepted that a limited goal, such as seeing the European paintings and some of the sculptures, is about all they can comfortably manage in one visit. And by the time the final pieces of the new Grand Louvre are installed, the museum space will be so huge that we may have to settle for even less. But that debate is far away in the future, in the mists of 1995.

Tuileries Gardens

The Arc de Triomphe du Carrousel (1806-8) is one of several monuments in Paris that mark Napoleon's victories in Germany in 1805. It is an extraordinarily busy piece of work, designed by Percier and Fontaine and modelled on the arch of Septimus severus in Rome in its early years the chariot group on top included four gilded bronze horses from St Mark's, Venice, which Napoleon appropriated and sent back to Paris. In 1815 the Allies made the French government return their Napoleonic lootings and some five thousand pieces, among them the Carrousel horses, went back to their former owners.

The arch stands in uninterrupted alignment with the obelisk in Place de la Concorde, the Arc de Triomphe and the Grande Arche at La Défense. When the Carrousel arch was built, the view was very different. The arch was in fact trapped inside the Louvre Palace and served as a lodge-cum-entrance to a vanished palace. This was the Renaissance Palais des Tuileries of Catherine de Médicis, which spanned the whole of the west side of the Louvre from the Pavillon de Marsan in the north to the Pavillon de Flore in the south. It was the chief residence of several rulers of France and survived until 1871 when it was set on fire during the Commune. The end pavilions were restored but the rest of the site was cleared to make the Parterres – a flower garden decorated with statues by Aristide Maillol.

We turn west to the Tuileries Gardens, a vast rectangular park laid out by Le Nôtre in 1664 in the formal French style which it retains today. *Pétanque* players have occupied the corner by the Place des Pyramides, and the Round Pond is now a place where children hire model sailing boats and launch them briskly to the other side of the world with a sponge-tipped prodder.

Stroll through the tree-lined central avenue or past the open-air cafés on the grass. The French passion for statues is nowhere more obvious than in these gardens. In a work by Maillol, a grandly proportioned nude is about to topple sideways into a pond; you may have seen her twin perform a similar act in the garden of the Museum of Modern Art in New York. On the terrace by the Rue de Castiglione are a fearsome pair of bronze animal statues by A. Cain (1882). On one side of the steps a huge green rhinoceros overpowers a tiger; on the other, a lion has killed a wild boar and is about to eat its leg, watched hungrily by a junior lion. The figures rather steamily evoke a *Boy's Own* version of French Colonial Africa, as seen from Paris.

On the terrace by the Place de la Concorde, and around the Octagonal Pond, are more statues and two large pavilions. On the south side, by the river, is the Musée de l'Orangerie (*Admission*), which houses the Collection of Jean Walter and Paul Guillaume with 144 works by modern masters; most prominent are Derain, Renoir, Soutine, Cézanne, Picasso, Matisse, Utrillo and Le Douanier Rousseau. In the museum's Salle des Nymphéas are waterlily paintings by Claude Monet; others are in the Musée Marmottan (*Walk 21*). The other pavilion is the Jeu de Paume, currently closed and formerly *the* museum in Paris for Impressionist paintings; as mentioned earlier, these have now crossed the river and are in the new Musée d'Orsay (*Walk 14*).

Walk 6 ☂

1er Palais Royal Antiques Tour

More smart antique shops are clustered along this route than anywhere else in Paris. Includes the Galerie Véro-Dodat, the Louvre des Antiquaires with 250 boutiques, the *galeries* of Palais Royal gardens, and a visit to the Musée des Arts Décoratifs.

Allow 4–5 hours.

Best times Not Monday or Tuesday, when Musée des Arts Décoratifs closed; from approx. 2nd Sunday in July to 1st Sunday in September, Louvre des Antiquaires closed Sunday, as well as Monday through year.

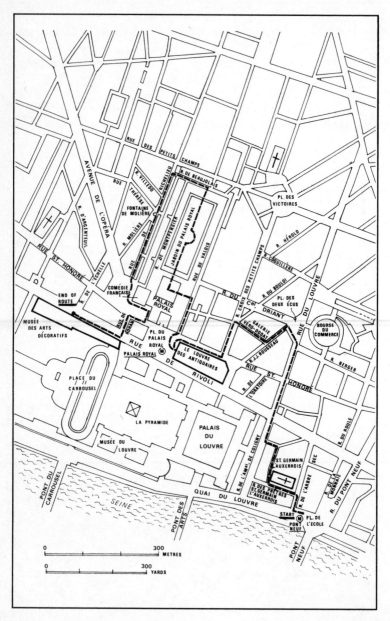

ROUTE

Begin at Ⓜ Pont Neuf. Nearest buses 24, 27, 58, 69, 70, 72. Exit on quayside, turn W along quayside by Samaritaine department store and 1st right into Rue de l'Arbre Sec. Take 1st left into Rue des Prêtres and walk round to front of Church of St Germain-l'Auxerrois ☜.

Leave church at W door and bear right by rose garden to Rue de Rivoli. Continue straight on in Rue du Louvre as far as Pl. des Deux Ecus, by circular Bourse du Commerce, then take 1st left into Rue J.-J. Rousseau. Halfway down on right is the Galerie Véro-Dodat; turn into arcade and follow to end, then turn left in Rue Croix des Petits Champs. Opposite in Rue St Honoré is Le Louvre des Antiquaires ☜; open Tuesday to Sunday 11.00 to 19.00, closed Monday. To enter turn right here and go in by main door round corner in Pl. du Palais Royal. Collect handsome free colour brochure at desk and explore boutiques on three levels. Bar, restaurant, *salon de thé*.

Leave by main door and turn right. Cross Rue St Honoré into Rue de Valois and at approx. 70 metres on left enter gardens of Palais Royal ☜. Turn right in courtyard with stripey pillboxes and stroll through gardens. In arcades to right and left are more specialist shops and café-restaurants. At top-left (NW) corner, exit from gardens into Rue de Beaujolais and turn left. At corner by theatre cross road and go up steps of Passage Beaujolais to Rue de Richelieu. Turn left and walk down to Molière Fountain.

Continue down Rue de Richelieu to Comédie Française. Walk round Pl. Colette to left of theatre and turn left into Rue de Rohan. Turn right into Rue de Rivoli and cross road to Musée des Arts Décoratifs ☜; open Wednesday to Saturday, 12.30 to 18.00, Sunday 11.30 to 17.30, closed Monday and Tuesday. *Admission*.

Walk ends here. Nearest refreshments not great (and much exhaust gas from tourist coaches in Rue de Rivoli); worth returning to Le Nemours in Pl. Colette. Nearest Ⓜ Palais Royal.

☔ **Wet Weather Route** Begin at Ⓜ Palais Royal. Exit on square and go straight into Le Louvre des Antiquaires, joining main Route. If wet weather persists, go directly to Musée des Arts Décoratifs in Rue de Rivoli.

Church of St Germain-l'Auxerrois

We begin at the Métro exit by Pont Neuf. Step past the ever-wagging doors of the Samaritaine department store and turn round the corner and into the shadow of the grey façade, overhung by gargoyles, of the Church of St Germain-l'Auxerrois. Although the west front stands opposite the old eastern entrance to the Palais du Louvre, where in pre-Pyramid times art pilgrims formed a snaking line across the forecourt well before the museum opened its doors, this church is somehow on the wrong side of the tracks and is scarcely noticed by visitors; a pity, for it is very old and deep in atmosphere.

A small oratory dedicated to St Germanus (380 – 488), bishop of Auxerre, stood here among fields and marshes in the eighth century. The present church is the fourth to occupy the site and was begun in the thirteenth century.

The porch, built in 1431–9 by the master mason Jean Gaussel, is particularly fine with richly decorated bays, Flamboyant vaulting and bands of carved figures forming triple pointed arcs above the doors. Until the eighteenth century a cloister connected with the porch but this was removed, together with much else including some fifteenth-century stained glass and a roodscreen by Pierre Lescot, with statues by Jean Goujon. Dating from 1539–45, it went the way of many roodscreens, stripped out to make space for processions through the church; fragments of the screen are preserved in the Louvre. In the Revolution the church was used as a barn and printing works; in 1831 it was ransacked, and later restorations by Lassus and Victor (Les Halles market pavilions) Baltard further damaged its medieval character and unity.

Despite the upheavals of recent centuries, there is much to marvel at in the semi-dark of the nave and side chapels: the stained glass in the rose windows and transept (15C); the pulpit and royal pew (17C), behind which is a carved wooden triptych with painted panels depicting *The Life of the Virgin* (16C); the Flemish retable (15C); the polychrome statue of the Virgin (13C) in the restored Parish Chapel, and a modern devotional tapestry across the rear wall. Several wood carvings by Albert Dubos (1889–1974) fit remarkably well with the mood of the interior. The organ, by Clicquot (1771), was brought here from the Sainte Chapelle; now restored, it can be heard at Sunday concerts of religious music. A notice on the railings outside the porch gives details.

Walking up to the Rue de Rivoli by the rose garden, you pass two 'latecomers' to the neighbourhood: Ballu's neo-Gothic belfry (1860) and Hittorf's neo-Renaissance Mairie of the 1st *arrondissement* (1859). You can hear the 38-bell carillon each Wednesday, 17.00 to 17.30 April to September, 13.30 to 14.00 October to March.

Galerie Véro-Dodat

This is a collector's item among the shopping arcades and *passages* of central Paris. Two butchers named Véro and Dodat founded it in 1826. The rich mahogany columns and shop fronts ooze a musty charm; wander and gaze. Above the shops a shuttered storey rises to meet a panelled roof interleaved with glazed sections; underfoot are black and white tiles, perhaps an echo of the founders' taste.

It is difficult to know what to recommend, or what will be open given the eccentric trading and holiday habits of some proprietors; then again, people come and go and today's picture framer may be tomorrow's stamp dealer. On present evidence Robert Capia occupies centre-stage at Nos. 24–26 and opposite at No.23. His main speciality is antique dolls, beautifully made and packaged with their own individual wardrobes; he also deals in photographs and old records and has a splendid miscellany of other bygones.

Le Louvre des Antiquaires

The clinical layout of the shops in this antiques hypermarket, founded in 1978, may not be to everyone's taste, especially bargain hunters for whom it is an essential part of the kick to tunnel in dusty back rooms piled with broken furniture and no-hope bric-à-brac. 'Too perfect,' complained a French visitor to his companion as they strolled the *allées* of Le Louvre des Antiquaires, where dust is unheard-of and the brochure tells us, with that fishy brightness you tend to find in company blurbs: 'Everything is conceived and designed to cultivate the purchaser's hedonism.'

It is possibly the most refined bazaar anywhere, everything contained in neat rectangular units, glazed from ceiling to floor, 1.5 kilometres from end to end. Many visitors, for all that, will find the displays gratifyingly pretty and tempting too, and surely no branch of the antiques business can be missing: furniture, paintings, silver, prints, china, glass, clocks and watches, jewellery, arms and armour, rugs, medals . . . If the list reads like a publisher's catalogue of pocket books for collectors, it is not altogether surprising; the two go glossily hand in hand. What rather staggers me is how much stuff there is about – simply masses of everything; can it all be simon-pure? The brochure says yes; and what is more, the dealer should give his customer a full history of every piece, including any changes it has undergone since it was made.

The shops are on three levels: jewellery is in the basement and the other specialities are on the ground and first floors. At the end of the first floor (Level 3) is a slick bar and exhibition room; in the basement they have a restaurant and *salon de thé*. The toilets are fabulous.

Gardens of Palais Royal

The gardens of Palais Royal are not at all what they used to be, and some say that is no bad thing. Today you find a charming sandy expanse lined with flower beds and avenues of trees leading up to a central not-very-energetic fountain. The atmosphere is that of a quiet provincial park. In the 1750s Denis Diderot, philosopher and chief editor of the *Encyclopédie*, liked its peaceful nature and mused there most afternoons on a bench beneath the trees. A hundred years later the poet Gérard de Nerval took daily walks in Palais Royal in the company of his pet lobster which he paraded on the end of a blue ribbon. It was what happened in the intervening years, between the happy promenades of Diderot and de Nerval, that gave the Palais Royal a very different reputation.

The palace was built in the 1630s for Cardinal Richelieu. After his death it came into the possession of the Duc d'Orléans, passing in 1780 to the fifth Duc, Louis-Philippe. He commissioned the architect Victor Louis to design the arcaded blocks surrounding the gardens and let them out as apartments, shops and cafés. Many were rapidly converted into gambling houses and brothels and the Palais Royal became the most notorious pleasure-ground in Paris, its galleries thick with soldiers, tarts, gamblers, thieves, gullible tourists and political plotters. The Duc forbade entry to the police and the vicious boys took over. William Wordsworth was sure that 'if a man be contented with sensual pleasures, there is not one which he may not gratify within the walls of this building'. Sir Walter Scott thought that the only way to control its traffic in 'the most hideous and unheard of debaucheries' was to level the whole thing to the ground. Heroes of fiction continued to lose fortunes or just save their skins on its roulette tables until 1838, when the gaming houses were closed down. The palace is now occupied by the Conseil d'Etat (Council of State) and the Ministry of Culture and is not open to the public.

The gracious main courtyard, galleried and with a double colonnade flanking the gardens, would be even more pleasing to the eye were it not now sprinkled with rows of 'burens'. These are children of the sculptor Daniel Buren and arrived in 1986: they are like stumps of columns, with black and white striped sides, and most are about a foot high; they remind me of liquorice allsorts and fill me with frustration and despair. Why muck up a beautifully proportioned old courtyard with these funny pills? Why rip up the original paving in the first place?

The true villains, it emerges, are the bureaucrats who allowed the courtyard to degenerate into an office car park. Supporters of the burens say it is now a much better place: children play there and a lot more people have taken to strolling in the gardens. My own view is that the floor of a courtyard should be in keeping with the buildings that surround it. Break up one element of the partnership and you destroy the whole. As a footnote to this argument, take a look at the fountains beyond the colonnade, their basins topped up with enormous silver balls. Grrr!

The authentic flavour of Palais Royal is to be found in the misty light of the arcades on either side of the garden: on the west side, the Galerie de Montpensier, on the east side the Galerie de Valois. In the former, La Caudriole (No. 47) offers a splendid setting for lunch, with tables along the edge of the gardens, and further along at No. 67 is Muscade Snack (smarter than it sounds, and meaning that you don't have to order a full meal); next door is the Théâtre du Palais Royal, also designed by Victor Louis and now in the business of light comedies. At the far end, officially at 17 Rue de Beaujolais, is a famous restaurant, Le Grand Véfour, an extraordinarily attractive room with a painted ceiling and red velvet banquettes.

We leave by the covered way next to the theatre and turn left into

Rue de Beaujolais. At the corner, look along the iron theatre balconies in Rue de Montpensier and then mount the steps of the Passage Beaujolais, emerging after a few seconds in the Rue de Richelieu. This is another favoured place for eating. On a fairly modest level you may like Juveniles Wine and Tapas Bar at No.47. DIY lunchers flock to Richard's delicatessen at No.41, queueing to buy little pots of salad, pâtés, vol-au-vents and stuffed things which they whisk back to the office – and which you may like to carry back to the Palais Royal for a *pique-nique* under the trees. A small fillet of bass, perhaps? Certainly. At Richard's they have all the goodies down to sliced carrot available in industrial quantities and priced by the kilo.

Comédie Française

Just here is the Molière Fountain. It occupies a rather cramped position, but it is aptly placed because the playwright lived in a house at No.40 Rue de Richelieu and this is where he died on the night of 17 February 1673 after being taken ill during a performance of *Le Malade Imaginaire* at a nearby theatre. The fountain was designed by Visconti and inaugurated in 1844; the statue of Molière is by Seurre and the lower figures representing Comedy are by Pradier. The shrewd dramatist, France's greatest inventor of comedies, sits beneath a shifting garland of pigeons which collect there by the score, clearly approving of the excellent choice of toeholds he gives them.

We come next to the Place André Malraux, formerly the Place du Théâtre Français. At the entrance to the square are the gunsmiths Fauré Le Page, founded in 1716, whose door is inscribed with the imperious word *Arquebusier* (arquebus-maker). The square is the home of the Comédie Française, named after a company of actors formed in 1680 who settled in this theatre in 1792; they acquired state patronage under Napoleon I and today the theatre continues to put on a traditional repertoire of classical French plays with some modern and foreign works. The current season's bill includes plays by Corneille, Molière, Racine, Marivaux and Samuel Beckett. In summer the theatre is closed for two months from mid-July to mid-September. In the foyer is the chair in which Molière was sitting on stage when he was taken fatally ill.

Around the corner in neighbouring Place Colette, named after the novelist who lived and worked for a period in an apartment in Palais Royal, is a favourite café, Le Nemours, with almost an arcade to itself; jostle for a table on its eighteenth-century terrace and enjoy a *croque monsieur* or a coffee at side-street prices.

Museum of Decorative Arts

The Musée des Arts Décoratifs is one of the most popular in Paris, and its special exhibitions are much admired. Despite being vastly improved by a five-year renovation plan which has given it a hundred rooms on six floors, it can still be a nightmare to find your way around. Whole chunks may be cordoned off, and it is difficult to see things in chronological sequence. Below I suggest a way of doing this, but give no guarantees that readers will score a clear round.

On the way in, collect your MAD badge and pin it where it cannot escape. Mine came off once: I was caught without it on the 3rd floor and *sent back* to the Front Desk.

Begin on the 2nd floor, which has a marvellously evocative collection of furniture, paintings, sculpture, tapestries, plate, enamels, etc from the 13th to 16th centuries (Middle Ages to Renaissance).

Go up to the 3rd floor (17C: Louis XIII to Louis XV; also Department of Toys and special exhibition rooms).

Go up to the 4th floor (18C: Louis XVI and Gold and Silver – *Orfèvrerie*; then 19C: Empire, Restoration, Louis-Philippe, Second Empire).

The 5th floor is optional, with specialist departments and 'documentation centres' for Drawings, Glass, Wallpapers, etc. Interesting, though, to peer down through one of the seven central wells to the floor beneath.

Go down to the 1st floor (20C: 1900–25 and Contemporary; also Decorative Arts at the Universal Exhibition of 1900, and the Jean Dubuffet Donation with paintings, drawings and sculptures by the artist from 1942 to 1966).

The Museum also runs art courses. It is an excellent institution and its collections give a fascinating view of French interior design and decoration across a span of eight hundred years. Be patient with its layout and it will reward you.

While you are here, and especially if fashion is your thing, try the small museum next door – the Musée des Arts de la Mode, 109–111 Rue de Rivoli; open Wednesday to Saturday 12.30 to 18.30, Sunday 11.00 to 18.00, closed Monday and Tuesday. *Admission.* On view in the revamped Pavillon de Marsan are clothes from the eighteenth century to the present, displayed in tableaux and through paintings and photographs. Many famous designers, e.g. Worth, Chanel, Schiaparelli, are on view. On the way out, the boutique has alluring accessories and jolly ephemera.

Walk 7

4^e The Marais

Once an almost secret world of narrow streets and run-down mansions, this revived and newly prosperous quarter has some of the finest houses in Paris. See the Place des Vosges, Carnavalet Museum, Picasso Museum and Historical Museum of France.

Allow 4–5 hours.

Best times Not Monday, Tuesday or holidays, when museums closed.

ROUTE

Begin at Ⓜ Bastille. Nearest buses 20, 29, 65, 69, 76, 86, 87, 91. Exit at Rue St Antoine and look round the great square. Walk N to Bd Beaumarchais and take 2nd left into Rue du Pas de la Mule. At Pl. des Vosges turn left and walk round three sides of square; Victor Hugo's house in SE corner (No.6); perhaps only for fans, open 10.00 to 17.40, closed Monday and holidays. *Admission (free Sunday)*.

Turn left at NW corner of square into Rue des Francs Bourgeois. At the second turning, Rue de Sévigné, is the Musée Carnavalet, devoted to the history of Paris 👁; open 10.00 to 17.40, closed Monday and holidays. *Admission*.

Exit on Rue de Sévigné and turn left, then left at end into Rue du Parc Royal. At Pl. de Thorigny bear right into Rue de Thorigny to

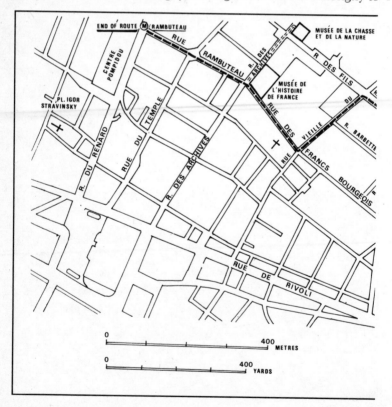

Musée Picasso at Hotel Salé 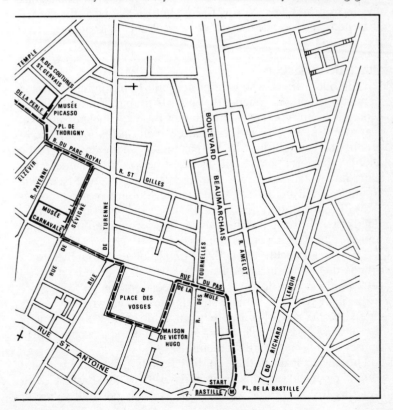; open 09.15 to 17.15, closed Tuesday, late night Wednesday to 22.00. *Admission.*

Exit and return to Pl. de Thorigny, then turn right into Rue de la Perle and 1st left into Rue Vieille du Temple. At Rue des Francs Bourgeois turn right to Musée de l'Histoire de France at Hôtel de Soubise ; open 14.00 to 17.00, closed Tuesday and holidays. *Admission.*

Diversion. On Rue des Francs Bourgeois, take 1st right into Rue des Archives and just after next crossroads visit Musée de la Chasse et de la Nature (Museum of Hunting and Nature) ; open 10.00 to 17.30, closed Tuesday and holidays. A marvellous array of hunting guns and trophies of almost everything you can shoot – big game includes stuffed crocodile, moose, bison, tigers, panthers and a huge polar bear with a splendidly fluffy coat that can only be the product of regular shampooing; hunting pictures by Rubens, Desportes, Monet and others, and a vast portrait of Zette, an aristocratic bitch from the royal kennels; plus dinner services, plate, prints, buttons and other hunting ephemera. Return to Rue des Francs-Bourgeois.

At exit turn right along Rue Rambuteau to Pompidou Centre. Walk ends here. Nearest refreshments all around; try for a table facing the pond in Pl. Igor Stravinsky to S of Centre and let the jumping water sculptures of Jean Tinguely and Niki de St Phalle draw that aching feeling from your feet. Nearest Ⓜ Rambuteau. See essay for alternative ending – a bus ride to the Parc des Buttes Chaumont.

Place de la Bastille

The Bastille district is where the professional trendspotters say it is all about to happen. As evidence they point to the prestigious new Opera House, a lumpy concrete fabrication by the Venezuelan-Canadian Carlos Ott now risen on the square, which opened on that most emotive of days, 14 July 1989, the bicentenary of the storming of the Bastille; they also point to the influx of new shops, galleries, rock clubs and restaurants in the quarter to the east around Rue de la Roquette and Rue de Lappe; and to the zooming rents and other signs of gentrification that mark this latest style migration, a short flight out of the neighbouring Marais, now too prosperous for some, and over the working-class frontiers of the 11th *arrondissement*.

They are probably right, those trendspotters, though there is little in the outwardly bland Place de la Bastille, beyond a done-up restaurant or two, to mark its new social standing. Nor, more surprisingly perhaps, is there anything to explain why the square should be *the* symbol of the Revolution, a shrine which France's Socialists will go to any lengths – even to building a people's opera house – to hug and guard for themselves.

The key to it all is the vanished Bastille prison, a huge and forbidding medieval hulk built in 1370–82 as the Bastion of St Antoine. It stood on the western or St Antoine side of the present square and, with its later barracks and arsenal, covered a vast area. Under Louis XIII it became a state prison where men could be detained by *lettre de cachet*, a form of warrant used to keep political undesirables locked up and out of the way indefinitely. In 1789, the revolutionary mob stormed the prison to get gunpowder for weapons they had stolen from the Invalides. Eighty were killed in the fight with the Swiss guards, and after its fall eight hundred workers joined in the task of dismembering the hated fortress. As the stronghold of despotism slowly disappeared it became transmogrified into the glorious fount of the Revolution.

In the middle of the square is the July Column (Colonne de Juillet). This too was born out of violence and commemorates French citizens killed in the riots of July 1830. More than five hundred were buried in vaults beneath the column; after the Revolution of 1848 the vaults were reopened to admit the dead from that struggle. The column, 51.5m (164 ft) high, bears the names of the victims and is surmounted by a bronze-gilt figure of Liberty. On 14 July each year it becomes a focus of nationalism, festooned with tricolours and triumphal banners and surrounded by wild crowds who dance through the night. If only for a day, the spirit of Revolution is ritually worshipped.

It was a great mistake to knock the old Bastille down. Had it survived it would probably now house a gigantic museum of arms and armour and be revered rather like the Tower of London. The July Column is a thin substitute when one is looking for symbols of Revolution. At least, though, it is more dignified than the 1802 plan which very nearly gave the square a monumental fountain crowned with an elephant.

Although we now leave the Place de la Bastille, the old prison will be a recurring image in our walk. The Rue du Pas de la Mule, into which we turn, is narrow and typically deceptive: a main artery of the Marais, it has nothing to say for itself until it tips us suddenly into the oldest square in Paris.

Place des Vosges

The pavement becomes a limestone arcade almost before you realise you are in it. Above, all round the square and in near-perfect unity, rise the two main storeys of rose-coloured brick and stone, then the mansards and the attics set in blue slate roofs. Thirty-six mansions in all make up this ancient and beautiful square, built in 1606–11 under the direction of the Duc de Sully.

Walk down the east side towards the house of Victor Hugo in the corner (No.6). At No.8 a plaque records that the poet Théophile Gautier lived there from 1824 to 1834. The low vaulting creates a feeling of intimacy, tickling the desire to come and eat at one of the elegant restaurants whose tables lap into the arcade. Other celebrated inhabitants of the square were Louis XIII, who staged his marriage there to Anne of Austria, and Mme de Sévigné, born at No.1 bis, whose letters make a fascinating portrait of life in the quarter. In the seventeenth century the square was the centre of Parisian social life, the scene of tournaments and flamboyant processions.

From 1833 to 1845 Victor Hugo lived in the house which is now his museum. Here he wrote Ruy Blas, three volumes of lyric poetry and several chapters of Les Misérables; the rooms display many of his drawings and illustrations to his novels, heavy with black ink and conveying a melancholy mood which his admirers will enjoy.

The Place des Vosges is in an interesting state. Massive restoration shows how it will all look in the not-too-distant future, but there is still a chance to view crumbling, untreated façades. Much of the Marais quarter fell into dilapidation after the Revolution, when the mansions were emptied of their aristocratic owners and the district became a hive of small craftsmen – jewellers, hatters, haberdashers, leather workers, candelabra-makers and fabricators of any small etcetera for which a market could be found. In the last fifteen years it has entered a new cycle of restoration and regeneration. Many buildings have been cleaned up, the shops are smarter and the prices are considerably higher; too high for some, hence the latest migration eastward to the Bastille of the designers and gallery-folk.

We continue along the Rue des Francs-Bourgeois. This is the main east-west street of the Marais, off which we divert occasionally. If your progress along this narrow thoroughfare coincides with that of a double-decker Cityrama Paris-Vision coach coming the other way, its roof slanted by the camber to almost scrape the house fronts, leaving the pedestrians a narrow triangular gap beside the wall, remember to keep your mouth shut and your head turned away as the exhaust fumes bellow out.

At the intersection with Rue de Sévigné, look to the left where the Classical façade and dome of the Church of St Paul-St Louis rear massively over the shadowy street.

Carnavalet Museum

The many museums of the Marais deal in subjects as diverse as locks, keys and doorknockers and the Oriental theatre. It would be insane to try to tour them all in a few hours and I have limited the choice to three essentials plus two optionals (the Victor Hugo and the Hunting and Nature).

The Musée Carnavalet is essential for several reasons: it is the museum of Paris itself, covering the city's history from François I (reigned 1515–47) to the Belle Epoque (1900s); it is housed in a Renaissance mansion altered in 1660 by the Classical hand of François Mansart . . . and it is a delight to visit.

So rich is the range of objects, displayed in a roughly chronological sequence, any brief list could never do the collection justice. The following is therefore a mere taster. It begins with a majestic portrait of François I, the king who re-established Paris as one of the court's main residences and launched major building projects at the Louvre, Hôtel de Ville and elsewhere. A diorama of the Ile de la Cité, dated 1527, is crude and dark but clearly shows how cramped the narrow streets were in the Middle Ages. A sixteenth-century view of the Church and Cemetery of the Holy Innocents makes a remarkable contrast with the fashionable place to idle which it is today (see *Walk 2*). The unexpected continually pops up in the finely furnished rooms: beneath rows of prints stand four grotesque, knobbly stone heads – mascarons from the Pont Neuf, the oldest surviving bridge in Paris, completed in 1607. On the 1st floor are cases of miniature portrait busts in polychrome wax and alabaster, including four of Voltaire; Boucher's exquisite *Study of a Foot for the Portrait of Mademoiselle O'Murphy*; the brilliant gilt and cream *lambris* (panelling) from the Café Militaire in the Rue St Honoré (1762). Here is a stove in the form of the Bastille prison, made by the potter Olliver and given by him to the Convention; this was recently part of a superb exhibition about the Revolution which has since received permanent space in the nearby Hôtel Le Peletier de St Fargeau, at 29 Rue de Sévigné.

You will find many references in the museum to Mme de Sévigné, who spent the last nineteen years of her life at the Hôtel Carnavalet, which she dearly loved. Stroll through the gardens before leaving. The Louis XIV statue in the main courtyard is by Antoine Coysevox; it is one of the few royal bronzes to escape being melted down in the Revolution.

In the next stage of our walk we sidle past one superb seventeenth-century mansion after another. Aiming for the pink building, the Hôtel Canillac at the end of Rue de Sévigné, we turn into Rue du Parc Royal and pass the immaculate frontage of the Hôtel Duret de Chevrey, now the registered office of the St Raphael drinks company. Next is the Hôtel Vigny, then the Hôtel Croisilles; all four look out on the small green space of the Square Léopold Achille. Continue a little further and, if refreshments are needed, try the charming Royal Bar.

At the Place de Thorigny we note that the Hôtel Libéral Bruant, which the architect of the Invalides built for himself in 1685, is now the home of the Musée Bricard, also called Musée de la Serrure, with its curious collection of keys, Gothic locks, Venetian knockers and other door furniture; open 10.00 to 12.00, 14.00 to 17.00, closed Sunday, Monday and holidays.

Picasso Museum

The Hôtel Salé is a spectacularly beautiful mansion, completed in 1659 for Pierre Aubert de Fontenay who made his fortune as a salt-tax collector, hence the name Salé or 'salted'. Between 1974 and 1980 the house was painstakingly restored and devoted to the vast Picasso collection, which after the artist's death in 1973 was made over to the State in lieu of death duties. It consists of more than two hundred paintings by the artist, also sculptures, ceramics and a mass of prints and drawings – as well as his private collection of works by other artists.

From the moment you cross the courtyard to begin the tour, there is a sense of something special. Then you climb the bright creamy-white stone staircase with its black wrought-ironwork and come to the first Picasso exhibit: a sculpture, *La Femme à l'Orange ou La Femme à la Pomme* (1934). The clash of forms is no clash at all; somehow a miraculous empathy exists between this serenely brilliant Classical house and the angular, challenging shapes and colours of the artist, a man who was decades ahead of his time for most of his life.

Wander through the chronologically ordered rooms with works from the Blue Period, Pink Period, the *Demoiselles d'Avignon*, etc. Take time out to see the views through the floor-to-ceiling windows. Work your way gradually down to the conservatory and pass through vaulted tunnels. Paintings, vases, sculptures, lithographs... the gloriously pagan *Goat* (1950), and a sculpted black cat which guards an archway, its tail alarmingly rigid and held at an angle of forty-five degrees. Are we to be sprayed in the name of art? Of course not, this place is much too well-mannered and ordered. Were the artist himself around, things might be different. It seems astonishing that he has been dead for so long.

Among the works by other artists are Vuillard's Intimist *La Berceuse* (1896), Modigliani's *Jeune Fille Brune, Assise* (1918), a Balthus, a Miró, two by Le Douanier Rousseau, and in the next room are Renoirs, Cézannes, Matisses – each a wonderful surprise.

Museum of French History

On our way back to the Rue des Francs-Bourgeois we pass the Hôtel Rohan, at one period inhabited by four cardinals of the Rohan family, one after the other, and now part of the National Archives, as is our next destination, the Hôtel Soubise.

This mansion is the headquarters of a vast store of historical documents which spills over into several adjoining *Hôtels*, including the smaller, grubbier-looking ones we have just passed. From the colonnaded courtyard we go up to the Musée de l'Histoire de France on the first floor. The house was acquired in 1700 by Mme de Soubise and this section became the apartment of the Princesse de Rohan-Soubise, beautifully decorated by Boucher, Van Loo, Natoire and others.

Documents on view include the Edict of Nantes (1598) and the Revocation of 1685, the will of Louis XVI and the page in his diary for 14 July 1789: he wrote '*rien*'. There are scrolls, engravings and maps, and a special exhibit on French Elections 1789–1939. The Bastille appears again, modelled from one of its original stones, together with the cell keys. At the bookstall are some interesting souvenirs. My personal weakness for maps meant completing this walk with a long tubular parcel: a reproduction of the *Plan de Paris* of 1676, ordered by Louis XIV and showing the latest building projects. The map is at once particularly fascinating and awkward to read because Paris is turned on its side, the river running north-south with the Ile St Louis at the top and the 'Chasteau des Tuileries' at the bottom. Our day's walk is charted in embryo: three hundred years ago the Bastille was surrounded by a broad grassy ditch, the Place des Vosges was the Place Royale, and we would at this moment be standing in an orchard, part of the 'Hostel de Guise'.

Bus ride

The Centre Pompidou is now just a couple of blocks away along Rue Rambuteau, as mentioned in the Route section above. Another idea, perhaps to round off the day, is to walk down the Rue des Archives to the No. 75 bus stop (not Sunday) and take a ride to the Parc des Buttes Chaumont. The journey goes via the old Temple quarter, Place de la République and a pretty section of the Canal St Martin (Quai de Jemmapes). Get off at the Mairie of the 19e *arrondissement* and walk down to the lake. The park is one of the happier remodellings of Prefect Haussmann and was converted in 1864–7. Journalists of the day called it 'The People's Tuileries'. Two bridges cross to the island and the park's centrepiece, the temple and belvedere, with splendid views across to that other *butte*, or mound: Montmartre, crowned by the Basilica of Sacré-Cœur.

Walk 8

4ᵉ The Two Islands

Where Paris began, on the Ile de la Cité. Begins with the Ile St Louis and includes the Deportation Memorial, Notre-Dame Cathedral, Bird and Flower Market, Sainte Chapelle, Place Dauphine.

Allow 5–6 hours.

Best times Morning to mid-afternoon; Ste Chapelle closes 16.30, between 1 April and 30 September closes 17.30, also closed 1 January, 1 and 8 May, 1 and 11 November and Christmas Day, as are Towers of Notre-Dame.

ROUTE

Begin at Ⓜ Pont Marie. Nearest bus 67. Cross quayside road and bridge to Ile St Louis. Turn left and follow Quai d'Anjou to eastern tip of island, crossing Bd Pont de Sully to Sq. Barye. Return along other side of island to Quai de Béthune, take 1st right into Rue de Breton-villiers and walk to Rue St Louis en l'Ile, the narrow main street which runs the length of the island.

To the right is the Hôtel Lambert (No.2). Turn left and visit 17C Church of St Louis en l'Ile ☞; open 09.30 to 12.00, 15.00 to 19.00, closed Monday also Sunday afternoon. Interesting shops and rest-aurants include Berthillon (No.31), Paris's leading ice-cream makers.

Turn left down Rue des Deux Ponts to quayside, turn right and walk to top of island, Notre-Dame ahead, then left across green metal bridge (Pont St Louis) to Ile de la Cité. Turn left into gardens and visit

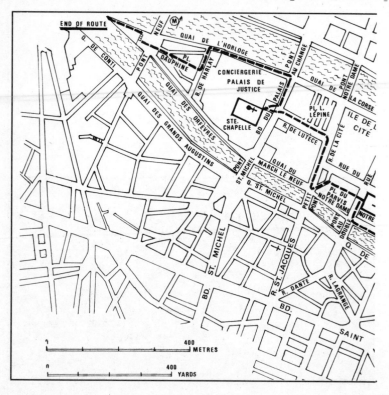

Deportation Memorial 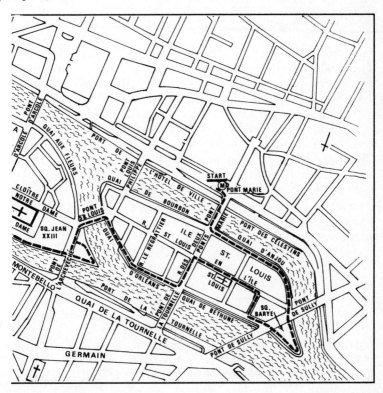 ; open 1 April to 30 September 10.00 to 12.00, 14.00 to 19.00, 1 October to 31 March closes 17.00.

Walk towards Notre-Dame through gardens of Sq. Jean XXIII, keeping to path by river for views of E and S façades of Cathedral. Walk round to W façade and enter . Treasury, in former Sacristy, open 10.00 to 18.00, opens 14.00 Sunday and holidays. *Admission.* For views, climb to top of towers, entrance on N side; open 10.00 to 17.30, closed on dates listed earlier. *Admission.*

Walk to end of Place du Parvis (forecourt), past Archaeological Crypt; open 10.00 to 18.00, 1 October to 31 March closes 17.30, closed holidays. *Admission.* Continuing W, cross Rue de la Cité, turn right and 1st left into pedestrianised Rue de Lutèce. On right is Pl. Louis Lépine, home of the Flower Market (Birds on Sunday). Walk through Rue de Lutèce to Bd du Palais. Cross road to entrance to Ste Chapelle ☞; open 10.00 to 16.30, 1 April to 30 September closes 17.30, closed on dates listed earlier. *Admission.*

Exit on Bd du Palais and turn left. Walk to quayside and turn left along Quai de l'Horloge. Entrance at 1st gate on left to Conciergerie, the old prison; open 10.00 to 17.00 *Admission*. Continue along quayside and turn left into Rue de Harlay. Triangular Pl. Dauphine is on right. Walk through to end, cross Pl. du Pont Neuf by Henri IV statue and go down steps to end of island in Sq. du Vert Galant.

Walk ends here. Nearest refreshments in Pl. Dauphine, Fanny-Tea or Bar du Caveau (Le Caveau du Palais restaurant next door). Nearest Ⓜ Pont Neuf.

Ile St Louis

In the tourist season the most visited places on this walk – Notre-Dame Cathedral and Ste Chapelle – are crowded by noon with lengthening queues after lunch, and an early start is recommended. To arrive on the Ile St Louis not long after breakfast is anyway no bad thing. It is a private, refreshing place of narrow streets and tall houses; much of it lives in perpetual shadow, and seems content to do so.

The Pont Marie, which we cross to the Ile St Louis, is named after the contractor responsible for developing it. In 1627, when Christophe Marie received his sixty-year lease from Louis XIII, he had two muddy islets to deal with: the 'Isle Notre-Dame' and the 'Isle aux Vaches' (Cow Island). He joined the two together and laid out a central street with nine side roads. Houses were built by the finest architects of the day, giving the island the marvellous Classical uniformity which it retains to this day.

Until the 1840s there was a third island, latterly known as the Ile Louviers, which housed a number of timber yards. It stood off the eastern end of the Ile St Louis before it was joined to the Right Bank along the line of the present Boulevard Morland. This accounts for the sudden kink in the river as you look east along the Quai d'Anjou.

Of the many fine *hôtels* (mansions) on the Quai d'Anjou the Hôtel de Lauzun (No.17) is perhaps the most famous. Now used by the Mayor of Paris for receptions, it is closed to casual visitors although you can apply to the Hôtel de Ville, 4ᵉ, to join a guided tour. Behind

Le Vau's severe façade (1650), decorated by a gilded iron balcony and fishhead drainpipes, is a luxurious interior with an extraordinarily vivid past. In 1682 the house was sold to the Comte de Lauzun, brother-in-law of the diarist Saint-Simon and a man of gargantuan tastes and nerve, who once listened under the bed while Louis XIV and Mme de Montespan made love, then astonished her with a word-by-word account of all that had been said. In the 1840s the poets Gautier and Baudelaire lived in the house, and the salon on the second floor became the headquarters of the Hashish Eaters' Club (*Club des Haschischins*), where artists and writers competed through the night to outdo each other in verbal brilliance, urged on by a coterie of strange and beautiful women.

As we cross the Pont de Sully the view to the left runs clear up to the July Column in the Place de la Bastille. We walk through a small park, the Square Barye, which terminates at the far end in a balcony rather like the stern-rail of a ship. Look out over the lower quay where in hot weather sunbathers bask beneath the south-facing wall. Close to my feet, one day in August, the mummified occupant of an aquamarine-coloured sleeping bag refused to acknowledge either my presence or even the arrival of daylight. It was 11.10. Across the river on the Left Bank, dogs were exercising their owners and children played in the sandpit by the Open Air Sculpture Museum (*Walk* 9). At the top of a slender mast the aluminium sails of one of the sculptures semaphored vaguely in the morning breeze. Upstream, two bridges merged into one, presenting the impossible spectacle of a Métro chasing cars across the Pont d'Austerlitz. Then the puzzle was resolved – the Métro was on the next bridge, the single-span iron bridge that crosses between the Gare d'Austerlitz and the Quai de la Rapée. A *bateau mouche* swung round the tip of the island at the furthest point of its journey and churned back beside the Quai d'Anjou.

After the park we walk up the Rue de Bretonvilliers and turn right into the island's main street to look at the façade of the Hôtel Lambert (No.2 Rue St Louis en l'Ile), which the art critic and writer John Russell called 'one of the most enviable town-houses in the world'. Voltaire once lived in this house which Le Vau built in about 1650; it remains in private ownership and, alas for us if not for the occupants, all we can see must be viewed from the street.

Church of St Louis en l'Ile

The island's church stands side-on to the main street, unobtrusive save for its openwork spire and the iron clock which overhangs the pavement. Enter by the steps at the first corner you come to (Rue Poulletier). The stained glass of the east windows, St Louis portrayed in the centre, has an extraordinary jewel-like richness: the deepest blues, the most glowing reds and ambers.

The church was designed by Le Vau and built between 1664 and 1726. The decoration of the interior is of a controlled ornateness, with pale carved woodwork, gilding and alabaster reliefs. The present altar was consecrated in 1804 by Pius VII while on his way to crown Napoleon – who at the last minute forestalled the Pope by crowning himself. If you climb through the débris behind the altar, you will come upon a small plaque commemorating the Pope's visit.

Out in the main street a queue may be forming at No. 31, the headquarters of Berthillon, the city's foremost ice-cream makers. The shop is open from 10.00 to 20.00 for takeaways, and in the afternoon you may eat inside the shop; they are closed on Monday and Tuesday, and for the whole of August and the first week in September. If desperate, you can buy a Berthillon ice at the Brasserie Louis IX on the next corner, or two doors along at Pom' Cannelle. The Brasserie, by the way, is a good refreshment stop; they cook tasty specials at lunchtime and there is much jolly banter among locals at the bar.

Turning left down Rue des Deux Ponts we face the Pont de la Tournelle and Landowski's extraordinary statue of Ste Geneviève, dating from 1928 when the bridge was last rebuilt. The figure faces upstream and from the Notre-Dame side the buttresses give the unfortunate impression that she is about to be rocketed into space.

The siting of the figure commemorates a river journey which the saint made to find food for the starving citizens of Paris. While the city was besieged by the Franks, she led a convoy to Troyes and pleaded successfully with Childeric, the Frankish leader. Ste Geneviève (c.420–c.500) is the patron saint of Paris and deserves a more worthy statue, though she is remembered elsewhere in the city. On the Left Bank, the area known as Montagne (Mount) Ste Geneviève was named after her in the Middle Ages, as are several buildings in the quarter.

From the Quai d'Orléans there are fine views of Notre-Dame Cathedral and its magnificent cluster of flying buttresses and chevet chapels, with the slender spire rising to a height of 96m (315 ft). We soon arrive on the Ile de la Cité, crossing the green-painted Pont St Louis where usually a busker or two is on duty. At midday it is likely to be a mournful lone guitarist; towards evening larger bands assemble and you may be honked on board the island to an iffy rendition of *Night in Tunisia*.

Deportation Memorial

Built on the site of the old morgue, this remarkable monument was opened in 1962. You go down a narrow flight of steps to a high-walled triangular courtyard barred at the tip of the island by a water-gate and a black wall-mounted sculpture like a line of medieval lances. To reach the inner memorial you almost have to squeeze between two straight-sided slabs of concrete. Inside, the Flame of Memory burns at the centre of a circular room. Carved on the concrete wall, an inscription explains that the monument exists to remember two hundred thousand French people exterminated in Nazi camps between 1940 and 1945. Names of the camps are inscribed in triangles on the walls of surrounding cell-like chambers, each barred at the end and offering no way out or through. In the longest chamber is the tomb of an unknown deportee, brought from the camp at Struthof, Alsace; the walls on either side are studded with two hundred thousand crystal beads, one for each victim; at the far end, thirty metres away, a candle burns in a black-painted recess.

Notre-Dame Cathedral

It can be almost as difficult to find a seat in the cathedral when nothing is going on as it is before a service. To experience a real crush, go to one of the free Sunday organ recitals. These begin at 17.45 and, in summer above all, the spectacle in the half-dark of the nave is amazing as the lucky seated cling to their chairs while hundreds more surge endlessly through the aisles, this way and that, searching for a square foot of woven rush whereon to park themselves; all this beneath a mist of incense that never quite disperses, in a temperature of ninety degrees, and still twenty minutes to go before the great organ rumbles into life. One senses a breath of near-medieval confusion. 'I find it difficult to pray in there,' an American priest from Brooklyn, in Paris on a working holiday, told me. I saw his point.

It is, for all that, the spiritual centre of Paris and of the nation: the church where French people gather to mark the pinnacles of their history. In modern times the most dramatic service was the Thanksgiving held on 26 August 1944 to celebrate the Liberation of Paris; even with the cathedral surrounded by troops of the FFI (French Forces of the Interior) and tanks of the 2nd Armoured Division, rifle shots cracked from the upper galleries and several of the congregation fell wounded.

It is, moreover, magnificent. Space here is too limited for more than a brief summary of the interior and the west front; you may anyway wish to buy one of the official illustrated guides to animate your memories of the place.

The present building was the inspiration of Bishop Maurice de Sully. Work began in 1163 under the master-builders Jean de Chelles and Pierre de Montreuil, and the cathedral was virtually completed by 1270. It was extensively restored in the nineteenth century by Viollet-le-Duc but is chiefly Gothic with Romanesque elements.

The best time to see the great nave is on a Monday morning, after the cleaners have taken out the chairs. Then you can look directly through to the chancel as well as up to the vaulted roof. The rose windows of the transept are both technically and aesthetically stunning; built in 1250–70, they are 13m (43 ft) in diameter and proclaim the extraordinary skills which flowered in the first age of cathedral-building. At the crossing is the revered fourteenth-century statue of the *Virgin and Child*. The choir is the oldest part of the building. Two spectacular friezes separate the ambulatory from the choir: Jean Ravy's scenes from *The Life of Christ* and *Apparitions of the Risen Christ*, carved in the fourteenth century and most recently restored and recoloured in 1963 for the eight hundredth anniversary of the cathedral. On the right of the choir is the treasury, built by Viollet-le-Duc in 1845–50. Depleted by lootings during the Revolution and in 1830 and 1831, it contains many precious objects and relics including what is claimed to be Christ's Crown of Thorns, now placed on view only on Friday in Lent and on Good Friday.

The towers of the west front are there to be climbed. The adventure is worth it for the views over Paris and the roof of the cathedral itself. Here you come face to face with the famous gargoyles, the much-photographed devils and a pack of perching stone animals – dog, pelican, lion, eagle. Then look eastward along the ridge of the nave to the standing bronze figures which rise through the valleys to the base of the spire. Walk across to the south tower and make your spiral descent. In the upper chapel of this tower is a bookshop-cum-video room, where you can see a film, *Les Grandes Heures de Notre-Dame*, disappointingly shown on two living-room-sized television sets. The video does, however, make a useful point to carry in the mind to the Parvis outside: that the west front was designed as a 'living book', a picture map of the Bible. At a time of mass illiteracy it showed the Christian story in a way that everyone would be able to follow.

Only when you look closely at the densely carved portals may you notice that all three are different: the gabled Portal of the Virgin on the left, the taller and broader Portal of the Last Judgment in the centre, and the pointed arch of the Portal of St Anne on the right. Above them the Gallery of Kings bridges the entire west front. The originals were destroyed in 1793 by Revolutionaries who mistook the twenty-eight Kings of Judea and Israel for Kings of France; copies were later made under the direction of Viollet-le-Duc. Then the eye meets the marvellous rose window and the towers, united by a great gallery of openwork arches. In the south tower is the cathedral's famous thirteen-ton bell: when it was recast in the seventeenth century, its sound was purified, so the story goes, by pious women who threw pieces of gold and silver jewellery into the molten bronze.

The first Parisians

About thirty metres from the west front of the cathedral, a plaque on the pavement marks the *Point zéro des routes de France* – the point from which all road distances in France are measured. The Parvis is an apt place to recall the very beginnings of the city: on this island the first settlers put up fortifications in the third century BC. They were Parisii, members of a Celtic tribe who joined forces with the Gallic leader Vercingetorix in the last efforts to keep the Romans at bay.

The turning point came in 52 BC when Julius Caesar defeated Vercingetorix at the Battle of Alesia (Alise-Ste Reine, near the source of the River Seine). The last Gallic resistance collapsed and the capital of the Parisii, which the Romans called Lutetia, became a meeting-point for commanders of the captured territories. Gradually a dual city evolved: the Gallic people remained on the Ile de la Cité while the Romans developed the nearby slopes on the Left Bank, building streets, baths, villas and a forum.

As we move west across the island, all evidence of the tumbledown medieval city that grew up after the Romans' departure has been crushed by mighty installations of the Law which cover its middle section. The Préfecture de Police and the Palais de Justice, as well as the resited Hôtel Dieu, straddle an enormous area, and between the first two runs the Boulevard du Palais, now ten times its original width. Twenty-five thousand people were turned out of their homes during these upheavals, among them the entire community of jewellers whose trade centred on the Quai des Orfèvres. The man responsible was Baron Haussmann, Prefect of the Seine under Napoleon III, who wrenched Paris into the Industrial Age; nowhere more than here was his hand more crudely felt. As we cut through to the Ste Chapelle along the newly pedestrianised Rue de Lutèce (the French form of Lutetia), the avenues of the Flower Market in the Place Louis Lépine make an agreeable interlude; on Sunday the market deals in cage-birds, traditional and cherished companions in this city of apartment-dwellers.

Sainte Chapelle

Since you are within the walls of the Palais de Justice it should come as no surprise to be greeted by a police bag and body search before they let you into the Ste Chapelle courtyard; but somehow it always does. There may be another temporary hold-up at the ticket desk, the longueurs of the queue made worse by people buying combination tickets for here and the Conciergerie, which somehow brings on the need for extensive debate with the cashier.

In 1239 St Louis, then Louis IX of France, acquired at vast cost from the Venetians a collection of holy relics, including the Crown of Thorns now in Notre-Dame. The Ste Chapelle was built in three short years to house the relics, and was consecrated in 1248. The building is a Gothic miracle of windowed space with almost no stone in between. Looked at from either the exterior or from inside the Upper Chapel, the impression is of enormous height and gracefulness. The building is narrow and not especially tall and achieves its astonishing visual effect through its perfect balance. The vaults are supported on groups of slender shafts held in position by simple external buttresses. All the more astonishing, therefore, to find that no one is sure who the architect was; Pierre de Montreuil is usually credited, though not with certainty. Between 1802 and 1827 the Chapel was used as an archive, and was restored between 1841 and 1867.

The Lower Chapel is smothered in nineteenth-century polychrome decorations which remind me of an overdone film set, perhaps a Hollywood version of Robin Hood's tent. At the bookstall you may like to buy the Ouest-France colour guide, *La Sainte Chapelle*, and use its key map and summary to identify the statues and subjects in the sixteen stained-glass windows of the Upper Chapel.

You emerge from the spiral staircase into a dazzling room lit by thirteenth-century windows 15m (49 ft) tall. The stained glass is the oldest in Paris. The windows portray more than 1,100 scenes from the Old and New Testaments, of which about 720 are the original glass; the others are nineteenth-century restorations. Their small scale makes them difficult to read even with a key map to help you; try focusing on one or two small sections at random, then move on to their immediate neighbours to see if a pattern emerges. In general, the sequence of scenes in each window should be read from left to right and from bottom to top; you begin, therefore, in the bottom left-hand corner. Remember to turn and see the rose window, decorated with scenes from the Apocalypse.

Contemplation of this brilliant sea of glass must have had an extraordinary effect on medieval congregations. Today among the constant moving press of visitors it is difficult to concentrate and find the necessary stillness. If the idea appeals, you may like to come back here one evening when there is a concert. These are held regularly in the Upper Chapel; see *Pariscope* for details. Before leaving, look down at the paving stones decorated with fleurs-de-lys, animals and foliage.

Conciergerie

On the next corner by the quayside is the Tour de l'Horloge. The splendid clock on the wall was the first public clock in Paris, restored several times since it was installed in 1370. This tower is one of four belonging to the Conciergerie, the old prison, and best seen from the other side of the river, as mentioned in *Walk 2: Les Halles.*

The Conciergerie was built in the fourteenth century by Philippe Le Bel and was soon transformed into a prison. During the Revolution, thousands spent their last night here before being led out to the guillotine. Of the rooms on the ground floor the Salle des Gens d'Armes is most impressive, a vast vaulted Gothic hall. On the right of the entrance hall, the Salle des Gardes, a spiral staircase winds up the Tour d'Argent. This was the route followed by Marie-Antoinette and countless other prisoners on their way to the scaffold.

Recent renovations have given the place a somewhat tacky, over-restored look. What is more, you are shown Marie-Antoinette's cell, then told it may not have been her cell. The tour includes the women's exercise yard, prisoners' gallery and *chapelle expiatoire.*

As you walk along the Quai de l'Horloge, look over the wall for signs of barge life. It is amazing what the skippers pack on to the decks of their rusting monsters: a complete open-air dining room with parasols, framed by potted plants; a jumble of bicycles on the wheel-house roof; even the family car gets craned on board and squashed in somehow.

Place Dauphine

Turn left at Rue de Harlay and enter one of the prettiest backwaters in Paris. The Place Dauphine was even quieter before 1874, when a third row of houses ran along the east side, completing the triangle; these were lost to make way for a new staircase in front of the Assize Court.

The Place Dauphine is named after the Dauphin (heir to the throne) who became Louis XIII, and was built in the 1600s as a uniform development of houses in brick and white stone with slate roofs. Most have now been altered considerably, though the houses at the narrow bottleneck leading to the Pont Neuf keep their original appearance. Try the view from a bench at the base of the isosceles triangle. The shadowy trunks of the chestnut trees stretch out in grove-like columns. Pigeons like it here, gathering in numbers and zooming aggressively through the air at very low altitude. It occurred to me in this square that French pigeons fly rather as French people drive their cars: from a standing start they aim directly at the oncoming traffic, as though this were the safest way to keep themselves on course, then they swerve past at the last moment, shaving your ear. Good refreshment stops at Fanny-Tea and the Bar du Caveau add to the recuperative charm of the Place Dauphine.

Square du Vert Galant

Finally, brave the whizzing traffic on the Pont Neuf, pass to one side of the Henry IV statue and go down to the tip of the island. Stone steps at the end of the upper terrace lead to a riverboat landing-stage and the leafy gardens of the Square du Vert Galant, named after Henri IV who by all accounts was a sprightly old thing.

Down here we are at the old level of the island before it was built up in the 1570s. A couple of boggy islets standing off the Ile de la Cité were joined to it at that time and form the present *square*. Fine views reach across to the Louvre on the Right Bank and the Mint (Hôtel des Monnaies) and Institut de France on the Left Bank. Ahead is the pedestrian Pont des Arts; beyond it, the Pont du Carrousel.

There was a sandy beach here in the eighteenth century, popular with local layabouts who passed the time lying naked in the sun, mischievously displaying themselves to washerwomen in the laundry boats which in those days were moored along the far bank.

Boat trip

Our walk ends in the gardens of the Square du Vert Galant. If the departure time is right, take a relaxing trip on a *Vedette du Pont Neuf*. In the afternoon, boats leave every half-hour up to 18.30. In the evening, between 15 April and 15 October, they run an Illuminations trip, leaving at 21.00.

102

Walk 9

5ᵉ Rue Mouffetard and Botanical Gardens

Many Left Bank favourites: the Rue Mouffetard street market, Gallo-Roman arena, the Mosque, Botanical Gardens (Jardin des Plantes), and Open Air Sculpture Museum by the river.
Allow 3–4 hours.
Best times Morning best for market; some parts of Botanical Gardens closed Tuesday and holidays.

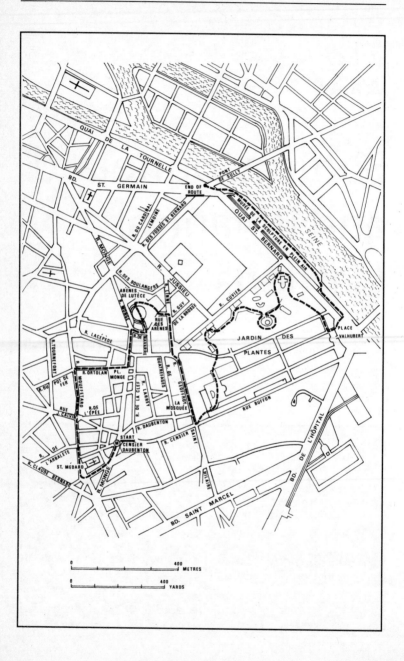

ROUTE

Begin at ⓂCensier Daubenton. Nearest buses 27, 47. Exit on Rue Monge, turn right and walk down to Square and Church of St Médard. Market begins nearby at foot of Rue Mouffetard; open daily. Walk up through market and Greek restaurant sector and turn right into Rue Ortolan. Continue to Pl. Monge; good market here, open Wednesday, Friday, Sunday.

Turn left at NE corner of square into Rue Monge. Take 2nd right into Rue de Navarre and on left enter gardens of Arènes de Lutèce ☞. Walk across middle of arena, then at far side go round to back and up steps to gardens; continue past stone bays overlooking arena, then exit left down steps to Square Capitan and Rue des Arènes. Turn left, then right into Rue Linné.

Keep straight on past shops and down hill (Rue Geoffroy-St Hilaire) keeping Jardin des Plantes on left. Entrance to Mosque garden is on corner of Rue Daubenton. Take mint tea and *baklava*, or what you will, in Moorish café or outside in tree-shaded courtyard; open 11.00 to 21.00.

Cross road and walk through arch into gardens of Jardin des Plantes ☞. Bookshop in courtyard. Turn left past palm houses to see famous Sequoia. Entrance here to Ménagerie; open 09.00 to 18.00 in summer, closes 17.30 in winter. *Admission*. Wander through – flamingoes, vivarium, bears, bison, monkeys, vultures, big cats, etc.

Leave Ménagerie at SE corner and exit gardens at main gate on Pl. Valhubert. Cross Quai St Bernard here and turn left. Walk down ramp to river and along quayside past sports centre to beginning of Open Air Sculpture Museum ☞. Walk through, looking at sculptures dotted about. Exit on Quai St Bernard near Pont Sully.

Walk ends here. Nearest refreshments: assorted cafés/brasseries in Bd St Germain, or try crossing Pont Sully to the Ile St Louis for ice cream at Berthillon, 31 Rue St Louis en l'Ile; open 10.00 to 20.00 for takeaways, service in shop in afternoon, closed Monday, Tuesday.

Rue Mouffetard

There are some places you just don't have much luck with. For me, Rue Mouffetard market seemed as if it was going to be one such. Whenever I went there it was so extraordinarily quiet. The market might be in full swing, but something enormous was missing. Where,

I wondered, was that quasi-medieval flavour that the travel writers go on about? Now I was there, I too wanted a piece of that Rabelaisian squalor, that fevered, many-tongued cacophony, that malodorous riot of yesterday's meat, fruit and veg. *Mais où sont les choux d'antan?* So clearly unavailable were they, it looked as though the good old 'Rue Mouffe' had suffered a drastic personality change.

And so it has, I later discovered. At one time it *was* something of a rumbustious stew, but that is an old image and few traces of it remain today outside those overblown descriptions I had been reading. You may well enjoy it, all the same, for the narrow uphill street does have a picturesque and lively market which begins near the Avenue des Gobelins and sprawls sideways into the Rue de l'Arbalète.

In the Middle Ages the Church of St Médard stood by the banks of the River Bièvre, a clear stream known for its freshwater shrimp. In the sixteenth and seventeenth centuries skinners, tanners and dyers moved into the district – the Gobelins tapestry works (see below) is a survivor of that age. Under fierce abuse from these new industries, the river became miserably polluted and in 1828 it was partly covered over to quell the fumes; in 1910 it was taken into the underground sewerage system and disappeared altogether.

In 1727 another event took place which added to the quarter's reputation for courting excess. A Jansenist deacon, François Pâris, died at the age of thirty-six, exhausted from a life of the severest self-denial. He was buried in the churchyard and declared a saint by the Jansenists, who laid a black marble stone over his grave. This became a shrine for fevered worshippers, many of whom were fanatical young girls – 'Convulsionists', who sought miraculous cures through such acts as eating dirt from the deacon's grave and submitting themselves to hideous torture and self-flagellation. In 1732 the government banned these near-orgies and the cemetery was walled in and locked. A notice appeared on the gate:

> De par le roi, défense à Dieu
> De faire miracle en ce lieu.*

The cult continued for more than thirty years, then gradually the mood of hysteria subsided.

---

* By King's command, let God no more
  Make miracles in this place.

The market continues as far as the Rue de l'Epée de Bois, then the street is transformed into an eating quarter dominated by a string of Greek restaurants.

A short walk along Rue Ortolan leads to Place Monge, where on Wednesday, Friday and Sunday you will find another market, varied and attractive, laid out on stalls in the centre of the square. Along with spectacular displays of fruit, vegetables, meat and fish are others of dried fruits, nuts and spices; cheap fashion jewellery and leather goods; cheeses in fine bloom; lace and embroidery from tablecloths to collars to sew on at home, and long racks of children's clothes, cotton blouses and nighties.

This walk passes several good picnic spots, by the way, in the Jardin des Plantes and beside the river, and the stalls of the Rue Monge would be just the place to assemble an outdoor menu. Around the corner, at No.66 Rue Monge, they sell bread and delicious pastries at Ch. Bahon. They sell ice creams too, from a fridge on the pavement: *cassis, abricot, passion, menthe, framboise, chocolat.* Pick a colour, and eat on the way to the Gallo-Roman arena.

Arènes de Lutèce

A notice declares that in the third century two thousand men took their leisure here, watching wild animal fights and gladiatorial battles. Difficult to believe? Try walking across the middle of the sandy gravel arena and see how the atmosphere takes you. In spite of the unsightly backs of houses in Rue Monge which rear above one side of the amphitheatre, this old Gallo-Roman sports stadium still has a certain presence. Today students bask on the arena steps and old men commandeer the benches on the side by the garden, adopting attitudes of lizard-like fixity in the face of the sun; and the only sport on view is *pétanque*, especially on Sunday.

The arena was originally in use from the end of the first century to about 280, when Lutetia was destroyed by the Barbarians. Stones from the site were later used to enclose part of the Ile de la Cité, and the amphitheatre became a burial ground.

The Arènes de Lutèce lay hidden for centuries until 1869, when a piece of the site was discovered at No.49 Rue Monge while foundations were being dug for a bus depot. The Franco-Prussian

War of 1870–71 intervened and further excavation work was delayed until 1883, then was continued in 1917–18 by Dr Capitan, after whom the gardens of Square Capitan are named. The Arènes and the baths at Cluny Museum (see *Walk 10: Latin Quarter*) are the only on-site remains in Paris of the Roman occupation.

The Mosque

We have been lucky on this walk with foodsellers, and the prospect of another good snack looms at La Mosquée. In its pale green and white walled courtyard, those in the know sit at tables under tall ash trees fitted with mosaic-faced seats, drinking Moorish coffee or mint tea and nibbling at *baklava* or *corne de gazelle*. If the weather is chilly, the indoor café is the place to go. Turkish baths are also available; open 10.00 to 19.00, women on Monday, Thursday, Saturday, men on Friday, Sunday. The whole establishment is closed from the end of July until early September.

A guided tour of the mosque may prove somewhat lengthy, though you can look round the patios and gardens; open 09.00 to 12.00, 14.00 to 18.00, closed Friday and Muslim holidays. The formal name of the Mosque is the Institut Franco-Musulman. Decorated in Hispanic-Moorish style, it was opened in 1925 to serve the growing Muslim community in Paris, offering a place to worship and relax.

Jardin des Plantes

These gardens are a favourite place for Parisians to stroll in the sun. They began in 1626 as a physic garden for medicinal herbs and were expanded greatly after 1739 when the Comte de Buffon, a great botanist, became keeper of the Jardin du Roi. He founded the Ménagerie, and his work was continued by Napoleon who ordered a bearpit to be built, and a Rotunda in the form of the badge of the Legion of Honour.

Along the south side of the gardens are various scientific galleries which natural historians may well want to visit: Zoological, Mineralogical, Palaeobotanical, Entomological annexe (across Rue Buffon), Botanical and Palaeontological. The last-named has a massive gallery with models of prehistoric animals and fossils; it is situated close to the exit gates so could be visited after this walk has finished its tour of the Zoo (Ménagerie) which is the principal attraction for most.

The galleries are open in the afternoon, usually from 13.30 to 16.30 or 16.50, closed Tuesday and holidays. The snag is that each charges its own *Admission*, so selective visiting may be best for families on a budget.

Wander as you will through the gardens. Our suggested route calls first at the bookshop by the entrance, then we turn left past the Zoological Gallery and walk up between the glasshouses and the Winter Garden (also open 13.30 to 16.50) to the northern perimeter, following signs to the Sequoia.

This is an extraordinary exhibit: a slice of sequoia tree presented in 1927 to the soldiers of France by the people of California. The tree from which it was taken was two thousand years old, and small plaques radiating from its centre mark world events that took place in its lifetime. The slice is presented resting on its side: about 15 cm (6 in) from the centre is the Birth of Christ; then underneath the AD 1 plaque is another for the Destruction of Pompeii (AD 79). After a gap of some 23 cm (9 in) it is the year 460 (Saxons invade England). Then the tree quietly grew in girth while Western man waxed very little during the Dark Ages, and there are no plaques. By the year 1215 (Magna Carta), something very curious has become apparent. The annual outward growth of the tree has slowed down, just at the moment when the rate of human progress has begun to speed up. The plaques for events in the Middle Ages are already close to the edge of the tree, and the rest of human history has to be crammed into a narrow outer ring.

Although it makes little sense to compare the growth rate of a tree with the development of Western civilisation, just for a moment one does perceive a slightly nutty parable. Twelve hundred wasted years while the tree grew and we did not!

A few paces from the Sequoia is one of the entrances to the Ménagerie (*Admission*). At the gate they give you a plan which has to be turned upside-down before you can really see what is where. You are at the 'Mᵒ Jussieu' gate, and should aim to finish your visit in the opposite corner, labelled 'Gare d'Austerlitz'. In between are all sorts of joys and you will have your own favourites. My own include the nearby flamingoes (H on plan, *Volière* = aviary); the unbelievable hulks of the American Bison, all born here at the Ménagerie (8); then the bears romping in their pools, deadly and cuddly all at once (11); the monkeys in their *Singerie* (A); the big cats in the *Fauverie* (B), and the wolves by the exit (1).

Open Air Sculpture Museum

I would not like to be accused of nannying the reader, but when you cross the Quai St Bernard it is safer to do so at the traffic lights opposite the gates of the Jardin des Plantes. The quayside road is a *racetrack*, and if you leave it till the next crossing, down by the Ménagerie fence, the cars will be going at 130 km/h (80 mph) and may or may not be able to stop. The first time I tried it, the drivers on this stretch of riverine flyway were so astonished at having to stop, several nearly broke their necks from standing on the brakes so hard, black smoke spurted up from the rear wheels of fully half a dozen cars, and three onlooking dromedaries and four giant turtles froze in horror.

The Open Air Sculpture Museum is a splendid place for a picnic. Some of the sculptures may be less than brilliant, but the quayside and the grassy banks behind it are big enough to absorb comfortably some forty works from the second half of the twentieth century.

The gardens housing the Museum were opened in 1975 and are known as the Jardin Tino Rossi in memory of the celebrated Corsican singer. The first exhibit you may see is Michael Noble's marble *Bird Bath* (1969–71). Then a scruffy rusted thing that stands by the river, Michel Guino's *La Porte Eclatée* (1965). Never mind. Sit on the grass for a moment and watch the barge life between the Pont d'Austerlitz on the right and the Ile St Louis. These gardens are a haven for dog-walkers and the occasional tramp. On we go past several spheroid or cuboid or flag-shaped sculptures. The largest piece is a striking chrome scaffold bearing a series of wind-blown giant shaving mirrors mounted on a 2m (6 ft) concrete tub. This is Nicolas Schoffer's *Chronos 10*, and alas, the last time I saw it, it was besmirched with black graffiti. The morons responsible had even gone to the trouble of climbing up the scaffold to daub the mirrors on top. If this kind of thing turns you mauve with rage, you may be consoled to learn that the other sculptures had been spared.

Some of these pieces must look impressive from the river; for instance Kiyomizu's *Belt II* which shelters in its own piece of walled-off quayside, reached by broad shallow steps. On one of the upper levels is an interesting group. A tall chrome mast with twelve semaphore blades (*Ailes Brillantes* by Iida Yoshikuni, 1981) is more fun when a good breeze is blowing. Next to it, Claude Cehes's *Torse Rouge* is smooth and warm despite undertones of butchery, and Albert Féraud's *Sans Titre* (1979) is an amazing mess – a three-car smash at least. When I worked in a certain publisher's office (not the good Hodder & Stoughton) we passed the time by holding paperclip sculpture competitions. The Féraud reminds me of that period.

At the far end, as we approach the Pont de Sully, is Zadkine's *Naissance des Formes* (1958). If you like Zadkine, there is a museum in Paris devoted to his works. It is at 100 *bis*, Rue d'Assas, 6ᵉ, not far from the Observatory Fountain, nearest Ⓜ Vavin; open 10.00 to 17.50, closed Monday and holidays. *Admission*.

Ice cream or tapestries

Here are two ideas for passing an hour or so at the end of this walk. As noted in the Route section above, Berthillon's famous ice-cream shop is only a short step away on the Ile St Louis. They shut in August, but you can still buy their ices at the Brasserie Louis IX on the next corner or two doors down at Pom' Cannelle.

Alternatively, pay an afternoon visit to Les Gobelins tapestry works at 42 Avenue des Gobelins, 13ᵉ; open Tuesday, Wednesday, Thursday 14.15 to 15.30. *Admission*. To get there, cross the Quai St Bernard, and go straight ahead down the Rue des Fossés St Bernard, then left along the Rue Jussieu to Ⓜ Jussieu. Take the *Direction Kremlin-Bicêtre* to Les Gobelins (three stops).

Walk 10

5e Latin Quarter

Medieval Paris in the students' quarter; a tour of quiet streets and beautiful churches. Includes the Bd St Michel, Cluny Museum, Panthéon, Police Museum, Churches of St Etienne du Mont, St Julien le Pauvre and St Séverin.
Allow 5–6 hours.
Best times Morning to mid-afternoon best. Not Tuesday or holidays, when Cluny Museum closed. Church of St Etienne du Mont closed Monday and at lunchtime 12.00 to 15.30, Sunday 12.15 to 16.00.

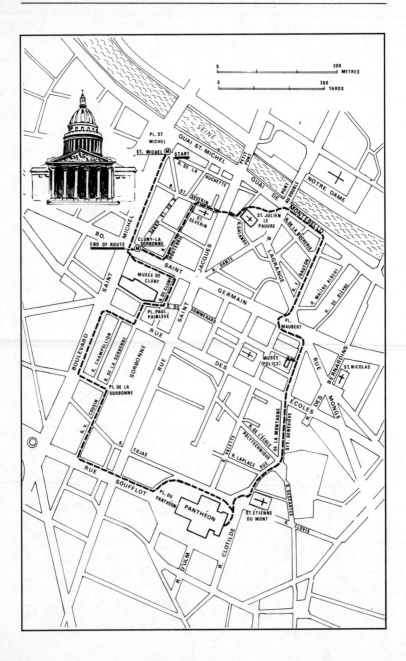

ROUTE

Begin at Ⓜ St Michel. Nearest buses 21, 24, 27, 38, 85, 96. Emerge on Pl. St Michel and look round. Walk up Bd St Michel, cross Bd St Germain and enter gardens of Hôtel de Cluny. Walk through to far end, exit and turn right up Rue de Cluny, right at Pl. Paul Painlevé and enter courtyard of Cluny Museum☞ ;open 09.45 to 12.30, 14.00 to 17.15, closed Tuesday and holidays. *Admission.*

Exit museum, bear right across Rue du Sommerard, then turn right in Rue des Ecoles and walk to Bd St Michel. Turn left up Bd and 1st left into Pl. de la Sorbonne. At far end turn right into Rue Victor Cousin and 2nd left into Rue Soufflot to face Panthéon.

Walk left round Pl. du Panthéon, past Bibliothèque Ste Geneviève, and enter Panthéon at rear ☞; open 10.30 to 17.30, closed lunchtime in winter and all day some holidays. Nave closed but two other 'circuits' offered. *Admission.* Exit to Pl. Ste Geneviève and enter Church of St Etienne du Mont☞ ; open 09.30 to 12.00, 15.30 to 19.15, Sunday 09.00 to 12.15, 16.00 to 19.30, closed Monday. (If necessary to avoid midday closure, visit church *before* Panthéon.)

Exit church, turn right into Rue de la Montagne Ste Geneviève and follow down hill towards Pl. Maubert. Just before Pl. Maubert, turn left at Police Headquarters of 5ᶜ *arrondissement* and visit Police Museum☞ ;open weekdays 09.00 to 17.00, Friday closes 16.30.

Cross Pl. Maubert and go down Rue Frédéric Sauton to river. Turn left along Quai de Montebello to Sq. René Viviani, walk diagonally across gardens to Church of St Julien le Pauvre . Exit and turn left across Rue Galande, cross Rue St Jacques to Rue St Séverin and enter Church of St Séverin☞ ; open 11.00 to 19.30 Sunday 09.00 to 20.00.

Walk ends in garden of church. Nearest refreshments not pleasant (Greasy Spoon quarter). Avoid by turning left along Rue des Prêtres St Séverin and walk up to Bd St Germain. Turn right to better cafés; best of these is Café Cluny on opposite corner of Bd St Michel. Nearest Ⓜ Cluny-la Sorbonne.

Place St Michel

The Place St Michel has an international reputation as the centre of the student quarter which it does extremely little to sustain apart from offering the chance of a good rummage in Gibert Jeune's bookshop. People nevertheless swarm there, presumably because it is so famous, then seem to stand around thinking 'Well, this is meant to be *it*', and hoping something will happen. On an average day the only thing likely to happen in the Place St Michel would be if the bikers and other hairy nomads by the fountain started a scrap and the neatly dressed boys in the CRS van parked across the street had to get down and do some normalising.

Davioud's fountain (1860) is large and fairly undistinguished, though if you like spouting chimeras here are two healthy specimens: lion-headed, ram-horned and fish-tailed. Plaques on their bases commemorate the people of the 5^e and 6^e *arrondissements* who on 19–25 August 1944, after fifty months of occupation, rose against the Germans and were killed. Those of short memory pollute the pool daily with their empty beer and wine bottles.

We now move up the tree-shaded boulevard. On the left are bargain clothes in every known acid colour, on the right are shops devoted to *bandes dessinées*, those comic adventure strips which are such a cult in France.

Hôtel de Cluny

If you have not been to Paris for a while, you may not know about the Métro station on the next corner, Cluny-la Sorbonne, which was closed in 1939 and reopened in 1988 on the line between Odéon and Maubert Mutualité. We walk through the gardens of the Hôtel de Cluny on our way round to the entrance to the Museum. Railed off behind a row of laurel bushes are the gaunt-faced original statues from the top of the Tour St Jacques (see *Walk 2: Les Halles*). Next to them are two porches mounted on the façade of the chapel. The larger came from a church in nearby Rue St Jacques, St Benoît le Bétourné, which was pulled down to make way for the Rue des Ecoles when it was built.

The Hôtel de Cluny encloses a rare group of buildings: the partly restored Roman baths, the former residence of the Abbots of Cluny and a museum based on the medieval collections of Dr Alexandre du

Sommerard. The Palais des Thermes measures 100m × 65m and was the largest bath-house in Gallo-Roman Lutetia. After the baths were destroyed by the Barbarians in the third century, the site was abandoned, then bought in about 1340 by the Abbot of Cluny en Bourgogne who wanted to build a Paris residence for visiting abbots; the present buildings are rather later, completed around 1500.

The State took over the residence during the Revolution. It had a number of occupants before Dr Sommerard arrived in 1833. On his death in 1842 the State bought his collections, and two years later opened the Musée des Thermes et Hôtel de Cluny.

Its treasures are housed on two floors and may well occupy you for an hour or so. The colour guide on sale at the bookstall is steeply priced but you may eventually feel you have to have it, such is the mesmeric charm of the objects on view. As a temporary measure, collect a plastic card-plan at the entrance to each room and let it be your guide.

The objects range from large wall hangings to tiny domestic bits and pieces: brushes and boxes and drawers full of buttons. Some highlights are: Room II, tapestries of *La Vie Seigneuriale* – how the lord and lady of the manor spent their days at hunting, embroidery, bathing, etc. Room VI, stained glass, including thirteenth-century originals from Ste Chapelle. Room VIII, sculpted heads in the 'Gallery of Kings'. Room XII, the *Frigidarium* (cold room) of the Baths, with ancient stone friezes, columns and carved blocks from the Gallo-Roman period. Upstairs in Room XI, a magical series of tapestries, *The Lady and the Unicorn*; in one of them, *La Vue*, the lady shows the unicorn its reflection in a mirror and a discernible grin has crossed the unicorn's face. Room XIV, painted panels and polychrome sculptures. Room XX, the chapel.

The Sorbonne

On leaving the courtyard of the Hôtel de Cluny, we face the north end of a huge rectangle occupied by the Sorbonne. This remarkable institution grew from a college for sixteen students of theology to become the University of Paris. In recent reforms it lost its unique status as *the* University, and is now occupied by two of the thirteen autonomous universities in the Paris area: Universities III and IV.

Most of the present buildings were built at the end of the nineteenth century. They include twenty-two lecture halls, sixteen examinations halls, more than two hundred laboratories, a physics tower, etc, which we may not visit except by special application. The oldest building is the domed Church of Ste Ursule de la Sorbonne, built by Lemercier from 1635; on our walk we approach it from the far end of the Place de la Sorbonne, passing the often-defaced statue of Auguste Comte. Defaced because he was the founder of sociology and Positivism? Unlikely; the spray can people are seldom choosy about their targets. The church, too, is not open to visitors except during special exhibitions or cultural events. One way and another, academic Paris keeps its face turned away from the street, and its doors locked to the casual visitor.

Place du Panthéon

The gentle incline of the Rue Soufflot, named after the architect of the Panthéon, is the ideal place to consider the great dome, 83m (272 ft) high, and portico modelled on the Pantheon in Rome. It was begun as a massive church, built in 1758–89 in the shape of a Greek cross to accommodate the shrine of Ste Geneviève, patron saint of Paris, then buried in the semi-ruined Abbey Church nearby. In the Revolution the Panthéon was converted into a national shrine for the great men of France. Thus the inscription on the pediment: 'AUX GRANDS HOMMES PATRIE RECONNAISSANTE' (To the Great Men, their country acknowledges them).

As we enter the Place du Panthéon, we reach the crest of the Montagne Ste Geneviève. The Romans were the first to settle the mount, followed in the Middle Ages by the student population which migrated there in the twelfth century from the Ile de la Cité. Many buildings here are dedicated to the saint, among them the great library on the north side of the square.

The Bibliothèque Ste Geneviève was built in 1844–50 by Labrouste on the site of a notorious institution, the Collège Montaigu. More scathingly known as the 'Hôtel des Haricots', it was a place of such austerity that the students were half-starved and had to sleep on the floor, attacked by bugs, lice and vermin. Along the exterior walls of the second storey the names of distinguished authors are inscribed on stone tablets: thirty names to each tablet, nineteen tablets along this façade and more round the corner in Rue Valette. The nineteenth-century selectors leaned heavily in favour of the Ancients, and only on the twelfth tablet do writers of the modern era make their first appearance with Roger Bacon, Boccaccio, Chaucer, Froissart, *et al*. By the nineteenth tablet we have reached Pope, Sterne, Richardson and J.-B. Rousseau; round the corner, the roll-call tails off somewhat with Geoffroy St-Hilaire, Chateaubriand and Berzelius.

As you look along the pavement on this side of the square, the irregular shape ahead is the Church of St Etienne du Mont; to its right, behind the walls of the Lycée Henri IV, is the Tower of Clovis, one of the last surviving elements of the Abbey Church of Ste Geneviève, demolished in the Revolution. Here too is a good view of one of the blank side walls of the Panthéon; these were originally pierced by forty-two windows before the Constituent Assembly ordered them to be blocked up. More than anything else, these blind walls set the Panthéon apart, giving it a cold magnificence unique in the architecture of Paris.

'*Le Panthéon est malade,*' said a sign, part of a temporary display in the crypt which showed how the building has suffered from the effects of water damage which, for instance, has bent and rotted metal windows, produced cracks in vaults and condensation on the murals in the nave. For the next two years or so the nave will be closed and admirers of Puvis de Chavannes and his mural decorations will have to seek him elsewhere, perhaps on canvas at the d'Orsay Museum.

Until the Panthéon is cured, visitors are offered the choice of a simple tour of the crypt or a more ambitious route said to last forty minutes and taking you up two hundred and fifty steps. This can be done in easy stages, the first of which leads to a stone model of the Panthéon in a circular domed side-room. Here too is a sight of the roped-off nave with Puvis's *Ste Geneviève* available for viewing at an angle.

A further flight leads to the Tribune, with a view down to the centre of the nave and the circular mosaic on the floor. A notice warns: '*Risque de Vertige*'. Up more steps to a terrace, then you walk across the roof and climb a narrow flight of steps into the Dome. Seen from street level, you are now a small moving speck behind the columns in the lower gallery. A long way beneath the dome, but a long way up, too. If you are like me you are also slightly terrified at this moment, because the gallery floor slopes in a quite pronounced way down to the low outer balcony, beyond which oblivion appears to lie. This is enough to start me clinging uncomfortably to the inner wall and edging crablike round the gallery to the next door and vanishing down the staircase. Usually I am all right on tall buildings, but on the Panthéon I had a clear feeling of being exposed to danger. Perhaps if they had not warned me about the risk of getting vertigo, I would have thought less about it and so been happier. Perhaps. I am not sure about that. Here is another perhaps: perhaps the Panthéon is better after lunch.

Timing is, in fact, all-important in this section of the walk, partly because of lunch and partly for reasons I will explain in a moment. We first descend to the crypt where a graphic display, made audiovisual by the addition of sombre canned music, explains the origins of the Panthéon. We then wander the dim passageways past cells containing the tombs of France's 'Great Men'. Near the entrance are Voltaire and J.-J. Rousseau, two spiritual fathers of the Revolution, and Soufflot, architect of the building. Elsewhere you may find the tombs of Marshal Lannes, Victor Hugo, Emile Zola and many others. One curious aspect of being panthéonised is that an eminent Frenchman can seem to be buried in more than one place. Zola, for instance, also has a large monumental tomb in Montmartre Cemetery (see *Walk 22*). Where, then, is the real Zola?

The solution is simple enough when you know it. In 1908, six years after the author's death, his ashes were transferred from the cemetery to the Panthéon in a grand ceremony at which Captain Alfred Dreyfus was twice shot and narrowly escaped assassination. Passions were still running dangerously high over the Dreyfus Affair and Zola's part in supporting the beleaguered Jewish officer. The Zola tomb in Montmartre Cemetery is now occupied by members of the writer's family.

It is now time to think about personal restoration, the when and the where. The key to any decision is the midday closure of the Church of St Etienne du Mont, from 12.00 to 15.30 on weekdays, 12.15 to 16.00 on Sunday. If you begin this walk around 09.30, reaching the Cluny Museum shortly after opening time, you may have time to go round the Church of St Etienne before it closes at noon; in which case the Panthéon can be left until after lunch (and with a glass of wine on board the lofty gallery may be easier to circle). At other times I think it is logical, if not chronological, to go round the Panthéon before the Church of St Etienne. The main reason is that by far the best way to approach the Panthéon is along the Rue Soufflot, after which it would be rather quaint to suppress further thoughts of it and try somehow to slide past it and visit another building.

As for the where of lunch, Au Vieux Paris in the north-east corner of the square has extensive menus, fine views of both church and Panthéon, and a wonderful swan's head tap in the loo. Other restaurants just round the corner would also be very adequate, in fact the Rue de la Montagne Ste Geneviève is something of a restaurant street, the menus for the most part in the modest-to-medium price range.

Church of St Etienne du Mont

This church has recently emerged from an extensive restoration programme. In its newly cleaned state the golden stone of the nave looks quarry-fresh, lighting the stained-glass windows to brilliant effect. Even on a dull winter's day the transformation is extraordinary.

The church is an unusual mixture of styles, its eccentricity proclaimed by the tall clock and bell tower and by the Renaissance west façade which is out of period with the rest and actually stands out of line with the nave. The present building replaced an earlier church which was no longer big enough for the parish's needs. It was begun in 1492 in the Flamboyant Gothic style and completed in the early seventeenth century, hence the variation in styles. Queen Marguerite de Navarre, wife of Henri IV, laid the first stone of the west façade in 1610 and the church was consecrated in 1626. Its greatest architectural treasures are the stained-glass windows, the pulpit of 1650, the ornately carved organ case and the magnificent *jubé* (roodscreen), a masterpiece of the stone-cutter's art made by Antoine Beaucorps in 1521-5 and now the only surviving *jubé* in Paris. Near the pillars at the entrance to the Lady Chapel are the tombs of Pascal and Racine, which has led at least one writer to say that this building is the true Panthéon.

Most important of all is the shrine to Ste Geneviève, to the south of the chancel. A gilded casket encloses a fragment of the sarcophagus in which the saint was originally buried in the nearby Abbey Church. In the Revolution the mob exhumed her remains and burnt them on the Place de Grève (now the Place de l'Hôtel de Ville). The present shrine dates from 1853, and is a place of annual pilgrimage.

Police Museum

Close to the foot of the Rue de la Montagne Ste Geneviève, just before the horse butcher's, is a squat slab of a building which houses the Police Headquarters of the 5e *arrondissement* and, on the second floor, the fascinating Museum of the Prefecture of Police. The museum moved here in 1974 from the Quai des Orfèvres; it documents in fine and occasionally gruesome detail the history of the police in Paris, going back in time as far as 1610 with the gaol-book from the Conciergerie prison recording the incarceration of Ravaillac, murderer of Henri IV. The Revolutionary period is richly documented; this section includes the order to arrest Dr Guillotin himself on the *16 vendémiaire an IV* (8 October 1795).

Murder and the science of detection are the strongest themes. Here you can see a reproduction of Fieschi's twenty-five-barrelled '*machine*' which killed nineteen in an ambush in 1835; glass cases filled with murder weapons – pistols, knives, a pastrycook's rolling pin, a cobbler's hammer, and the grim tools used by Landru. This celebrated fiend, executed in 1922, recruited his victims through small ads suggesting marriage and killed eleven women, one with a pair of curling tongs. Also here is the pistol used in 1932 by the Russian, Gorguleff, to assassinate President Doumer.

Among the scientific items are Alphonse Berthillon's 1914 camera for taking improved mugshots, and the *tableau synoptique* developed to describe in detail the many variations of the human face, assembling a 'spoken portrait' (*portrait parlé*) for use by police officers on the lookout for wanted criminals. It is compelling stuff, and well worth a tour. Small brochures in English are available.

To the quayside

Place Maubert is a shabby square bisected by the Boulevard St

Germain, with butchers' shops along the south side and a small fruit and vegetable market three days a week. The square ('la Maube') was a gathering place for popular uprisings; today President Mitterrand lives in one of the narrow medieval streets running between the square and the river: Rue de Bièvre, barricaded round the clock to traffic and guarded by police, though you may walk through. From here each morning, the President commutes to the Elysée Palace.

We set off along another narrow street on the north side, the Rue Frédéric Sauton; its continuation, the Rue du Haut Pavé meets the Quai de Montebello opposite Notre-Dame Cathedral. This is a good eating quarter, though in summer it is tightly packed with tourists, which can have a limiting effect on menus. I recently overheard this conversation on one of the pretty terraces nearby:

French customer, waving menu: 'I can't see much here. Haven't you got anything more interesting?'

Waiter: 'It's for the tourists. It's all right for them.'

Along the quayside is the Square René Viviani, a charming garden with one of the oldest trees in Paris: a geriatric Robinia or acacia, now sadly bent and heavily propped, which dates from 1680.

The Church of St Julien le Pauvre is small, quiet, beautiful, and very different from other churches in Paris. Although one of the oldest, built between 1170 and 1250, it has been the Melchite (Greek Catholic) church since 1889 and is decorated in a Byzantine manner, including a distinctive screen across the choir surmounted by a cross. The church is a regular venue for concerts; see *Pariscope* for details.

On the other side of the Rue St Jacques, just a few steps from the porch of St Julien le Pauvre, is one of the most famous views in Paris: the gabled and buttressed east end of the Church of St Séverin. This is primarily a Gothic church, dating from the thirteenth century and partly rebuilt in 1450 after a fire. The porch is from the earlier period but belonged originally to the Church of St Pierre aux Bœufs on the Ile de la Cité. When that church was demolished in the early nineteenth century, the porch was dismantled and reassembled here in 1839.

The double ambulatory is a striking feature of the interior, especially the central pillar with its 'palm tree' decoration, though the modern stained-glass windows by Jean Bazaine (1970) are too splashy in pattern and colouring for the rest of the interior. Outside is a garden on the site of the old cemetery, shaded by a vast chestnut tree which on one side laps up to the gargoyles of the church and on the other side touches the roof of the old charnel-house galleries.

On leaving the church, take care not to continue along the Rue St Séverin, for this is now part of the loathsome and smelly Greasy Spoon quarter, a steaming inferno of greco-vietnamese eateries which has also wrecked the Rue de la Harpe and the Rue de la Huchette and which up to now we have been careful to avoid. If you agree with even some of this, flee south to the Boulevard St Germain and perhaps the Café Cluny, as suggested earlier, or some other bustling brasserie. To order one of those large and wicked ice creams, ask for the *menu des glaces*.

Walk 11

6ᵉ Luxembourg Gardens and Val de Grâce

Through the elegant streets of the Odéon to the Luxembourg Palace and Gardens. See the Médicis Fountain, the Pond and the Orangerie. Stroll through to the Observatory Fountain and visit the Church and Gardens of Val de Grâce. Walk along the Bd Montparnasse with its famous cafés.

Allow 4 hours.

Best times Not Sunday and holidays, when Church of Val de Grâce closed; also closes weekdays 12.00 to 14.00.

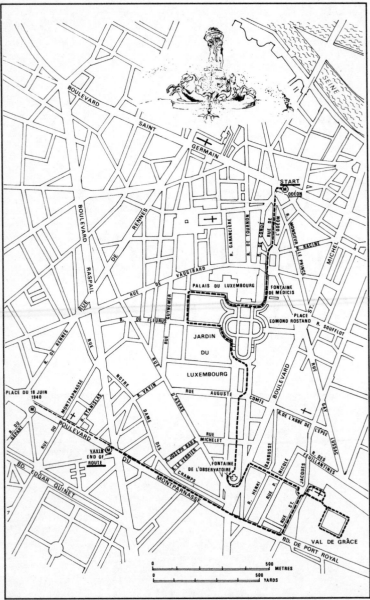

ROUTE

Begin at Ⓜ Odéon. Nearest buses 58, 63, 70, 86, 87, 96. Exit on Pl. Henri Mondor, turn left to Carrefour de l'Odéon and take middle street ahead up to Théâtre National de l'Odéon. Walk round square to right and enter Luxembourg Gardens ☞ .

Kiosk on left shows main places of interest. Just up on left is Médicis Fountain. Walk round by pond and garden front of Palace to Orangerie, where special exhibitions held. On W side of gardens are Théâtre des Marionnettes, tennis courts and nurseries.

Leave gardens on S side, cross Rue Auguste Comte to Jardin Cavalier de la Salle and continue through Jardin Marco Polo to Observatory Fountain. At left of garden exit, cross Av. de l'Observatoire and Bd St Michel and turn left, then 1st right into Rue du Val de Grâce ☞ ; church open 10.00 to 12.00, 14.00 to 17.00, closed Sunday and holidays. Cloisters and medical museum closed for long-term restoration work. Meanwhile, after visiting church, ask at guard room on right to see exterior of cloisters and gardens of military hospital. Access is controlled, and the soldier on duty may be cooperative or he may not.

Leave front courtyard, turn left into Rue St Jacques, walk to Bd de Port Royal and turn right. Keep straight on to Bd du Montparnasse and stroll past famous cafés, choosing the one to end your walk in: Closerie des Lilas (No.171), La Rotonde (No.105), Le Dôme (No.108), La Coupole (No.102), Le Sélect (No.99).

Walk ends here. Nearest Ⓜ Vavin, or continue to Place du 18 Juin 1940. *Walk 12* begins nearby with ride to top of Montparnasse Tower for excellent views.

Odéon

This is a calm restoring walk, in green surroundings for much of the way. We arrive on the traffic island by the Danton statue, then immediately quit the clamour of the boulevard for the sloping, dozing street of publishers and booksellers that leads to the Odéon Theatre, the pale golden temple of the Comédie Française.

Playwrights are remembered in the street names here – Racine, Corneille, Crébillon, Claudel – and at No.12 Rue de l'Odéon, in 1922, Sylvia Beach published the first edition of James Joyce's *Ulysses*, from her bookshop Shakespeare and Company.

Luxembourg Gardens

At the gates to the Jardin du Luxembourg a sign advertises the Marionnettes theatre; every afternoon at four. Another sign explains that your dog may only enter 'authorised' parts of the gardens via specified entrances – and this is not one of them. To reinforce the point, the accompanying picture looks like an ancient mosaic – a Roman *cave canem* – and portrays just the kind of half-wild creature, tongue crookedly out between open jaws, that should be banned for life from the Luxembourg Gardens.

Next to the Palace, workmen are building a temporary extension for office staff while restoration work goes on inside. Then, the authorities promise, the extension will disappear and the gardens be put back as they were.

The Palace was built in 1615 by Saloman de Brosse for Marie de Médicis, then the widow of Henri IV, and was modelled on the Pitti Palace in Florence. Since the Revolution it has served various official functions and today is the home of the Senate, the French Upper House. The interior is luxurious but unexciting, the victim of a nineteenth-century remake by Chalgrin. At one time a gallery contained the series by Rubens celebrating the life of Marie de Médicis which now has its own room in the Louvre (*Walk 5*). The Palace may be visited, by appointment, at times dictated by whether the Senate is in session. The determined may ring 42.34.20.60 for details.

We are off to sit by the Fontaine de Médicis, a wonderful murky place, damp and cool under a canopy of plane trees. Pigeons love it here. While we bag a garden seat by the long narrow pool, pigeons paddle and bathe in the tinkling water beneath Ottin's statue of Acis and Galatea. There lie the couple, so very much in love. But wait! What is that bearded hulk doing on the overhanging rock above their heads? It is the jealous giant Polyphemus, and in the myth he is about to crush them both. There is more than one version of what happened next, though it is generally agreed that Galatea, a sea nymph, escaped, and her shepherd lover did not.

Sit here and let your eyes focus on some distant point beyond the grassy bank to the south, between two lines of trees, a view dominated by leaves. Paying a visit to this frond-covered water mansion is like spending a quiet hour with a friend who owns an antique shop, and doesn't mind if you fold yourself into one of his slightly rotting velvet sofas and fall into a dream. It was George Moore who 'loitered in the Gardens to watch the birds and the sunlight, and they seemed to understand each other so well that I threw myself on a bench and began to wonder if there was anything better in the world worth doing than to sit in an alley of clipped limes smoking, thinking of Paris and of myself '. Even today, when cigarettes and introspection are so unfashionable, Moore's words pin down the mood of the place.

Cross when ready to the front of the Palace and look across the formal terraces around the octagonal pond, the Grand Bassin. As the sun climbs higher, people turn their garden chairs to face it and then bask like lizards for hours on end, hauling up shirts and skirts to admit the rays, eyes shut till tea-time.

As long ago as 1890 the editors of *Paris-Atlas* wondered if there were not too many statues in the Gardens. What with the Queens of France and other 'illustrious women' lining the terraces, and the tradition of commemorating artists and writers – Watteau, Delacroix, Murger, Sainte-Beuve, Leconte de Lisle and others – where would it end? My own feeling is that these twenty-three hectares (fifty-seven acres) are well able to cope with all this decorative masonry, and some pieces merit a special look, in particular Dalou's portrait of Delacroix. This stands to the west side of the Palace in front of the Petit Luxembourg, now the residence of the President of the Senate.

Along here is the charming Orangerie. If an art exhibition is being held there, do go in. The art may be banal, but the exhibition room is like no other. Beneath the high conservatory roof you walk on the same pea gravel used to cover the path outside; because, to keep the dust down, it is watered from time to time it imparts a sensation, for me unique among art museums, of marching through a vast tray of cat-litter. Not to be missed.

The western half of the gardens embraces much more than trees, statues and strollers. In its relaxed way it is the Left Bank's largest outdoor playground with tennis courts and donkey rides, a children's playground and the Théâtre des Marionnettes. Joggers jog and groups of martial artistes perform mysterious exercises. Further along are the nurseries, where apples and pears are trained on wire and stick frames and in season the ripening fruit are encased in white bags to protect them from the birds. How nice to see the English Peasgood's Nonsuch doing so well.

Following the Revolution the gardens were extended along the Avenue de l'Observatoire, opening out a splendid vista through the chestnut-lined gardens of the Cavalier de la Salle, who claimed the Mississippi Basin for France and named it Louisiana; and of Marco Polo, who needs no introduction. At the end is the marvellously expressive Observatory Fountain (1873), designed by Davioud and crowned by Carpeaux's sculpture: four athletic girls, the four 'quarters of the world', hold up a celestial sphere banded by the signs of the Zodiac; around the base are four pairs of prancing fish-tailed horses; four wide-mouthed fish spray water into the surrounding pool, and eight turtles stationed in the water fire fierce jets up and over the horses.

To the south rises the dome of the Observatory. Begun in 1667, the building stands on the line of the Paris Meridian, from which longitude was calculated on French maps until 1912. Today it houses the International Time Bureau which broadcasts the official time; in its basement a speaking clock is said to be accurate to one-millionth of a second.

Val de Grâce

If time is against being able to tour the Val de Grâce before it closes for lunch at midday, turn down the Rue St Jacques to the Boulevard Port Royal and take your pick of the local cafés and restaurants. At No. 342 Rue St Jacques is a tea-room with the beguiling name Thé des Brumes. On the corner, Le Marigny is an amiable café with *plats du jour*. I can report that the Salade du Chef is surprisingly accompanied by a plate of toasted cheese. 'Oui, oui, ça marche avec la salade,' says the waiter. And so it does.

The statue of Baron Larrey in the front courtyard announces the work of the Val de Grâce, which in 1793 became a military hospital. Larrey (1766–1842) was Inspector General of the Military Health Service and the bronze reliefs on the base of the statue record lively battle scenes from Beresina, the Pyramids, Sommo-Sierra and Austerlitz, with, for a change, the wounded in the foreground and the customary glorious waves of bayonets and bearskins relegated to a supporting role.

The magnificent church was endowed by Anne of Austria in

gratitude for being able to give birth to a child after twenty-three years of marriage. In 1638, after the arrival of the future Louis XIV, she commissioned François Mansart to plan the building which Lemercier completed in 1665. The influence of St Peter's, Rome, is clear to see in the fine ribbed dome, the grandeur of which is nowadays difficult to appreciate amid the huddle of surrounding streets; when built, the church and the adjoining abbey looked out over acres of nursery fields.

Inside the church look towards the six twisted marble columns of the *baldaquin* (canopy) surmounted by cherubs and censer-bearers, then by the ball and cross above the altar. In the dome is a famous fresco by Pierre Mignard, newly restored, with a tier-like arrangement of figures on clouds – two hundred altogether, and three times life-size, they include Anne of Austria offering a model of the church to God.

To the right of the church a large doorway leads to the cloisters, a museum of military medicine and the military hospital on the far side of the gardens. Both cloisters and museum are closed for restoration and unlikely to reopen until well into the 1990s. It may still be possible to have a look at the gardens and the exterior of the cloisters. At the guard room, a soldier in red medical epaulettes may say no, it's private, or he may remind you that the far building is a military hospital and ask you to be quiet. Patients sit on benches beside the flower beds and talk in low voices to their visitors, some of whom cannot conceal a parent's anxiety; in the centre of the garden is an impressive statue of stretcher-bearers in the First World War, a monument to the dead of the Service de Santé Militaire.

Cafés of Montparnasse

We now make for the boulevard. Beyond the iron-framed pavilion of Port Royal station is the statue by Rude of Marshal Ney. The figure of Napoleon's fiery marshal, Duc d'Elchingen and Prince de la Moskowa, the Bravest of the Brave, bristles with aggression. After Waterloo he was captured, brought back to Paris and executed by firing squad near this spot. His crime – renouncing the Bourbons after Napoleon's return from Elba – and his dignity minutes before his death, made him a hero among opponents of the Restoration.

The Boulevard du Montparnasse begins at the Closerie des Lilas. The awnings of this famous watering-hole stretch tentlike around the corner building and along to a congenial arbour where further awnings are concertina-ed back and forth on rails, if necessary maintaining the customers in perpetual shade.

This walk, having in any case no fixed destination, may well end here for some. From now on the idea is to find which of the celebrated artistic/literary cafés along this boulevard you favour, and go in. The Closerie des Lilas, frequented at various times by such writers as Baudelaire, Verlaine, Jarry, Apollinaire and Gide, and by such painters as Modigliani, Picasso and Derain, would feature high on many lists. We, however, must first defer to the grass-is-always-greener principle, for there are several others to be seen.

It is nonsense, of course, to maintain that one prefers, say, La Rotonde to other cafés simply because it was Hemingway's place or Henry Miller's. By and large, writers of that period, especially expatriate writers, went where they thought the action was, caring little which café was the current venue. Going to one place just made it easier to remember the next time, as a Jean Rhys character might have said. If nothing was happening at the Dôme, they went across to La Rotonde, and if that was no good they went somewhere else. Hemingway, it is true, wrote much of *The Sun Also Rises* at the Closerie des Lilas; but then again, there were few cafés to which he did not go.

Why did all these people congregate in Montparnasse? A slow migration began before the First World War, when artists began to drift down from Montmartre to the Left Bank. After the war, a fresh wave of expatriates arrived, Americans to the fore, and they fixed on Montparnasse as the place to be. It already had a well-developed café life, and the long opening hours suited the erratic pattern of their days and nights.

Of all these establishments, the Closerie has evolved more than the others. At one time a *guinguette* (open-air dance hall), then a café, it became an informal meeting-place for artists and writers who came down from St Germain des Prés and the Latin Quarter as well as along from Montparnasse. Today, although you can just pop into the bar for a drink – best of all in the evening – the Closerie des Lilas looks and feels more like a restaurant than a café.

On the broad pavements of the boulevard the *flâneur* (stroller) can make gentle uninterrupted headway beneath the plane trees, perhaps wondering what to eat if money were no object. Would it be lobster at La Langousterie (No.145), or would it be worth crossing the road to La Créole (No.122), a sumptuous white-painted restaurant serving de-luxe *Antillais* (Caribbean) food at tables decorated with hibiscus flowers?

At the crossing with Boulevard Raspail, the pagoda-ish gold and black of Le Dôme may beckon, or perhaps you prefer the red and gold of Brasserie La Rotonde across the road. Both have splendid terraces for drinks, and the restaurant part of the Dôme specialises in fish. Next is Le Sélect-American Bar (No.99), its awnings in Autobus-green and white. Perhaps most loved of all is the Coupole, by repute the most romantic of the Montparnasse cafés with the nuttiest, most variegated clientèle. Recent efforts to rejig the Coupole have now produced a version not all that far from how it was in its prime at the turn of the century.

So there they are, the cafés of the Boulevard du Montparnasse. Make your selection. Take no notice of me, by the way, I am off back to the Dôme, and a round-backed basket chair in the fourth row of the terrace. This is a built terrace, a semi-indoor affair, where only a single line of chairs and tables in the front row has any contact with the pavement. I suggested at the beginning that this was a calm restoring walk, and here under the pink light shades hung with six glass pendants apiece is no end of a good place to contemplate the drawing-on of evening.

Walk 12

6ᵉ Montparnasse to St Sulpice

A ride to the roof of the Montparnasse Tower – views up to 40 km (25 miles). Visit the Musée Hébert; window-shop in Rue St Placide and Rue du Cherche Midi, and walk through Au Bon Marché store. On to Pl. St Sulpice and its famous church.

Allow 4 hours.

Best times Shopping hours; not Sunday, or Tuesday when Musée Hébert closed, open other days 14.00 to 17.45.

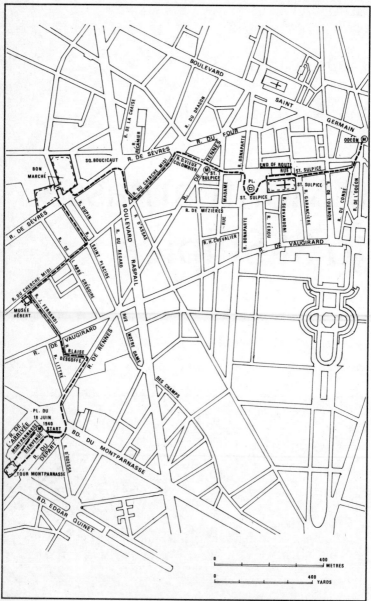

ROUTE

Begin at Ⓜ Montparnasse Bienvenüe. Nearest buses 28, 48, 58, 82, 89, 95, 96. Follow signs to 'Tour Montparnasse', up from platform and through shopping centre to ticket office at rear of Tower 👁; open 09.30 to 23.30 1 April to 30 September, 10.00 to 22.00 1 October to 31 March. *Admission.* Take express lift to 56th floor, walk round observation gallery, stairs up to unrestricted views on roof.

Back on ground floor, turn right from lift and walk through Centre Commercial to Pl. du 18 Juin 1940. Cross square to right and enter Rue de Rennes. Between Tati and FNAC, turn left into Rue Blaise Desgoffe, cross Rue de Vaugirard to Rue Jean Ferrandi. At next corner is Musée Hébert 👁. *Admission.*

Exit museum and turn right into Rue du Cherche Midi. Take 2nd left into Rue St Placide and walk down to Au Bon Marché, the Left Bank's department store. Walk through store, crossing bridge to main building, exit on Rue de Sèvres and turn left to Sq. Boucicaut.

Cross Bd Raspail by Hôtel Lutétia, turn right then left into Rue du Cherche Midi. At Carrefour de la Croix Rouge, take 1st right into Rue du Vieux Colombier and continue to Pl. St Sulpice. Walk past fountain to church 👁.

Walk ends here. Nearest Ⓜ St Sulpice. Nearest refreshments Café de la Mairie in square. Or walk along Rue St Sulpice on N side of church, then 3rd left down Rue de Condé to Odéon. See essay for further suggestions.

Montparnasse Tower

Parisians hated it even before it was built. By 1974, when it was finished, a great chunk of the old quarter by the station had been ripped out and replaced by a shopping centre, a new station and the tallest office block in Europe, 209m (686 ft) high, where seven thousand people go to work each day. The best thing about this charcoal pillar is the view from the top, after which we travel north and are not obliged to give it a second glance.

The journey up from the Métro to the piazza and beyond can be irritating. First an orange sign opposite C & A points to the '*Centre Commercial*', then others say '*Vers Tour*' (Towards Tower), then the supply peters out. After walking some distance through the shopping centre, following what signs are available, you find yourself out in the street. Is something funny going on? No, actually it's part of the plan. You then go up some steps to the ticket office at the rear of the tower.

The express lift registers the floors as 'X' until the 43rd, then the numbers tick off to the 56th. The observation gallery here offers views all round, with orientation maps to help, also a twenty-minute video of scenic Paris in a small comfortable cinema, refreshments at Bar le 56, and a souvenir shop. You can also come here in the evening for dinner in the *restaurant panoramique*.

For the best all-round views, walk up the stairs to the roof. To the east, near the foot of the tower, is Montparnasse Cemetery; in those long rows of tombs lie Jean-Paul Sartre, Baudelaire, Maupassant, Sainte-Beuve, Zadkine, Saint-Saëns, César Franck, André Citroën. Looking beyond the cemetery, the huge eastern suburb is Vincennes, with the woods of the Bois de Vincennes to the right of the towers. The tall building behind the Panthéon is the university tower at Jussieu, on the site of the old Halle aux Vins next to the Botanical Gardens. To the north are several new or newish landmarks. Behind the Arc de Triomphe and to the left is the Palais des Congrès; to the north-west beyond the Eiffel Tower are the blocks of La Défense; to the left of the Eiffel Tower is the Centre Beaugrenelle, another office district. Running between the last two, a stretch of the overground Métro seems like a toy train, the tiny blue carriages edging into and out of a series of identical sheds, the stations between Sèvres-Lecourbe and Passy. To the south-west is the mainline railway from the Gare Montparnasse, the traditional entry-point for Breton immigrants who more than a century ago began arriving by train and settling in this part of Paris.

Back on the ground we cross the square, leaving the bus station on our left. This is a lively district in the evening, with plenty of bistros and brasseries and an impressive concentration of cinemas. Two fish and seafood specialists are the Taverne de Maître Kanter and Chez Hansi, where you can pick and crack your way through the iced tiers of a *petit* or *grand mareyeur*, a sort of cakestand for crustaceans.

Along the Rue de Rennes shoppers mill outside the branches of Tati, an extraordinary pink and white bazaar crammed with bargain clothes, and FNAC, for cameras, videos and sound systems. We turn at this corner into the instant quiet of a residential street. As you walk through these nineteenth-century canyons, turn your mind to painting. What would have been the taste of the new middle-classes who occupied these apartments in a period roughly equivalent to the High Victorian age in Britain? Unadventurous, for the most part, would you not think, certainly preferring a safe academic diet of portraits and landscapes spiced perhaps with melancholy and exotic settings, to the strange new spotty painting being shown at the *Salon des Refusés*.

Musée Hébert

Now visit the Hôtel Montmorency, a restored eighteenth-century mansion devoted to the paintings and drawings of Ernest Hébert (1817–1908). Hébert never lived in this house, but the setting seems just right for this eminently Establishment artist, member of the Institut, professor at the Ecole des Beaux Arts, who spent much of his working life in Italy, studying at the Académie de France à Rome and later serving two spells there as its Director.

This is polite poetic realism, very much of its time. Hébert painted soulful portraits of bourgeois ladies, peasant girls and gypsies, Ophelias, sultanas, and once or twice ventured into harp-plucking temptresses – though never quite giving them the heavy sensuousness of a Rossetti or that other-wordly air which the Symbolists were to cultivate. Of his better-known contemporaries, he was perhaps closest to Théodore Chassériau, who died in 1856 at the age of thirty-seven, and with whose passing a line of artistic development also died until it was taken up by one of his pupils, Gustave Moreau. It is in a way odd that Hébert, a resolutely minor figure, should have a Paris museum to himself. Mysterious are the ways of Establishment art.

Au Bon Marché

The Rue du Cherche Midi is a jolly bric-à-brac street full of small antique shops, a few art galleries, a poster shop and several others selling novelties such as Les Contes de Thé, packed with all the clutter you would need for a full-blown tea party. The Rue St Placide deals mainly in cheap, i.e. last season's fashion, offering permanent sales (*soldes*) at boutiques with names like Boom-Sold, King Soldes and Lovely. For children's clothes, try the Mouton à Cinq Pattes. Elsewhere are those indispensable little places where residents of the quarter go for *le pressing, le brushing, le shampooing*, and, to adjust essential contours, *le lift modeling*.

At the end of Rue St Placide are the columns and eau-de-nil frontage of Au Bon Marché, the oldest department store in Paris, founded in 1852. '*La Grande Epicerie de Paris*,' says a banner, and there is indeed a gigantic food department on the ground floor. Go up to the first floor for antiques and restaurants, then across the bridge to the main building. On this side of the floor they sell men's and children's clothes. The tone is middle Oxford Street, the selection vast, e.g. racks fully thirty metres long devoted to socks. Women's dresses, suits and separates are on the other side. On the ground floor are perfumes, gifts and lingerie (for which Au Bon Marché is quietly renowned).

At the corner by the Square Boucicaut (Aristide Boucicaut was the founder of Au Bon Marché), we swerve past the curvy luxuriousness of the Hôtel Lutétia (renovations directed by Sonia Rykiel) and rejoin the Rue du Cherche Midi. This is a better-heeled part of the 6^c *arrondissement* and the shops grow a little smarter all the way – clothes, antiques, décor, and so on. At No.13 is Au Chat Dormant, which stocks everything cat-shaped you can imagine. More than just a novelty shop, it is a local notice board as well. Pussy-shaped cards next to the door announce cats available – '*cherche maître et jardin*', and lost and found – *'J'ai été trouvé Samedi 19, Rue de Sèvres. Je suis chat, adulte, blanc avec des taches gris souris. Je ne suis pas sauvage. Où êtes-vous? Tel. . . .'*

Church of St Sulpice

The liturgical bookshops of the Rue du Vieux Colombier prepare us in some way for the grandeurs of St Sulpice. Then the view of the north tower broadens into the striding double colonnade of the west façade and we arrive before one of the largest churches on the Left Bank, if not the most admired.

Between 1646 and 1777 six architects laboured to produce a pleasing and coherent design, but the span of styles between Le Vau and Chalgrin has proved to be against them. The result is monumental but ponderous. Although the west façade was not begun until 1732, Servandoni's original design was severely modified by his successors and the south tower was left unfinished. Writers have been unkind enough to compare the towers to a pair of clarinets and to 'municipal inkwells'.

Inside there is much to see. In the nave are two great conches presented to François I by the Republic of Venice, set on marble mounts carved by Pigalle with seaweed and octopus tentacles. In the north transept is an obelisk, precisely positioned in 1744 to receive a ray of sunshine which at certain times of the year passes through a small hole in a window of the south transept, then travels along a copper band laid in the floor to strike points on the obelisk at precisely midday.

The Lady Chapel behind the altar at the east end of the church is decorated with a *Virgin and Child* by Pigalle. There are paintings here by Van Loo, but so dark you can barely make them out. Lemoyne's fresco in the dome is oddly framed so that you observe it as through a gilded 'hole'. The finest pictorial decorations are those by Delacroix in the first chapel on the south side. On the right, in a scene of great swirling action is *Heliodorus Driven from the Temple*: avenging angels wheel violently through the air armed with *fasces* (bundles of sticks). On the facing wall is *Jacob Wrestling with the Angel*, and on the vaulting above, *St Michael Slays the Dragon*.

At the souvenir stand outside the sacristy they sell an interesting local magazine, *Nouvelles Rive Gauche*, subtitled 'The Christian monthly of the 5^c and 6^c *arrondissements*'. Interesting because it has features on local history and 'characters', like 'Jeanne the Pigeon Lady', for instance, that it would be hard to find elsewhere.

Out on the pretty square, fringed by a double row of chestnut trees, is a large though unimposing fountain by Visconti, dating from 1844. Beneath the recessed statues of four bishops, two octagonal tiers carry water down to the bottom pool, into which fading summer visitors cannot resist dipping their feet.

Our walk ends in the square. For local refreshment, the Café de la Mairie is popular and friendly. As for the next move, at least four immediate possibilities come to mind. To the north, walk along the Rue de Canette – now trading in cowboy boots at roughly three times the price in Texas – and keep going until you reach St Germain des

Prés (where *Walk 13* begins). Or, as suggested in the 'Route' above, walk through to Odéon (where *Walk 11* begins). Or, quickest of all, walk south to the Luxembourg Gardens and write postcards under the trees. Finally, six bus routes pass through the square, bound for all parts.

Walk 13

6ᵉ St Germain des Prés

The Church and cafés of St Germain des Prés, followed by a tour of local streets, visiting the Delacroix Museum and the market in Rue de Buci. Walk up to the river, see the Mint and the Institut, and return via the antique shops of Rue Bonaparte.

Allow 3 hours.

Best times Not Tuesday or some holidays, when Delacroix Museum closed. Coin Museum closed Saturday and Sunday, though shop selling coins, medals, etc, open Saturday 09.00 to 11.45.

ROUTE

Begin at Ⓜ St Germain des Prés. Nearest buses 39, 48, 63, 70, 86, 95. Emerge on S side in Pl. du Québec and see *Embâcle* sculpture and fountain. Cross main square and visit Church of St Germain des Prés 👁.

Exit and walk W along Bd St Germain, past the Café des Deux Magots, etc. Take 2nd right at gardens of Ukrainian Church into Rue des Saints Pères, go past Faculty of Medicine and turn right into Rue Jacob. Stroll along to Rue de Furstemberg (3rd right) and in corner on right of tiny square visit Delacroix Museum 👁; open 09.45 to 17.15, closed Tuesday and some holidays. *Admission.*

Walk to far end of Rue Furstemberg, turn left and keep straight on via Rues de l'Abbaye and de Bourbon le Château to Rue de Buci. Turn left into street market. At Carrefour Buci take 2nd left into Rue

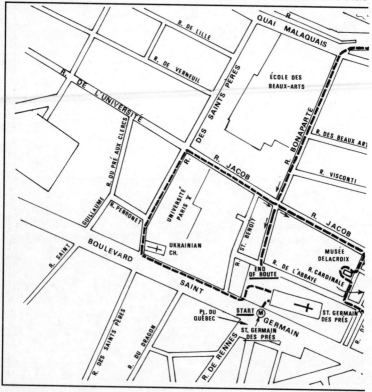

Dauphine, then 1st left into Rue de Nesle and 1st right into Rue de Nevers. Walk down to river, turn left and visit Mint (Hôtel des Monnaies) 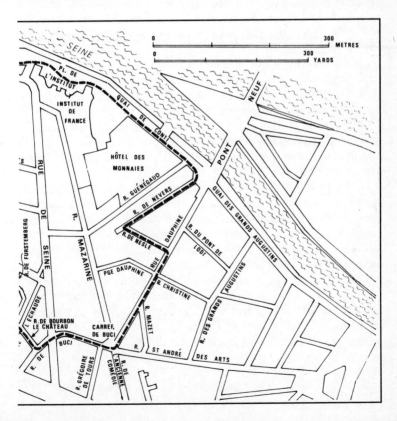. Coin Museum open 11.00 to 17.00, closed Saturday, Sunday; shop at 2 Rue Guénégaud open 09.00 to 17.45, closes 11.45 Saturday, closed Sunday and holidays.

Continue along Quai de Conti past Institut de France, to Rue Bonaparte. Turn left here or first visit Ecole des Beaux-Arts if special exhibition showing. Return along Rue Bonaparte to Pl. St Germain des Prés and garden of Sq. Laurent-Prache, containing Picasso bust of Apollinaire.

Walk ends here. Nearest refreshments all around. Nearest Ⓜ St Germain des Prés.

A strange eruption

To begin on a happy note, look out for the strange erupted-pavement sculpture in Place du Québec, on the south side of the boulevard. Called *Embâcle*, it is by Charles Daudelin and was presented by the City of Quebec in 1984. The shape is intriguing enough, with bronze 'paving slabs' bursting upwards, clearly in the wake of some mighty subterranean explosion, to reveal a fountain gurgling beneath. To add to the fun, someone has added this graffito on the pavement: *'Dis, t'as vu ce que notre nuit d'amour sous terre a érigé hier?'*

Church of St Germain des Prés

The church and the abbot's palace are all that remain of a powerful Benedictine abbey which by the eighteenth century covered several acres with gardens, stables, a considerable library, cloisters, refectory and outbuildings; the domain of the abbey extended as far west as the Champ de Mars. In the bookshop at the church you can buy postcards showing how the abbey buildings looked at the end of the sixteenth century – a moated medieval stronghold surrounded by crenellated walls and conical towers – and how the property grew outwards in the next two hundred years until it occupied the whole of a rectangle bounded by Rue Jacob, Rue de l'Echaudé, Rue Gozlin (a scrap of which remains on the far side of the boulevard) and Rue St Benoît. The abbey was then at the peak of its powers, virtually a town in its own right.

In the Revolution it was suppressed. More than three hundred priests and monks were massacred, the church became a saltpetre store, the twin towers at the transept were demolished and the library confiscated. Two years later an explosion destroyed more of the interior, and heavy restoration work from 1822 has further distorted the Romanesque character of the original.

Today the interior is a curious blend of Romanesque nave with seventeenth-century restorations, Gothic choir and polychrome decorations liberally applied in 1842-64, many of them by Hippolyte Flandrin, a pupil of Ingres. The bell tower is the oldest in Paris, though only the stonework is original (11C). Among the memorials in

---

* 'Hey, have you seen what our night of underground love erected yesterday?'

the side chapels are the black marble tombstone of the poet and critic, Nicolas Boileau, and the tombstone of the mathematician and philosopher Descartes, flanked by those of the Benedictine scholars Mabillon and Bernard de Montfaucon.

Around the sixth

In the square we face the terrace of the Café des Deux Magots, for generations a centre of intellectual gossip, ideas and argument. Its neighbour, the Café de Flore, has an equally rarefied reputation and in 1940 became a second home to Jean-Paul Sartre and Simone de Beauvoir, who moved up there from the Dôme in Montparnasse when it became at once popular with the enemy and difficult to get to at night without street lighting. Across the road is the Brasserie Lipp, famed for its two-party system: if you're *in*, you get a table on the ground floor, if not, you are sent upstairs. Alas it was closed for summer holidays last time I called; for devotees that meant twenty-five days without, to quote the lettering on the wall, '*Choucroute, Jambon d'York, Saucisses de Strasbourg, Harengs Marinés, Plat du Jour, Vins et Produits d'Alsace*'.

Among the well-heeled shops in this stretch of the boulevard, Façonnable (No.174) supplies English-style fashions for men and well-brushed juveniles. At Shu Uemura – L'Art de la Beauté (No.176) they have created a kind of 'studio of the face'; earnest seminars take place beyond windows decorated with millions of delicate brushes for powder and blusher, in pale blue, pink, green, yellow and champagne; also sticks, applicators, pluckers, and sharpeners for eyeliner pencils.

The Ukrainian poet, Taras Chevtchenko (1814–61), is remembered in the gardens of the Ukrainian Church, where we must turn into the Rue des Saints Pères and brave the yucky orange façade of the Faculty of Medicine (University of Paris V), arriving with still-wrinkled nose in the charming Rue Jacob.

This is where the English like to stay – at hotels such as, what else, the Angleterre, also Les Marronniers and the Isly. When No.56 Rue Jacob was the Hôtel d'York, it was the Paris residence of David Hartley, King George III's representative in France, who on 3 September 1783 signed peace documents with Benjamin Franklin recognising the independence of the United States.

Rue Jacob is a genteel street of antique shops and galleries; they sell scientific instruments at Alain Brieux (No.48) and Brocante Store (No.31); there are bookshops to nose through, and small restaurants with tables on the pavement, decked in pink cloths. It is light, bright and wholesome, a kind of inner-city Dordogne – or so I rationalise its attraction to the English holidaymaker.

House of Delacroix

The Rue de Furstemberg prolongs the air of gentility with luxurious wallpaper and fabric shops, then in a corner of the tiny Place de Furstemberg we visit the house where Eugène Delacroix lived. The Romantic painter arrived here in 1857, six years before his death, and had a studio built overlooking the small leafy garden. The museum is modest in size, consisting of four small rooms in the apartment – an antechamber, the bedroom where he died, a salon and a small library – and the *atelier*, reached down a flight of steps. Here he conceived several late works such as *The Abduction of Rebecca* and *Hamlet and Horatio in the Graveyard*, both now in the Louvre, and continued with his decorative works in the Church of St Sulpice (see *Walk 12*). It was this commission that initially brought Delacroix to the Place de Furstemberg: his health was failing and he could no longer make the daily journey from his old studio in Rue Notre-Dame de Lorette. Once installed in the new apartment, he was much happier. 'My hermit's retreat pleases me more and more,' he wrote to a cousin, 'and although I have been ill again since I last wrote to you, I have been able to enjoy my little garden . . .'

After his death the artist's furniture was dispersed, but luckily an inventory of his effects survived and thanks to patient detective work by the Society of Friends of Eugène Delacroix, founded in 1929, some pieces were recovered. These, together with paintings, drawings, lithographs, letters and photographs, form the basis of the collection now on view.

Rue de Buci

At the top of the road is the abbot's palace, built in 1589 and redesigned in 1699 by Cardinal de Furstemberg. We turn here and burrow through ancient alleyways, briefly glimpsing the towers of St Sulpice on the right, then arrive in the Rue de Buci, there to find the heartening sight of three immaculately starched waiters poised and ready for the lunchtime gallop at Le Muniche, most stylish of the local eateries. The market here is popular and lively, though much smaller than some effusive accounts of it might have led you to believe. It also gives off a rather quaint folksy atmosphere that I suppose you could get used to: in the street outside their premises, some shops keep an old-fashioned cart in the gutter to sell ice creams, pastries or whatever. La Charcuterie Alsacienne goes further than most: its immaculate pale wood shopfittings are precisely echoed in the twin carts in the street, and its female assistants wear a uniform of long maid's apron and white clogs – dangerously close, I would have said, to Noddyland.

The market continues to the right in the Rue de Seine, and the main part ends at the Carrefour de Buci. If you had stood here seven hundred years ago, you would have been outside the new city wall, built between 1180 and 1210 by order of King Philippe-Auguste. Paris in those days was still a tiny lozenge centred on the Ile de la Cité. On the Right Bank the new wall ran from the Louvre to the north of Les Halles market, crossed the river between the two as-yet-unjoined halves of the Ile St Louis, enclosed the Abbey of St Geneviève (near the Panthéon) and returned to the river at the Tour de Nesle, opposite the Louvre.

The Tour de Nesle, since demolished, is remembered as a place of high scandal. As the story goes, not one but two Queens of France – Marguerite, wife of Louis X, and Jeanne of Burgundy, wife of Philippe V – lured philosophers from the university to their rooms, then in the morning had them put in sacks and thrown in the river.

A few yards from the Carrefour de Buci stood one of the gates in the new wall, the 'Porte Bussi'. We walk on towards the river, and in the Rue de Nevers find the south end of the street barred by a house wall which stands on the line of the old Philippe-Auguste fortification. The roadway here is barely one cart's width, plus a token kerbstone on each side for pedestrians. Little has changed here in centuries: ancient walls bulge, sag and flake, and rotting drainpipes hint of gruesome plumbing arrangements within. At the top of the road an arch admits us to the Quai de Conti by the Pont Neuf.

Mint and Institut

The Mint (Hôtel des Monnaies) was commissioned by Louis XV, and designed by Jacques-Denis Antoine. The mansion and workshops were built in 1771–5. Although the main business of coin production is now handled at a new mint, set up in 1973 at Pessac near Bordeaux, they still keep the security tight at the old building. Twice a week only, from 14.15 to 15.00 on Monday and Wednesday, does the enthusiast have a chance to be escorted round the *ateliers* (workshops) in the second courtyard, and see medals and decorations being made.

Also in the mansion is a Coin Museum, reached by an imposing double staircase, which has displays of medals from the Renaissance to the present day and an exhibition illustrating the history of French currency from the age of the Merovingian Kings (476–751). The Mint's attractive shop is round the corner in Rue Guénégaud.

We walk along by the river to the Institut. One of the special pleasures of the Paris quayside is browsing among the stalls of the *bouquinistes*. Old maps and city guides, novels, histories, poetry, posters and postcards – the mix is nearly the same from one stall to the next, but never quite the same. Prices are negotiable.

The Tour de Nesle occupied part of the site of the present Institut, home since 1806 of the Académie Française, and four other academies too, and the Bibliothèque Mazarine. The august crescent and superb dome were originally built to fulfil a bequest by Cardinal Mazarin who wished to found a college for sixty students from France's new provinces – Alsace, Flanders, Piedmont and Roussillon. The Collège des Quatre Nations was built from 1662 to plans by Le Vau and opened in 1668. It closed in 1790, then the building was given to the Institut which moved itself across the river from the Louvre.

The Académie Française is the most famous of the Institut's five academies. Membership is restricted to forty, and these wise souls, their bodies cloaked in green robes on ceremonial occasions, are responsible for producing the *Dictionary of the French Language*. Always a most sensitive task, it is particularly so today when the prosperity of French is being undermined by the apparent unceasing advance of Anglo-American words and phrases in fields as diverse as international trade and rock music. The *Immortels*, as they are commonly and often unkindly known, are now hard-pressed to limit further damage to the language of their predecessors.

Just along the quay is the Ecole Nationale Supérieure des Beaux-Arts which from time to time holds special exhibitions. In 1987 its 'Matisse – Le Rythme et La Ligne' was splendidly done, and offered a rare opportunity to look through one of the three great bull's-eye windows at the top of the building which give a marvellous elevated view of the Palais du Louvre. The courtyard of the Ecole and some relics of the old Museum of French Monuments may be visited at 14 Rue Bonaparte, through the gate guarded by portrait busts of the artists Pierre Puget and Nicolas Poussin. Against the wall of the neighbouring Académie de Médecine is a coloured tile picture of *The Eternal Blessing the World*, alas part of it obliterated by time and the weather.

Square Laurent-Prache

The Rue Bonaparte lies on the eastern fringe of the Left Bank's antique district. Enjoy the opulent displays on the way back to Place St Germain des Prés, where this walk ends in the Square Laurent-Prache. Monsieur Prache was a Deputy of Paris at the turn of the century and the little garden that bears his name is leafy and calm. It is a fitting place to sit for a moment on a green-painted bench and collect one's thoughts. Here too, beside fragments of the Lady Chapel removed from the church in 1802, is Picasso's portrait bust of Guillaume Apollinaire, whose *Voyage à Paris* is likely to live for ever:

Ah! la charmante chose
Quitter un pays morose
Pour Paris
Paris joli . . .

When the need for liquid refreshment returns to the mind, risk your savings at the Deux Magots or the Flore, or live less dangerously at the superbrassy Drugstore Publicis across the road.

Walk 14

7ᵉ Quai d'Orsay to Rodin Museum

A Left Bank walk from the Esplanade des Invalides to the Musée d'Orsay, down past the mansions of St Germain to the house and gardens of the Hôtel Biron, now devoted to the remarkable sculptures of Auguste Rodin.
Allow   3–4 hours.
Best times   Not Monday when Musée d'Orsay closed or Tuesday when Musée Rodin closed.

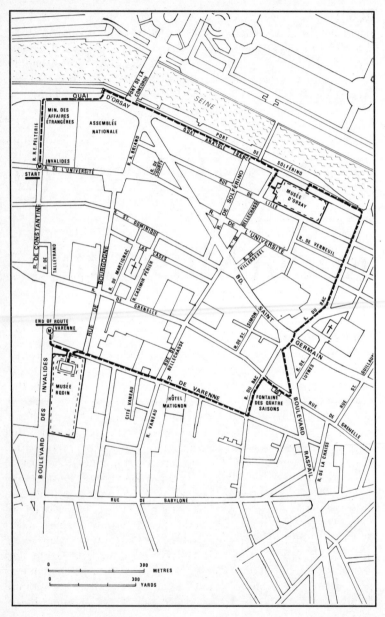

ROUTE

Begin at Ⓜ Invalides. Nearest buses 63, 69, 83. Walk up to river along Rue Robert Esnault-Pelterie, cross to quayside and turn right. Continue past Ministry of Foreign Affairs and National Assembly (French House of Commons), and keep straight on to Musée d'Orsay ☞ ; open 10.00 to 18.00, opens 09.00 Sunday, late night Thursday until 21.45, closed Monday. *Admission.*

At exit, continue along Quai Anatole France, then take 1st right into Rue du Bac. Walk down past antique shops to Bd St Germain, cross at junction and go down Bd Raspail to Rue de Grenelle (1st right). See Fountain of the Four Seasons, take 1st left into Rue du Bac and 1st right into Rue de Varenne.

Continue past Hôtel Matignon (Paris residence of the Prime Minister) to the Hôtel Biron and Musée Rodin ☞; open 10.00 to 18.00 1 April to 30 September, closes 17.00 1 October to 31 March, closed Tuesday. *Admission.*

Walk ends here. Nearest refreshments in garden, at Café du Musée around corner in Bd des Invalides, or at pretty Chinese garden at La Pagode, 57 *bis* Rue de Babylone. Nearest Ⓜ Varenne.

Ministerial Paris

From the front of the Air France terminal building we set off on a circumnavigation of the diplomatic and governmental quarter. At No. 1 Rue Robert Esnault-Pelterie, the massive entrance gate to the Ministry of Foreign Affairs glides electronically open to admit a chauffeured limousine and shuts before you could push so much as a bicycle in behind it. A plaque on the wall records an attack on the Ministry building, then in German hands, made by French FFI troops on 25 August 1944. The French tank 'Quimper' took part in the assault, but was hit and several soldiers 'found a glorious death'.

The quayside pavement is best for views to north and south, so cross the road leaving the gilded ornaments of Pont Alexandre III on your left. Around an angle in the road is the Assemblée Nationale. Five tricolor-bearing flagpoles front the building, properly known as the Palais Bourbon, which, after Napoleon's downfall, became the seat of the Chambre des Députés. In this year of the Bicentenary, 1989, there can be few cleaner buildings in Paris. The antique columns of Poyet's 1807 façade gleam with a special whiter-than-whiteness, and with the deeply carved pediment suggest a logo of unimpeachable quality, the political equivalent of a Rolls-Royce radiator.

Possibly you did not think to bring your swimming togs on this walk, but suddenly here we are at 'La Plage de Paris', the Piscine Deligny, moored opposite 25 Quai Anatole France and offering all-year swimming, solarium, use of mattresses, parasols, bar and *guingette* (open-air café), ping-pong, *babyfoot* (table football) and courses in *musculation*.

D'Orsay Museum

Next to the elegant rotunda of the Palais de la Légion d'Honneur is one of the most successful conversions in Paris. On 1 December 1986 President Mitterrand inaugurated the new art museum in the pavilion of the Gare d'Orsay. A current moan among art critics is that some of the newer museum buildings are more popular than the pictures and sculptures. Well, you could hardly come here and ignore the setting.

Enter through the vestibule at the west end, and pick up a free 'Brief Guide' in the language of your choice. This suggests a route through the museum and labels galleries from A to Z. The period covered is from 1850 to the early 1900s: 'A' is for Ingres and 'Ingrisme', Delacroix, Chassériau, History Painting and the Portrait 1850–1880; 'B' is for Daumier, Millet, Rousseau, Corot, Realism, Courbet – and so on. The labelling is well-intentioned but imperfect, and does not find room for the main concourse on the ground floor which offers a splendid collection of sculpture from 1850 to 1870, including Carpeaux's original plaster model for the statue on the Observatory Fountain (*Walk 11*) and others for the Pavillon de Flore at the Louvre (*Walk 5*). You are, however, unlikely to miss them; the chief problem may be in deciding whether to try to see everything in the museum or skip some parts. In general, the temporary exhibitions seem more missable than the permanent galleries.

It amounts to a feast of quite bewildering size, and everyone will have their favourites in a three-level tour that includes Puvis de Chavannes, Moreau, Manet, Monet, Renoir, Pissarro, Sisley, Degas, Van Gogh, Cézanne, Seurat, Signac, Toulouse-Lautrec,

Gauguin, Bonnard, Vuillard, and a large space devoted to Art Nouveau. Bunching among the spectators is inevitable from time to time, but with patience and cunning can be avoided. For instance, you arrive in 'D' to find fourteen thousand overseas visitors being introduced to Manet's *Déjeuner sur l'Herbe*. No worries. Pop into the room next door, spend half a minute looking at something else, go back and – they've disappeared! With luck you never have to see them again.

An unexpected highlight of the ground floor is 'E': a huge underfloor model of the Paris Opera House. On the upper level, the view across the river looking through the great clock is extraordinary; stay there a minute or so and the big hand creaks through a very large arc indeed. The clock has a twin further down the river façade in the Rooftop Café (Café des Hauteurs). Nearby, the side galleries of 'L' are half-dark, apparently because some of the Lautrecs are in a fragile state, especially the pastels. On the middle level is a preview, as it were, of the Musée Rodin we visit shortly: a plaster model of the Balzac statue ordered in 1891 by the Société des Gens de Lettres. This is a thinned-down Balzac, close to the state of the final version.

Also on the middle level is a restaurant, open for lunch 11.30 to 14.30, tea 16.00 to 17.30 and dinner on Thursday 19.00 to 21.30, closed Sunday.

Faubourg St Germain

Leave the museum through the large and elegantly panelled bookshop (*librairie*), and turn right along the Quai Anatole France. In the courtyard of the next building, the Caisse des Dépôts, is a large stripey sculpture by Dubuffet, *Le Réséda*, which would probably look better outside a bank in downtown Houston.

The Rue du Bac is part of the antiques district, though not every window is devoted to furniture. At Christian Constant (No. 26) are succulent pastries and jams, flowers at Jean Vassal (No. 28) and artistic rugs at Giannesini next door, tableware and ceramics at Laure Japy (No. 34). At Nos 42-46 the Galerie Maeght has a very watchable window decked out with Steinberg lithographs.

Just before reaching Bouchardon's Fountain of the Four Seasons in Rue de Grenelle, it may be difficult not to spend some minutes looking at or visiting the wonderful shop of Roland Barthélmy, who supplies cheeses to customers such as the Elysée Palace and Harrods. To explain the famous but enigmatic and rather gloomy fountain: it was made in 1739–45 and features the central figure of Paris flanked by others representing the Seine and the Marne; on either side of the fountain, figures in niches represent the Seasons and, beneath them, bas-reliefs show bunches of cherubs at work on seasonal tasks – cutting corn, lighting a fire, eating grapes and, I rather thought, slaughtering a sheep.

The Rue de Varenne has a misleadingly modest appearance. For a street of so many great classical mansions the frontages seem oddly low and unassertive; so much sky is visible as you look along to the far end. The reason, of course, is simple: what you first see is not the house but the walled entrance to a spacious courtyard, cobbled or gravelled and a little bit countrified. The mansions stand on the far side of each courtyard, set well back from the road.

This is one of the finest streets in the Faubourg St Germain, a district spurred into being after 1670 by Libéral Bruant's Hôtel des Invalides. Architects and their patrons built fine town-houses on a speculative basis, letting them to visiting aristocrats and diplomats. In this way the Faubourg, roughly the area between the Invalides and the Quai Malaquais, filled up and took its place as one of the most distinctive quarters in Paris: underpopulated, exclusive, now charmingly out of date with enormous hidden gardens that must be the envy of anyone who knows of their existence.

On the left at No.47 is the Hôtel de Boisgelin, now the Italian Embassy, then the police presence thickens around the residence of France's Prime Minister, the Hôtel Matignon (No.57), built in 1721. Other mansions of special note are the Hôtel de Gouffier de Thoix (No.56) and the Hôtel de Villeroy (Nos 78–80) which houses the Ministry of Agriculture.

Rodin Museum

You know you are arriving at the Hôtel Biron when the backs of the *Burghers of Calais* present themselves through glass panels let into the wall. Pay at the gate and walk up through the gardens. Two of Rodin's most famous sculptures, *The Thinker* (1880) and the standing figure of

Balzac (1891–7) are off to the right, the latter in its own private hedged-in space.

The mansion dates from 1728 and in the 1750s it came into the hands of Marshal Biron and took his name. In later years the gardens were hired out for dances and firework displays, and the house served as the residence of the papal legate, then of the Turkish ambassador. Later it was turned into a convent school, then a State residence for artists. The poet Rainer Maria Rilke came to live in the *hôtel*, recommended it to Rodin, and eventually the sculptor settled there until his death in 1917. The mansion became a national museum in 1919.

The museum is on two floors in the house with more works in the gardens. There is a simple black and white brochure which helps to highlight one's progress through the rooms beginning on the ground floor at Salle 1. Here are *The Man with the Broken Nose* (1864, marble 1875) and the wondrously delicate *Girl with Flowered Hat* (1865–70). In Salle 4 is the *Hand of God* or *The Creation* (1898), in Salle 5 *The Kiss* (1886) and the joined hands of *The Cathedral* (1908). On the first floor are numerous groups, portraits and studies for some of the artist's most famous works: *The Gate of Hell*, the *Burghers of Calais* and the *Balzac* monument for which Rodin produced many clothed and other remarkably pot-bellied nude models before he settled on the final, pared-down figure that was so unpopular when revealed to the public, but which is now thought one of the great masterpieces of modern sculpture.

After the profusion of works in the house the garden seems thinly populated. Wander by all means to the bottom but the few sculptures are poorly labelled, if at all, and helpful signs for visitors are limited to instructions like 'Don't Throw Anything in the Pond'. Returning towards the house there is more to see on the right-hand or eastern side: a gallery of heavy marble sculptures; *The Gate of Hell* (cast in 1937), more than 4 metres high; *Adam* and *Eve* and the *Burghers of Calais* (1895), which brings you back to the entrance.

Unless you have lots of energy left, a tour of the Invalides (*Walk 17*) is not recommended at this stage in the day. The Army Museum is so large and, I think, full of interest, it is worth more than a half-day visit and is best begun on fresh legs. This part of Paris, no doubt because of its opulence and self-sufficient way of life, is not well served by buses. It may be best to leave via Ⓜ Varenne, either south to Montparnasse or north to the Champs Elysées, etc.

Walk 15 ☂

7ᵉ Swiss Village to Palais de Chaillot

An unusual walk which includes a Métro ride along the elevated section near the Eiffel Tower. Includes the Swiss Village antique market and a choice of four museums and a cinema at the Palais de Chaillot.

Allow 4–5 hours to full day.

Best times Not Tuesday and holidays, when museums closed. Swiss Village closed Tuesday and Wednesday, shops open other days 11.00 to 19.00.

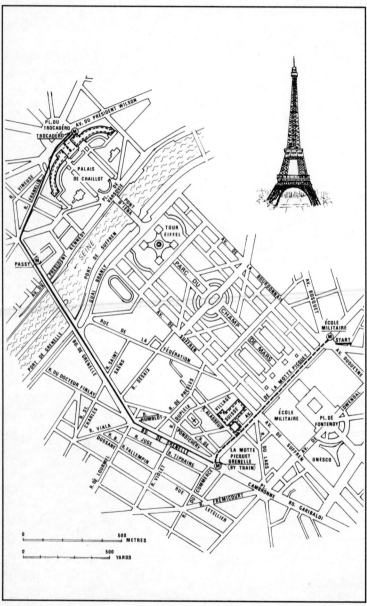

ROUTE

Begin at Ⓜ Ecole Militaire. Nearest buses 28, 49, 80, 82, 87, 92. Cross Av. Duquesne to front of Ecole Militaire. Continue on Av. de la Motte Picquet, crossing Av. de Suffren. Blocks of Swiss Village are on right and off street behind (Av. de Champaubert)👁 ; open as above.

Return to Av. de la Motte-Picquet, turn right and walk down to Ⓜ La Motte-Picquet Grenelle. Catch train to Trocadéro (*Direction Ch. de Gaulle-Etoile*). Take Palais de Chaillot exit and walk across terrace between pavilions for view at balcony. Return to front of Palace and choose museum(s) to visit.

In S wing, on right facing terrace, are:

Maritime Museum (Musée de la Marine); open 10.00 to 18.00, closed Tuesday and holidays. Ground floor.

Museum of Mankind (Musée de l'Homme); open 09.45 to 17.15, closed Tuesday and holidays. 1st and 2nd floors.

In N wing, on left facing terrace, are:

Henri Langlois Cinema Museum (Musée du Cinéma Henri Langlois); guided tours only, begin at entrance at 10.00, 11.00, 14.00, 15.00, 16.00, closed Tuesday. Ground floor (steps down to basement).

Museum of French Monuments (Musée des Monuments Français); open 09.45 to 12.30, 14.00 to 17.15, closed Tuesday and holidays. Ground and upper floors.

Some tactical points to note:

All museums charge admission. The Museum of French Monuments closes at lunchtime, so morning visits should begin not later than 11.45. The Cinema Museum may only be entered at the specific times listed above.

Walk ends at Palais de Chaillot. Nearest refreshments on far side of Place du Trocadéro. Best-value brasserie is Café Kléber, or try Carette, more a tea-room and popular with *BCBG* types (see *Walk 21*). Nearest Ⓜ Trocadéro.

🏹 **Wet Weather Route** Go straight to Ⓜ Trocadéro, preferably via elevated stretch of Métro described, and join walk there.

Champ de Mars

The walk across the front of the Ecole Militaire gives an excellent long view up the Champ de Mars to the Eiffel Tower and a glimpse of the Palais de Chaillot across the river. In about half an hour, unless waylaid by soft-tongued antique dealers, we shall be on the terrace at the Palais de Chaillot, seeing the view from the other side.

At various times the vast open rectangle of the Champ de Mars has been the setting for horse races, balloon flights, national celebrations and a series of Universal Exhibitions held in 1867, 1878, 1889, 1900 and 1937 (see also *Walk 16: Eiffel Tower and Champ de Mars*). The Eiffel Tower was built for the 1889 Exhibition and the Palais de Chaillot in 1937 for the last in the series, replacing another exhibition building, the Palais du Trocadéro built by Davioud and Bourdais for the *Exposition* of 1878.

The London *Daily Telegraph* sent a man to the 1878 Exhibition, George Augustus Sala. He was quite bemused by the scene, describing it as 'the enormous Bazaar at the foot of the Bridge of Jena'. Closer to, it was 'an immense parallelogram intersected at right angles by innumerable avenues between blocks of glass cases full of the most ingenious and the most highly finished specimens imaginable . . .' Everything he came across was so admirable – the steam-hammers, sewing machines, pictures, marble statues, carved bedsteads, toothpicks, embroidered petticoats, iron safes, anchors, crystal chandeliers, tapestries, colossal looking-glasses, pickle bottles, etc. In his exhaustion, he compared touring the exhibition ground to walking, on a very warm day, with a lady on his arm, from Oxford Circus to Mile End and Bow, looking in at every shop window on each side of the road. Would his readers be prepared to do the same? he demanded.

All that industry and commercial bedlam seems both resistible and very remote as we look at the present orderly lines of shrubs and pathways. The Eiffel Tower remains, of course, a masterpiece of Exhibition architecture, and we are grateful for that, but thank goodness they dismantled the rest.

The Champ de Mars was originally a parade ground, laid out in 1765 for drilling young officer-cadets at the Ecole Militaire. Now a staff college, the Ecole was designed by Jacques-Ange Gabriel in 1752 and completed in 1770. It is not open to the public, though a guided tour can be arranged if you apply in writing.

Swiss Village

The boutiques of the Swiss Village market are a sort of bland remake of Mr Sala's 1878 Exhibition. Row upon row of antique rugs, desks, vases, glass, fireguards, screens . . . If you have already been to the Louvre des Antiquaires (*Walk* 6) the pattern here will be familiar though the scale is much smaller. Some shops have branches in both locations, for example La Fille du Pirate at No. 38, selling marine paintings, model ships, sextants, globes and telescopes. The general emphasis is on furniture, attractively displayed by dealers happy to let you browse your way round. Views about Swiss Village prices vary between those who say expensive and others who say not bad compared with London.

There are several stretches of elevated Métro line in Paris, but the one between Pasteur and Passy has the most remarkable scenery. Just after the station at Dupleix the train angles towards the Eiffel Tower, and from our elevated position we catch a dramatic side-on view that demonstrates how surprisingly sturdy, almost squat, the base of the Tower really is – a long way from the 'tapering pylon' image that photographers like to give us. Then, as the train prepares to rattle across the Pont de Bir-Hakeim, the creamy wings of the Palais de Chaillot come briefly into the frame, then vanish behind buildings on Chaillot Hill. The carriages plunge into the tunnel after Passy station and we see no further daylight until we reach the pavement at the rear of the Palais de Chaillot.

Palais de Chaillot

This view of the Palais is very different from the side-on sighting we had in the train. From here, the Palace seems an altogether changed building, or rather, two buildings – a pair of long curving pavilion wings with an empty space in between; its evident lack of a central block seems most extraordinary. In fact, it *does* have a middle – a large hall beneath the terrace which houses the Chaillot National Theatre – but this is visible only from the river front. If you look at the Palace from that side, standing somewhere near the far end of the long pool, everything falls into place. The central block fits into the hillside and makes a harmonious bridge with the two pavilions.

We now walk across to the balcony for an exceptional view across the river to the Eiffel Tower and the Ecole Militaire beyond. The pool in the centre of the Palace gardens is lined by a battery of powerful fountains which are tremendously spectacular when floodlit, the high point of any Tour of the Illuminations (see page 269).

I mentioned earlier the Palais du Trocadéro that was installed for the 1878 Exhibition and demolished to make way for the present Palace. It is a pity that it has been so comprehensively wiped from the scene, for it was a hugely impressive circular building flanked by a pair of Moorish-looking towers and long wings like the present ones. It was designed to house and promote interest in Muslim art, and old photographs reveal a sumptuous creation, not exactly St Sophia, Istanbul with two of its Turkish minarets, but something of the sort. The name Trocadéro comes from a Spanish fort near Cadiz which French troops captured in 1823, quelling a rebellion which had deposed the Spanish monarchy. Four years later the event was restaged at a military tournament on Chaillot Hill, then in 1858 the present square was laid out and called the Place du Trocadéro.

Maritime Museum

If you have been to the Army Museum at the Invalides (*Walk 17*) and visited the Musée des Plans-Reliefs with its models of fortified towns ordered by Louis XIV's war minister, you will appreciate the link between that collection and the ship models here in the Maritime Museum. In 1678 Colbert, Secretary of State for the Navy, commissioned models to be made of the French fleet, to be used for instructional purposes at the naval ports. Some of the finest models were sent to the French court, and meanwhile, on the side, several private collections came into being in the next few years, one of which was presented to Louis XV and installed in the Louvre.

There the collection remained for many years, more than a hundred magnificently fashioned model ships waiting for some special event or benefactor to come along and found a proper museum. The event that finally prompted action was the Battle of Navarino in 1827. Just as the victory at Fort Trocadéro revitalised the spirits of the French Army and helped to efface the memory of Waterloo, so the French Navy restored its reputation when Admiral de Rigny's ships-of-the-line helped the Allies to defeat the Egyptian-Turkish fleet at Navarino.

In recognition of the Navy's success, Charles X signed an order to set up a maritime museum in the Louvre. It opened there in 1830 and was transferred to the Palais de Chaillot after the Second World War. In 1972 it became a national establishment, supervised by the Ministry of Defence.

Today there is much more to the museum than those early models. The coverage extends to all kinds of ship types, to minutely detailed dioramas of dockyards and equipment, to marine paintings, the history of merchant shipping and underwater exploration. It is also very popular with squeaky French school parties. 'Ne courez pas, s'il vous plaît,' says the voice on the loudspeaker, with only the faintest hint of having said it before, many times.

One of the most fascinating exhibits shows how Pasha Mehemet Ali's gift to France made the journey from Luxor, on the Upper Nile, to the middle of the Place de la Concorde. In 1831 the great obelisk, more than 3,300 years old, was taken down from its site in the desert and dragged to the Nile. The bow of a special barge was cut away and the 23 m (75 ft) obelisk was slipped into its hold, then the barge was resealed and towed to Rouen by the paddlesteamer *Sphinx*. On 25 October 1836 teams of sailors and gunners hauled the obelisk into place (see *Walk 19*).

The range of the museum is impressively broad: Joseph Vernet's series of paintings, *The Ports of France*; Ferdinand de Lesseps and the Suez Canal; the expeditions of Jean-Baptiste Charcot, polar explorer; developments in diving and underwater exploration. At the end of the room, climb a metal ladder to the bridge of the *Ailette*, an Iceland cod-fishing protection vessel of the Thirties. On the way back to the entrance, see the workshop where the museum's own craftsmen restore the model ships.

Museum of Mankind

This museum covers three disciplines. *Anthropology* deals with fossil man (palaeoanthropology) and mankind today. *Ethnology* is the study of human civilisations today, and *Prehistory* studies how men lived in the past. Once that is clear, you rise up a steep stairway which feels like the entrance to an Aztec temple.

One of the first exhibits shows mummified heads and bodies

immortalised for the after-life. The sight of them has several French students in fits. 'Tu le connais?' they ask each other, pointing at a particularly gruesome severed head.

This part of the 1st floor has a series of showcases on early man and the scientific study and measurement of people. Walk on through high-ceilinged dingy galleries dealing with African art, head-dresses, model villages, statues of gods. It was in this section of the old Ethnographical Collection, then housed in the Palais du Trocadéro, that Picasso pursued his interest in African sculpture in 1907. What he saw here may have led him – though he denied it – to add the distorted 'mask heads' to the two right-hand figures in his revolutionary *Demoiselles d'Avignon*.

The next cases illustrate European folk customs, no less exotic. See the Kukeri from Bulgaria and the Slovenian carnival mask which turns its wearer into an eerie birdman in a fur coat, by his side a wooden plough. Rooms on the 2nd floor are devoted to peoples of the Arctic, Asia, Oceania and America. There are rooms of musical instruments – an excellent collection from Java; a model of a Hopi village; and dazzling costumes in the Far Eastern rooms. Coverage of several themes was patchy, however, on my last visit and made worse by the fact that a large area of the 2nd floor was closed off while a big 'Eskimo' exhibition was being prepared.

The Musée de l'Homme is popular with the French who take their anthropology more seriously than some nations. I think it would have even greater appeal if it were given a considerable facelift. In some galleries the bright Thirties quality of the Palais de Chaillot has faded to a kind of East European austerity.

Museum of French Monuments

Before 1937 this unusual collection was called the Museum of Comparative Sculpture, which explains its function rather better than the present vague title. It opened in the Palais du Trocadéro in 1882, three years after the death of the architect Viollet-le-Duc who had been pressing for more than a quarter of a century for just such a museum to be founded.

It is rare to find a museum that contains not a single original work. Its purpose is almost entirely educational, and its tools are same-size casts of sculptures, models of buildings and copies of mural paintings. In the space of three floors it demonstrates the progress of French monumental art from region to region and from period to period: from Chartres to Paris to Amiens, for instance, and from the thirteenth to the fourteenth century, continuing as far as the nineteenth. Each cast is carefully coloured to reproduce in plaster the tone, marble, wood or bronze of the original.

To see how it works, walk past the bookstall (*librairie*) to the *Accueil* and collect a plan of the exhibits. In Room 2 you can pick up an audio commentary on the South Portal of the Abbey of Moissac, explaining some forty elements of the richly carved doorway and tympanum.

In all, the sculpture galleries include one room of pre-Romanesque casts, five Romanesque rooms, fifteen Gothic and eight covering the Renaissance to the nineteenth century. The section on mural painting was begun in 1937 and is much smaller, but has examples of Romanesque painting and Gothic works from the thirteenth century to the beginning of the Renaissance. As you go round, you come across lots of students drawing the casts and models; this is a marvellous place to learn about the history and mechanics of architecture.

The Museum of French Monuments is strangely fascinating and well worth a tour. It extends the full length of the north wing on two floors, with more on the 3rd floor, so leave plenty of time to cover the ground. The museum produces an excellent educational catalogue (*Dossier pour les Enseignants*), which includes detailed commentaries on six of the casts, including the Abbey of Moissac.

Henri Langlois Cinema Museum

This is the biggest cinema museum in the world, with more than five thousand exhibits. The curators are very security-minded, and visitors must wait outside the entrance door which is unlocked to admit the next tour and locked again behind them.

Each tour is guided, and with a passion rare among museum guides. Much of the first part is devoted to the development of photography through Niepce and Daguerre, as exposure times were reduced from ten to twelve hours to thirty minutes, and innovators sought ways of filming movement, e.g. Muybridge with his line of cameras and Marey with his 'bird gun' for taking rapid-fire shots of birds in flight; prints were then mounted close together to show how a man or a horse runs, or a bird flies. We see Reynaud's Optical Theatre of 1888, praxinoscopes and then the early cinematograph of the Lumière brothers and the fantastic illusions captured on film by Georges Méliès. We see stills from early films of every genre, with posters, set designs and costumes.

The earliest posters were hand-drawn, seeking to attract the public with an arresting image coupled to the name of the film and the company responsible. Actors had no status then; cinema was impersonal. The public came to see the train hurtle down the track and cared nothing for who drove the engine or was tied to the rails. Only later, when cinema became more respectable and, in France, actors from the Comédie Française consented to take part, did anything resembling a 'star' system begin to take shape. Then in the USA people like Sennett, Charlie Chaplin and Fatty Arbuckle began making their name, and film-makers hurried west to Los Angeles, mainly to avoid paying royalties to Thomas Edison on his patented equipment.

Pinned on the wall is a swimming costume worn by Esther Williams. In its flattened form it looks the opposite of romantic, but there it is. Elsewhere the dress that Martine Carol wore in *Lola Montez* still looks glamorous, but today's woman could not get into it, we hear. The new diet, and more physical exercise, develops '*une musculation*'; people today are larger anyway, and tiny waists like Carol's – barely a double handspan – are now a feature of yesteryear. (The presentation, you will gather, is very French in tone.)

The exhibits move more quickly through the Talkies era, demonstrating film styles through *Citizen Kane*, *Ossessione* (Italian Neo-Realism), and Fellini's designs for *La Strada*. James Bond is there, and *Rebel Without a Cause*; Chabrol's *Le Boucher*, Truffaut's *Tirez sur le Pianiste* and Hitchcock's *Psycho*. A prized object is the head of Norman Bates's mother. It arrived one day at the museum in a parcel, with no explanation. Henri Langlois, the museum's founder, opened it, blanched and quickly put it on one side. Three days later he received a letter from Alfred Hitchcock. 'I hope you liked my present,' wrote the master of suspense.

Our walk ends at the Palais de Chaillot. They have a cinema here, too, the Cinémathèque, at the far end of the north block. Each day it shows three or four different films, usually classics of one kind or another, and is one of the great meeting-places of film buffs. Check with *Pariscope* to see what's on.

For refreshments, the brasseries and restaurants on the other side of the Place du Trocadéro are all very competent. You will pay a good deal less at the Café Kléber, however. Next door is Carette, where the *Bon Chic, Bon Genre* meet – sort of French Sloane Rangers, noted for wonderful all-year tans, beautifully coiffed hair and perfect teeth (see *Walk 21*). You can either go into Carette and watch them there, or spy on them from the terrace at the Kléber.

Walk 16

7ᵉ Eiffel Tower and Champ de Mars

Rise slowly through the girders of Gustave Eiffel's enormous iron candlestick and see Paris displayed beneath. Stroll through the Champ de Mars, visit the Rue Cler market (one of the best in the city) and see a traditional puppet show at the Théâtre des Marionnettes.

Allow 5–6 hours (including 2 hours at Eiffel Tower).

Best times Morning recommended at Eiffel Tower, continuing to puppet show in afternoon. Tower open daily 10.00 to 23.00, 24.00 in July, August. Puppet shows are on Wednesday, Saturday and Sunday, 15.15 and 16.15, and every day in school holidays. Rue Cler market open Tuesday to Saturday.

ROUTE

Begin at Ⓜ Bir-Hakeim. Nearest buses 42, 82. Walk along Quai Branly to Eiffel Tower 👁 . *Admission.* Go up Tower as high as you care to. Stairs and lifts to 1st and 2nd floors; lift to 3rd floor; many amenities, including restaurants, post office, and free audio-visual show on history of Tower at Cinémax (1st floor).

Back on ground, walk SE towards Ecole Militaire across gardens of Champ de Mars. At central pond and fountain (Place Jacques Rueff) turn left along Av. Joseph Bouvard to Place du Général Gouraud. Cross two streets on the right of the square and enter Rue St Dominique, an elegant street with good food shops. Pass the picturesque square by the Mars Fountain (Fontaine de Mars), continue across Av. Bosquet and turn 1st right into Rue Cler.

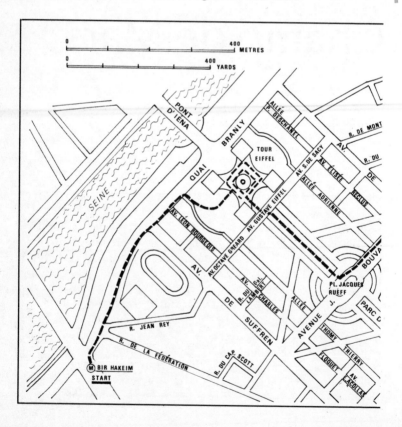

Diversion Continue along Rue St Dominique, take 3rd left into Rue Surcouf and at No.12 visit the Musée SEITA (SEITA Museum) which records the history of tobacco and its uses. Many exhibits of pipes, pouches, snuff boxes, cigarette and cigar-smoking equipment. Open 11.00 to 18.00, closed Sunday and holidays. Return to Rue Cler.

The market begins at the intersection with Rue de Grenelle. Wander among the shops and stalls with their mountain ranges of fruit and vegetables, flowers, pastries and chocolates. At end of Rue Cler, turn right by Post Office into Av. de la Motte-Picquet. For lunch, try one of the cafés/brasseries on Place de l'Ecole Militaire.

Cross the square and walk up through the Champ de Mars to the

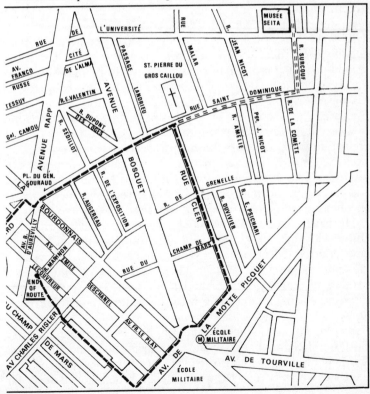

Théâtre des Marionnettes, situated in a woodland pavilion on the right, near the end of Av. Barbey-d'Aurevilly. Someone rings a hand-bell several minutes before each show to tempt and guide visitors to the theatre. *Admission*. Performances last about 40 minutes. Check *Pariscope* for what's on.

Walk ends here. Nearest Ⓜ and refreshments Ecole Militaire.

Eiffel Tower

On the elevated platforms at Bir-Hakeim Métro station, helpful signs point the way to the 'Tour Eiffel'. You step down to street level and so begins one of the easiest direction-finding exercises in the history of human exploration, for as you turn along the Quai Branly the great structure soars in front of your eyes, as big as the descending spaceship in *Close Encounters*.

It is a shock, almost, to see it suddenly so close, so tall and tapering, engulfing the mind yet curving away from the eye as far as the second-floor platform, where it straightens for the ultimate surge into the sky.

Unlike, say, the Washington Monument or the Empire State Building, where you speed upwards in an enclosed lift shaft and the viewing only begins when you are at, or almost at, the top, the ascent of the Eiffel Tower is one of the most magical parts of the experience. You rise through the open structure of the building in a series of windowed lifts, struck by the simple beauty of the interlaced girders and perhaps by the thought that, a hundred years ago, men perched and dangled out there, just beyond your nose, bolting it together.

The Eiffel Tower was a revolutionary concept, built to furnish the Universal Exhibition in 1889 with a crowning symbol of France's new-found confidence after the years of deflation which followed the Prussian conquest of 1870–71. There had been other Universal Exhibitions in Paris, in 1867 and 1878, but that of 1889 had the extra ingredient of coinciding with the centenary of the French Revolution.

A competition was held to build a 'tower of a thousand feet'. Gustave Eiffel was a bridge-builder of renown and France's foremost exponent of large-scale construction in metal, and it was his engineer associates who produced the winning plan. When built, it would far outstrip the Washington Monument, completed in 1885 and at 169 m (555 ft) the tallest building in the world at that time.

The Tower is a paradise for statisticians: 300.5 m (986 ft) high at its inauguration; 320.7 m (1,053 ft) high today, with the television transmitter added in 1957; 7,000 tons of iron used in the structure, 12,000 pieces of metal and 2.5 million rivets; the four pillars at the base incline to the centre at 54° . . . It took just over two years to build (January 1887 to May 1889) and the safety record was immaculate. No lives were lost on the construction of the Tower, even though by November 1888, as they edged towards the third platform, the 'sky carpenters' were working at greater heights than any man before them.

It was an extraordinary victory against the wind. In his design Eiffel boldly reduced the supporting elements of the Tower's openwork structure so that the wind would have as little as possible to tear at. Odd though it may seem, the strength of the building lies as much in its voids as in its iron; even in the stormiest weather it is said to sway no more than 15 cm (4½ in).

The question now is, how far up it will you go? There are three positive options: the first floor, which is at 57 m (187 ft); the 2nd floor, at 115 m (377 ft), and the 3rd floor, at 274 m (899 ft). I strongly recommend going to the top if you can bear to, then visiting the 2nd and 1st floors on the way down. If you are lucky with the weather, the views from the 3rd floor extend for more than 64 km (40 miles). The best light is usually one hour before sunset; however, the Tower is far more crowded in the afternoon and I feel that morning is the best time to go, preferably your first morning in Paris and preferably soon after the Tower opens at 10.00.

Among the brave who have bought their tickets to the top and entered the upper storey of the two-decker lift, not a few feel a lurch of panic when the doors close and they stand waiting to leave on their journey to the clouds, perhaps holding their breath. Nothing happens for quite a while, or is it the briefest of pauses that just seems like ten minutes? The face of the lift attendant gives nothing away. Then without warning the lift begins a rapid upward glide, the ground of the Champ de Mars falls away in a rush, then the chestnut trees and the roofs of the houses on the Avenue Elisée-Reclus. We are aloft, immediate fears forgotten.

The lift stops at the 1st floor to discharge and reload passengers in the lower storey; the journey resumes to the 2nd floor, a steeper, less sideways ascent, then it's time to change for '*Le Sommet*'. Naughty-looking bellhops in Harrods-green uniforms scuttle about in bursts of activity, ushering the queue down a passageway and urging the next sausage-slice of humanity into the 3rd-floor lift when at last it comes. Queueing is almost unavoidable up here, the press of voyagers always exceeding the thinned-out lift capacity on the final leg.

The ascent to the top is slower, majestically vertical and provides the first unimpeded, all-round views over the city. This part of the journey is, mercifully, a non-stop ride, a great improvement on the state of affairs when I made my first journey to the top in 1950 and passengers had to transfer somewhere in mid-air to another lift for the final trip to the 3rd-floor platform. The gap over which we stepped was no more than three inches wide, but in that moment all Paris gaped beneath and it seemed entirely possible that unknown forces might suddenly suck one's body through the fissure, like a passenger in the punctured cabin of an aircraft.

Arriving at the 3rd-floor platform, you spill out on to a kind of nautical structure like the bridge of a warship. The platform is an enclosed pillbox with lookout windows around the circumference; beneath the windows, at waist level, is a photographic panorama of what, weather permitting, you should be able to see by looking directly ahead. The panorama extends in six-foot stages around the platform and bears numbered points of reference: the Arc de Triomphe is No. 1, the Palais Galliéra No. 2, the Palais d'Art Moderne No. 3, and so on.

Set above the lookout windows is an intriguing survey of more distant points which line up with the buildings and monuments of Paris. While looking, say, towards Sacré-Cœur you can refer to this upper tier and find, beside a coloured flag of the USSR, the words 'MINSK Bielorussie 1,835 km' (1,140 miles). This has the makings of a great game, a form of heroic geography. Thanks to the plotters of the Institut Géographique National, who worked out the orientations and distances, we come upon an undreamt-of link between the Pompidou Centre and 'RANGOON Birmanie 8,899 km' (5,529 miles). Here is another. Stand facing the charcoal-grey lump of the Montparnasse Tower and the same sight-line will bring you after a journey of 7,140 km (4,446 miles) to the shimmering white towers of Dar es Salaam, Tanzania.

Out, now, to the open air and the Point de Vue platform, reached by stairs (non-vertiginous). One of the most compelling views is to the north-west. Behind the quaint 1937 pavilions of the Palais de Chaillot, built for the Universal Exhibition of that year, the skyline is dominated by the towers of La Défense, the suburb of the future, some say. If you have never seen it before, you could not escape seeing it from the top of the Eiffel Tower. Some Parisians will speak up for it, justifying the need for a massive new development on the outskirts of the capital, but I suspect it makes many more people miserable than happy. To me it is a glowering Darth Vaderland of black and showily tinted office blocks, biting great chunks out of the sky. Behind the offices are clumps of tubular and other high-rise apartment blocks, the whole forming a hideous environment for 50,000 people (see also end of *Walk 19*).

Altogether more agreeable is the downward view to the Seine beneath, where a *bateau mouche* slides under the Pont d'Iéna. Or look downstream to the long thin island called the Allée des Cygnes (Swans' Walk), at the far end of which stands a small-scale version of Bartholdi's Statue of Liberty, presented to the city in 1889 by the expatriate 'Paris Colony' living in the United States.

Up above, and fortunately difficult to see, a space-age mass of wires and antennae serving the television transmitter stick mainly upwards. One should not complain; without scientific equipment, in particular radio, the Tower might not be here today. At the time of its conception it was certainly not seen as anything other than a temporary structure. In July 1886 Eiffel signed a contract with the State and the City of Paris. Edouard Lockroy, the Minister of Commerce and Industry, signed for the State and the City was represented by its Prefect of Police, a certain Monsieur Poubelle whose name has entered the language after the dustbins which he introduced. By this agreement, Eiffel obtained a grant of 1.5 million francs and the right to build and then run the Tower as profitably as he could for 20 years, after which it would become the property of the State.

In 1909 the Palais des Machines, last vestige of the 1889 Exhibition apart from the Tower, was demolished and it seemed that Eiffel's creation must go the same way. It was saved because its use for radio telegraphy had already alerted civil and military strategists to its potential. Today it serves as a meteorological and radio station, and as a centre for the International Time Service, and its new crown of TV transmission equipment has increased the height of the Tower by 20.2 m (67 ft).

It hardly needs saying that the Eiffel Tower is *the* symbol by which both France and Paris are known throughout the world. Each year its fame and popularity are reinforced by four million visitors and a constant outpouring of images relayed by press, advertising, television and the souvenir industry. One of the latter's major trading posts is the 2nd floor of the Tower.

If the 3rd floor is for enchantment, a communion of town and cloud, the 2nd floor is a shrine of hard commerce dedicated to the sale of anything tower-shaped or tower-printable. To list the variety of objects on sale would not be interesting, and I limit my observations to saying that I could not find a decent guidebook about the Tower, and that the large model Towers, 25 cm (10 in) high or so with thermometer mounted on exterior, were not wholly repulsive but, along the line of them that I saw, the temperatures fluctuated between 20° and 24°C (in Fahrenheit a difference of more than 7°).

Across the way, at Photo Express, there are facilities for inserting your head through a painted scene; seconds later, polaroided, you emerge from the shop with a view of yourself floating flapperishly above Paris, or clutching the Tower from the outside, or, having fallen off it, lying in the grass with your legs in the air.

Enough of fantasy, let's look down at the real world. On the sunlit football pitch by the Quai Branly, where we walked from the Métro station, a footballer two millimetres tall prepares to take a penalty. No sound comes up to us as he strikes the ball and the goalkeeper, of similar height and also perfectly formed, leaps high to his left and saves.

The 1st floor seems vast after the upper ones. A brasserie and a fast-food restaurant, a post office where you can buy special covers, and the Salle Gustave Eiffel, a plush-looking pavilion which from the outside is mysteriously unforthcoming about its purpose. Is it a restaurant or what? I push inside and come upon a squad of about twenty North African workers doing nothing very much at the far end of a vast spread of mauve carpet.

'What is it for, this room?' I ask.

One of them comes over. He wears a blue overall coat and looks at me with a sad expression. '*C'est une salle de réunions,*' he says.

'Ah,' I nod, enlightened. Functions are its function; conferences, parties, receptions, that kind of thing.

He looks at me again, perhaps more sadly. '*C'est pas à toi,*' he says, and from this and a faint sideways lean of his body I understand that he wishes to see me off the premises. There is little point in objecting. For an outsider to be welcome at the Salle Gustave Eiffel he needs several things that I did not have: a suit and tie, for instance; shiny black shoes and perhaps a white carnation; and, of course, a function.

More rewarding is Cinémax. In its small comfortable cinema, alone save for a French family in the fourth row who, to my surprise, had brought their dog with them, I watched a film about the history of the Tower. The doomy bits were easily the most gripping, as you often find with this kind of institutional documentary.

Poor Monsieur Reichel. In 1911 this all-time loser, a tailor from Longjumeau near Paris, dressed himself in a kind of tented raincoat which had metal struts holding the material away from his body to form an airbag. He was convinced that this would catch the wind and cause him to glide through the air when he jumped from the 1st floor of the Eiffel Tower. To glide like a bird – *planer* – was his dream and obsession. To test his costume, he jumped 4m (14 ft) from the top of his house into a pile of straw. He twisted both ankles but said afterwards, 'I must have glided, as I am not dead.'

Why no one tried harder to restrain him on the day of his jump from the Eiffel Tower is not clear, although we know he was being egged on by two business associates who hoped to make a fortune out of him. The 1st floor, you will recall, is 57 m (187 ft) above the ground. As Reichel prepared for take-off, he looked hugely absurd, a man in an eiderdown trying to pass himself off as a pigeon. Film cameras were present when he stepped into space. He went down like a stone and the newspapers reported with clinical zeal that his body made a hollow 37 cm (14 in) deep in the frozen ground.

The Cinémax film also showed the Tower as seen by famous painters, and in René Clair's *Paris Qui Dort* and other movies; being climbed by mountaineers, flown round by Santos-Dumont in his

airship, cycled down and visited by the famous. None of these
spectacles could compare, I felt, with the dizzying feats of Rose Gold,
who in 1951 performed a trapeze act from the girders. It was a dottily
brilliant move to bring the circus to the Tower, itself a monarch of
show-business architecture, and it was wholly terrifying to watch. We
also saw the unveiling of Bourdelle's bust of Gustave Eiffel which
now stands by the North Pillar. As the cloth fell and Eiffel appeared,
the dog in the fourth row barked.

And so down to earth. You may take the lift or you may walk. I
opted for the lift, recalling a description by the nineteenth-century
diarist Edmond de Goncourt of how he made the descent one night
after dining on the Tower: '. . . a quite peculiar sensation, like sticking
your head into the infinite, the sensation of coming down those
openwork steps in the darkness, as though diving this way and that
into unbounded space, making you feel like an ant coming down the
rigging of a warship, whose rigging was made of iron'.

For the next part of our Slow Walk we take a stroll across the
Champ de Mars towards the eighteenth-century façade of the Ecole
Militaire. At the pond in the middle of the gardens we turn left to the
Place du Général Gouraud. On the way we pass a riding-path, the
Allée Adrienne Lecouvreur, which a sign advises is 'Réservée aux
Cavaliers Allure Modérée'. It seemed strange to restrict riders from
having too much, or possibly too little, allure; checking with the
dictionary, I found it means speed.

Rue St Dominique

The Rue St Dominique, which we enter after crossing the Place du
Général Gouraud, is a calm, elegant street of golden stone buildings
and smart food shops and boutiques. They build high mounds of
grapes, peaches, plums and cauliflowers, etc, at Les 4 Saisons,
just past the corner, and Charles (No.135) is a famous place for
charcuterie. At the Mars Fountain (Fontaine de Mars), step round
the flat-topped monument into the tiny open courtyard, most of
which is occupied by the terraces of two restaurants, La Fontaine de
Mars and La Croque au Sel. Both are splendid for sitting outside on a
warm evening; remember to reserve in advance, or be there by 20.00,
or else.

As for bakers and pastrymakers, rest assured you will not go short along here. Across the Av. Bosquet, Millet at No. 103 is excellent for chocolates and pastries, and on the corner of Rue Cler is La Cour du Sablé. On the fascia it says: *'Pâtissier – Boulanger – Confiseur – Chocolats – Lunchs'*. A kind of alimentary love-call. Pause here from thoughts of food to admire the simple four-columned portico of the Church of St Pierre du Gros Caillou, built in 1822–3 by an architect called Godde.

Rue Cler market

The market is a paved precinct which begins at the intersection with Rue de Grenelle and runs south to Av. de la Motte-Picquet. It is more a series of permanent shops fronted by stalls than a market where stalls stand in the roadway. It is open from Tuesday to Saturday, is liveliest in the morning, somnolent after lunch and returns to brisk action in the early evening. Although it is designed for pedestrian shoppers, an extraordinary number of drivers either have, or wish to assert, the right to travel up, down or across it by car or van; mind your toes.

Visually, the market is dominated by big greengrocery shops which sit next to other food shops, neighbourhood cafés, pharmacies and shops selling books, shoes and household goods. I have seen towering displays of monster flat-sided strawberries in April, and in September tray upon tray of melons and avocados piled by the hundredweight. In the window of Tarte Julie (No. 28) are delicious tarts, quiches and clafoutis. At Les Vertes Saisons (No. 40) they build rivers with cut flowers in vases, the stacked-up display flowing out from the shop and along the paving in either direction. Opposite, at No. 47, Le Lutin Gourmand is one of those chocolate shops you feel like dismantling entirely and taking home with you.

The Rue Cler market is just the place to buy a jar of jam, a cool fruity *reine claude*, an *abricot*, *groseille* or *mirabelle*. If you are lucky enough to be staying in a hotel which serves lashings of jam for breakfast, perhaps in a pretty earthenware pot with a long spoon, then I suggest you keep the identity of that hotel to yourself. My own experience indicates that jam has fallen victim to the doctrine of portion control and is almost universally served in those measly packets which never go far enough, leaving you with several inches of crusty roll which must be eaten dry or not at all. Of course, if you breakfast downstairs, you may be able to procure another measly packet, but I am assuming you are upstairs in your room and too diffident to telephone for more of something so ridiculously small. Hence the need for a personal pot.

Ecole Militaire

If you went to the Eiffel Tower in the morning it will now be time for lunch, so, provided you have not already been seduced into stopping off at the Fontaine de Mars or some cosy bistro near the market, step round the corner by the Post Office to the Place de l'Ecole Militaire and try your luck at one of the brasseries. I happen to like La Terrasse, on the corner of Av. de la Motte-Picquet and Av. Bosquet, partly on the strength of a warming chocolate taken there one chilly Sunday morning when Paris was still waking up, few people were on the move outside and a seat on a bench upholstered in tobacco-coloured plush seemed a most reassuring place to be.

La Terrasse is not particularly cheap, but all the big metropolitan brasseries tend to exact their toll for the comfort and pleasant atmosphere which comes with the food. Another day I was on the terrace here when a bright red helicopter dipped suddenly into view across the trees just over the road, then vanished in a swirl of blades behind the walls of the Ecole Militaire.

The Ecole, or Military Academy, was founded in 1751 to train young gentlemen without means to become army officers. In 1777 the rules of entry were extended to embrace non-gentlemen from provincial military academies. Napoleon arrived there in 1784 and left as an officer in the Artillery. The buildings now serve as the staff college for French and allied officers attending the School of Advanced War Studies and the Higher School of National Defence.

Just as one is not able to wander at will through the grounds and buildings of Sandhurst, so the Ecole Militaire is not somewhere you can just stroll into. The chapel is open each day to worshippers, however. The north façade is a fine example of French Classical architecture. Look back to its quadrangular dome and low symmetrical wings as, dusting off the crumbs of lunch, you make your way across the Place de l'Ecole Militaire to the Champ de Mars.

The Academy buildings were designed by Jacques-Ange Gabriel in 1752 and completed in 1770. Also known as Ange-Jacques, he was chief architect to Louis XV and also designed, among others, the Petit Trianon at Versailles and the Place de la Concorde.

Market gardens ran down from the Ecole Militaire to the river before the Field of Mars (Champ de Mars) was laid out in 1765 as a parade ground. Since then its long rectangle has served as a racecourse, as a launching ground for early hydrogen balloons, as the site for the Festival of Federation which in 1790 celebrated the first anniversary of the taking of the Bastille; and then it became the principal site for the Universal Exhibitions mentioned earlier.

Marionnettes du Champ de Mars

The small green-painted pavilion in the Champ de Mars is one of several theatres in Paris which put on traditional puppet shows throughout the year. They are mainly for children, but do not be put off from going because of age. The setting is charming, the performances well staged, and everyone I have seen there, whether above the age of six or below, seems to enjoy it tremendously.

Many of the shows feature a character called Guignol as the hero or prime mover of the action. Sometimes he appears in plays written specially for him, together with his wife, Madelon, and his companion, Gnafron, and sometimes he is grafted on to other traditional stories, starring in *Guignol Crusoe*, for instance, or, in one that I saw, as the saviour of Little Red Riding Hood in *Les Aventures du Petit Chaperon Rouge*.

Guignol was created as a puppet character in Lyon in the early nineteenth century. He is not to be confused with 'Grand Guignol' which is a type of short play with a violent or ghostly theme that was popular in the cabarets of nineteenth-century Paris. The name for this genre was probably inspired by the violence used by the puppet Guignol to beat up his enemies and in next to no time restore peace and happiness; in that sense Grand Guignol is 'Guignol for Grown-ups', through in every other aspect it is very different.

Inside the theatre, long chalet roof beams rise upwards to a point above the drawn curtains masking the stage. Parental heads dot the steadily filling rows, though most heads are much smaller and closer to bench level; they belong to young pre-school French children, many of them local, brought there by enlightened mums, aunts and grandparents. It is therefore tactful if large visiting persons sit towards the back.

The bell, which has been ringing outside for some fifteen minutes, stops. A clown, Dodo, appears in a pink spangled suit. Dodo can not only make his head turn sharply to right and left, he can make it spin the whole way round at alarming speeds. Cries of Ooh! from the front of the audience. Dodo finishes his act and the curtains part on a country lane where we meet, in turn, the Woodcutter and his Wife (*M. et Mme le Bûcheron*), Little Red Riding Hood (*Petit Chaperon Rouge*), Guignol, who in this production is her cousin, and the Wolf (*Grand Méchant Loup*). The Wolf is suitably frightening and keeps the oohs and other cries going until the interval, when the lights go up and an usherette sells bonbons from a tray.

In the second half the scene switches to the interior of Grandma's House, a creaky dark old cottage, lovingly constructed with cobwebs and all. The action of the play was resolved without too much further violence, and about forty minutes after the show had begun we were filing out of the theatre, the younger ones wearing thoughtful expressions, the adults smiling and beaming at each other. Any doubts they may have had about attending a mere children's show had long dispersed.

Our Slow Walk ends here. Should you be wondering what to do next, well, as long as there is Paris I hope there will always be pastries in the Rue St Dominique and the Rue Cler, whence it is a short walk to Ⓜ Ecole Militaire.

Boat trip

Alternatively, you may like to try an excursion on the river, a gracious and diverting way to fill in an hour or two before evening. Choose between a big *bateau mouche* or a smaller *bateau vedette*. *Bateaux mouches* leave from Pont de l'Alma on the Right Bank: go along the Avenue Rapp and cross the bridge. *Bateaux vedettes* leave from Port de Suffren on the Left Bank: go up the Champ de Mars and through the legs of the Eiffel Tower to the river. Trips last 1¼ hours. Check with *Pariscope* for timings and prices.

Walk 17 ☂

7^e Invalides and Army Museum

Walk down the Esplanade to the Hôtel des Invalides, the seventeenth-century home for disabled soldiers now best known as the repository of Napoleon's Tomb. For many, though, the real attraction is the splendid Army Museum, located in the front courtyards.

Allow 4–5 hours.

Best times Dome Church and Army Museum open all year except 1 January, 1 May, 1 November, 25 December; hours are 10.00 to 18.00 1 April to 30 September, 17.00 1 October to 31 March, Dome Church open until 19.00 June to August.

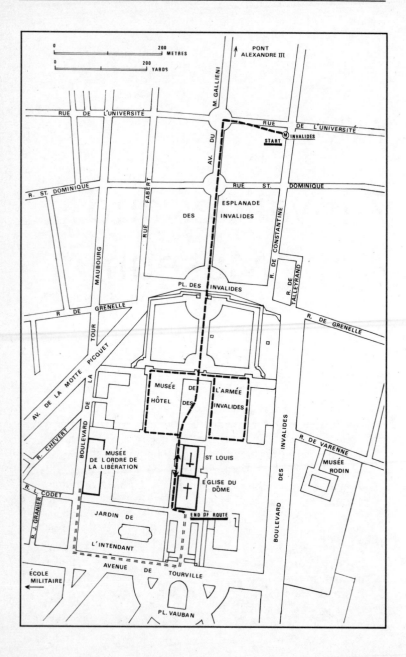

ROUTE

Begin at Ⓜ Invalides (RER). Nearest buses 49, 63, 83. Cross to centre of Esplanade, the Av. du Maréchal Gallieni which joins the Pont Alexandre III and the Hôtel des Invalides. Enter the Hôtel garden and walk through to the main courtyard (*cour d'honneur*), cross it and exit at the SW (top right) corner into a cloister. In garden on left are stones from Napoleon's tomb on St Helena. The cloister brings you to a courtyard next to the Dome Church. *Admission.*

Buy a combined ticket valid on two consecutive days for the Dome Church, Army Museum and Museum of Relief Maps (Eglise du Dôme, Musée de l'Armée, Musée des Plans-Reliefs). Visit the Dome Church and Napoleon's Tomb. Leaving the church, turn right and right again through the cloister to the main courtyard. Halfway down the left-hand side, enter the West block of the Army Museum and begin your tour with the arms and armour collections of the Salles François I and Henri IV. Walk through the Salle Préhistorique et Antiquité and the Salle Pauilhac to the galleries at the rear.

To continue the visit chronologically, return to main courtyard and cross it to the East block. Visit the ground-floor galleries and work your way up to the 3rd floor. This brings you up to 1914.

Now take a break from the Army Museum and visit the Soldiers' Church (Eglise de St Louis des Invalides), reached by turning left at East block entrance and walking through cloisters.

Leaving the Soldiers' Church, turn left and return to the West block of the Army Museum. On the 2nd floor (Level 2) visit the two World War rooms. Go up to the 4th floor and visit the fascinating Museum of Relief Maps, a collection of mainly seventeenth-century dioramas from the age of Vauban, master of the fortified town. Return to ground floor.

Diversion Also in the Invalides complex is the Museum of the Order of Liberation, commemorating an order set up by General de Gaulle at Brazzaville in 1940; other sections deal with deportation and campaigns of the French Resistance. Entrance on W side of Hôtel des Invalides at 51 *bis* Bd de la Tour Maubourg. Open Monday to Saturday, 14.00 to 17.00, closed Sunday, in August and on public holidays. *Admission.*

Walk ends in front of Dome Church. Nearest recommended

refreshments across Pl. Vauban at Le Vauban. Nearest Ⓜ St
François Xavier or Ecole Militaire.

𝄇 Wet Weather Route Begin at Ⓜ St François Xavier and walk directly
to Dome Church along Av. de Villars.

Esplanade des Invalides

The Route for this Slow Walk may seem a little eccentric at times but
it has its logic and as far as possible follows a chronological pattern.

The sequence begins in the reign of Louis XIV (1643–1715) who
ordered the building of the Esplanade and the entire mansion
complex of the Hôtel des Invalides, including the two back-to-back
churches, St Louis des Invalides and the Dome Church. It then
follows the story of Napoleon's death on St Helena in 1821 and the
eventual transfer of his remains in 1861 to the tomb in the Dome
Church. Finally, there is a tour of the Army Museum which was
established in 1905, uniting two earlier museums already based at the
Invalides.

As you set off towards the Av. du Maréchal Gallieni which runs
through the centre of the Esplanade des Invalides, turn towards the
river for a view of the flamboyant Pont Alexandre III and the huge
conservatory roof of the Grand Palais beyond. Both were built for the
World Exhibition of 1900, together with the more restrained Petit
Palais on the right.

Marshal Joseph-Simon Gallieni, whose Avenue you tread, was
military commander of Paris on the outbreak of World War I. An
energetic old soldier, who had successfully pacified and governed the
French Sudan and Madagascar, he came out of retirement only days
before the German armies swept across France in August 1914. The
French Sixth Army was less than thirty miles from Paris and falling
back before heavy German thrusts when Gallieni rounded up some
1,200 Paris taxicabs and rushed reinforcements to the front. Despite
extraordinary confusion on the roads, the men arrived in time to stop
the German advance. This dramatic and much-treasured rescue
mission is now popularly known as 'The Miracle of the Marne'.

Small wonder that Gallieni, its instigator, should be remembered
today with such a prime Avenue, in the heart of 'Military Paris'. In

1971, by the way, he also received a Métro station, a new terminus in eastern Paris, three stops after Père Lachaise.

To left and right along the Esplanade, rows of lime trees partly conceal dusty spaces where *pétanque* players spin and bomb the hours away. The Esplanade was laid out in 1704–20 by Robert de Cotte, brother-in-law of the architect Jules Hardouin-Mansart who designed the Dome Church and built much of the rest of the Hôtel des Invalides, completing the designs of Libéral Bruant.

Hôtel des Invalides

Cross the protractor-shaped Place des Invalides, preferably not at its widest part, and go in at the entrance to the garden, passing over the moat guarded by two gun batteries. Now the sweep of the Hôtel's north façade dominates every forward view. It is 196 m (645 ft) long and four storeys high; in the roofs of the two symmetrical wings are decorative dormers in the shape of trophies. Statues of Mars and Minerva flank the main entrance, and above them in the rounded arch is an equestrian bas-relief of Louis XIV supported by Prudence and Justice.

The Hôtel consists of fifteen rectangular courtyards. In the galleries overlooking the main courtyard (*cour d'honneur*) and in the four flanking courtyards are the collections of the Army Museum. The other courtyards, to the south, are used for administration and to house some seventy wounded soldiers. Originally, the entire hôtel was built to accommodate 4,000 *invalides* or old soldiers who before the 1670s were badly provided for when their fighting days were over.

Once inside the *cour d'honneur*, walk across the cobbled paving towards the entrance of the Church of St Louis des Invalides. There, beneath the ornately carved pediment, is Seurre's bronze statue of Napoleon which from 1833 to 1863 stood on top of the Column in the Place Vendôme (*Walk 1*). The Little Corporal registers his presence with a mean, glowering stare. In the context of what we are to see in a moment, it is appropriate.

In the cloister at the SW corner of the *cour d'honneur* we pass, on the left, a small garden. On the ground lies an undistinguished tomb consisting of three stone slabs. This is the reconstructed grave of Napoleon on St Helena, where he died in 1821. No epitaph marked this first grave. A notice on the cloister wall explains that the British were rigidly unforgiving towards the Emperor they had never officially recognised. The only wording they would allow on his tombstone was 'Le Général Bonaparte'. The French wanted something longer, plain but more informative. The British refused and the stones were left nameless, with only the words 'Ci Gît' (Here Lies).

In his will Napoleon had stated, 'I wish my ashes to rest on the banks of the Seine, in the midst of the French people I have loved so much . . .' To his successor in power, Louis XVIII, then enjoying his second restoration, this was a most unwelcome idea and it was ignored. It appealed still less to Charles X, who reigned from 1824 to 1830 and held extreme reactionary views. Not until the July Revolution of 1830, when Louis-Philippe, the 'Citizen King', came to the throne, was it permitted to show public enthusiasm for the Emperor. Then the tricolours emerged and Bonapartism was revitalised.

Negotiations began with the British government to bring back Napoleon's body to France, and eventually Louis-Philippe's son, the Prince de Joinville, sailed by warship to St Helena. He had the corpse exhumed, inspected it and saw the coffin re-sealed and loaded on board ship. On 15 December 1840 Paris lay under a snowstorm as Napoleon's hearse arrived back in the capital. Watched by 100,000 people, the cortège travelled through the Arc de Triomphe and down the Champs Elysées. The snow stopped and a pale sun shone through. A contemporary engraving depicts the extraordinary sight of the procession passing the Marly Horses to enter the Place de la Concorde. The funeral carriage – monumentally tall, exuberantly wreathed and carved – is drawn by sixteen plumed and barded horses, their heads masked in chamfrons pierced by large eye-holes which give them an other-worldly air, like messengers from beyond the grave.

Arriving at the Invalides, the coffin was placed beneath the Dome, then it rested in St Jérôme's Chapel while work went ahead to prepare the crypt and complete Visconti's design for a great sarcophagus. The reinterment ceremony was held in April 1861 and was attended by Napoleon III, a nephew of the first Emperor and himself Emperor of the French since 1852.

Napoleon's tomb

Even in death Napoleon Bonaparte stirred a turmoil which lasted forty years. When at last he was returned to his nation, he was reburied in the most grandiose tomb accorded to any Frenchman. The tomb was sited, moreover, in possibly the finest Classical building in French religious architecture. It is disappointing, therefore, to find the two so ill-suited to each other.

However fleeting the analysis, it is hard to look at the Dome Church today without seeing a place of two very distinct parts: in simple terms, the outside and the inside. When Louis XIV commissioned Hardouin-Mansart to design a chapel royal to complete the Invalides scheme, he was hoping for a building that would become a monument to his own greatness, an ecclesiastical equivalent of Versailles. The Dome Church was built in 1675–1706 and is widely regarded as a brilliant success. Seen from the forecourt, it is a supremely confident building. Doric columns surmounted by Corinthian columns, a high drum with paired columns and tall windows, then the massive ribbed and gilded dome, plump as a ripe half-orange, leading finally to the lantern, *flèche* (short spire), ball and cross, 107 m (350 ft) above the ground.

Inside the church the proportions are no less imposing but the building lost a great deal when it ceased to be a Jesuit church and became a military mausoleum. This happened in 1800 and the man responsible was Napoleon himself. He decided to transfer the remains of Marshal Turenne (1611–75) to the Invalides from St Denis, where he had been buried with the Kings of France. The role of the building was changed for ever. Today the incumbents of the Dome Church resemble an exclusive, erratically assembled Military Hall of Fame, the latest additions being Marshals Foch (1851–1929) and Lyautey (1854–1934) of whom more later, though not much.

By far the grandest memorial in the Dome Church is that of the Emperor. Visconti's tomb of red porphyry is sunk beneath the pavement in a circular crypt. The tomb is gigantic – 4 m (13 ft) long by 2 m (6 ft) wide and 4.5 m (14½ ft) high – and inside this mighty frame the Emperor is entombed in a nest of six coffins; the innermost is of tinplate, the next of mahogany, the third and fourth of lead, the fifth of ebony and the outermost of oak.

Everyone's first view of Napoleon's Tomb, unfortunately, is from the marble balustrade overlooking the crypt. You lean over, look down, and there it is, a very bulky wooden box with a scrolled top. You may well be disappointed by the sheer medium-brown mundanity of it, this bland hunk of timber in a colour reminiscent of the high-street dining suite you would never have in your house.

If it had to be done again, it is most unlikely that it would be done like this. The first error was to dig out the special circular crypt and place the tomb in an inferior position, beneath the viewer's eye-level. To see the tomb from a more impressive angle, go down the staircase to the entrance to the crypt. On the way you pass the large window that separates the Dome Church from the inner Church of St Louis des Invalides.

In the solemnity of the crypt it becomes clear that the French people of the mid-nineteenth century saw Napoleon above all as a warrior-conqueror, reaping Glory wherever he sowed a campaign. Twelve colossal statues by Pradier face the tomb and bear witness to the Emperor's chief exploits, from Italy in 1797 to Waterloo in 1815. Here too, writ large in a circle surrounding the tomb's pedestal of green granite, are the names of his most celebrated campaigns: 'RIVOLI – PYRAMIDES – MARENGO – AUSTERLITZ – IENA – FRIEDLAND – WAGRAM – MOSCOWA'.

There is not much else to hold you in this dusty palace of commemoration. The altar is framed by twisted columns and covered by a baldaquin (canopy) by Visconti. In the side chapels are the tombs of Joseph Bonaparte, King of Spain, Napoleon's elder brother; Jérôme Bonaparte, King of Westphalia, Napoleon's younger brother; Marshal Vauban, military engineer of genius who is better remembered in the Musée des Plan-Reliefs around the corner (his heart was brought to the Invalides at Napoleon's request); Marshal Foch, commander of the Allied forces in the last months of World War I – a better monument, this, the tomb borne aloft by eight soldiers; La Tour d'Auvergne, also represented here by his heart, who in 1800, the year of his death, was named the 'First Grenadier of the Republic'; Marshal Lyautey, resident general in Morocco between the two World Wars; and Marshal Turenne, most celebrated of Louis XIV's generals and the first occupant of the redesignated building.

When you leave, turn right and go back the way you came, past the pepperpot tower and into the cloister, past the little garden with the stones from St Helena. Perhaps, in their simplicity, they express more of the mystery of Napoleon than all the monumental masonry and that stout piece of carpentry in the Dome Church.

Army Museum: West and East blocks

Straight ahead is the West block of the Army Museum. This is not the main entrance but it is the best place to start. The present Museum is an amalgamation of two earlier ones, the Artillery Museum (Musée de l'Artillerie) and the Army History Museum (Musée Historique de l'Armée).

To avoid future confusion, it was decided that the Artillery Museum, which arrived in the West block in 1870, should concentrate on items of military hardware, mainly arms and armour, and the Army History Museum, in the East block (1896), should deal in a more rounded, historically minded way with events since 1569, when the first French infantry regiment was founded. To these two bodies a third was added, covering the activities of the Library, Archives and Print Collection.

Thus, in the Salle François I, to the right of the entrance to the West block, the past is conveyed through the objects on view: case upon case of early weapons and equipment from 1066 to the middle of the sixteenth century – daggers, swords, stirrups, spurs, pot helmets, body and horse armour, crossbows, longbows, maces and bombards (the earliest handguns).

Of the many fine exhibits in this hall of antiquarian delights, look out for the suit of Henri II (reigned 1547–59), decorated with his personal 'H' intertwined with the 'C' of Queen Catherine and the 'D' of his favourite, Diane de Poitiers; also the 'lion' armour made in 1540–45 in the Milanese style, probably for François I, and the vast suit assembled to fit the Friar Tuck frame of Count Otto Henri. The most talked-about piece is the gold sword of François I, taken from the King's tent at the Battle of Pavia (1525), where he was captured. The sword was taken off to Spain with the enemy; not until 1808, almost three hundred years later, was it recovered for France by Napoleon.

Cavalry armour is the dominant theme of the adjoining Salle Henri IV, but this is armour for amusement – the suits they wore for jousting and parading in the sixteenth and early seventeenth centuries. Around the walls large paintings attributed to Joseph Parrocel depict scenes from the Dutch Wars (1672–78); in their day they provided martial propaganda on a grand scale for Louis XIV's old soldiers, who ate their meals beneath them.

A central gallery leading to the rear of the West block contains a small Antiquities Room and the Salle Pauilhac, based on the arms and armour collection of Georges Pauilhac which the Museum acquired in 1965; then on to the Arsenal of Louis XIII (reigned 1601–43) and the Salle Louvois, named after Louis XIV's war minister. On either side of the central gallery are the open courtyards of the Cour d'Angoulême and the Cour de la Victoire, the resting-place for an extraordinary barrage of land and naval artillery pieces, from medieval and Renaissance cannon to mortars used in World War II. Strung along a wall of the Cour d'Angoulême is a rare item: the Danube Chain. In 1683 at the Siege of Vienna the Turks used this iron chain to bind together a bridge of boats and blockaded the Danube.

At the end of the Salle Louvois is an unusual collection of Oriental arms and armour, gathered from the Balkans and countries east as far as China and Japan: the helmet of the Ottoman Sultan Bajazet II, the war robes of an eighteenth-century Chinese emperor, turbans, daggers and other fearsome pieces. From this gallery you can make your way out to the main courtyard and prepare for a second round of rooms in the 'other museum' in the East block. Scattered through the cobbled yard is a random collection of guns from Europe, the Mediterranean and China; pieces with strange personal names that reek of soldiers' sardonic wit – the Doctor, the Sleeper, the Misanthropist, the Maniac.

Just through the entrance to the East block is a cinema showing films dealing, for the most part, with aspects of the two World Wars. Entrance is free with your museum ticket; check the noticeboard for details. In the room on the right, the Salle Turenne, is a display of regimental standards in the Age of the Tricolor: 'Honneur Et Patrie', 'Le Courage Ne Vieillit Pas', 'Valeur Et Discipline' – the mottoes resound from these walls.

In the Salle Vauban, on the left of the entrance, is an impressive line of life-sized cavalrymen, eighteen in all, mounted on very passable wood and plaster chargers, from a dragoon of 1803 to colonial and home cavalry of the mid-nineteenth century. A hussar of 1855 looks as madly brave as any of his sabre-waving predecessors, though soon the day of the machine gun would be upon him and his near-obsolete comrades, the dragoons, spahis and cuirassiers.

Time out

It would be a pity to rush the remaining rooms of the East block, the Soldiers' Church, the World War rooms across the courtyard and the excellent Musée des Plans-Reliefs; in short, a couple of hours' more viewing remains.

One civilised solution is to call a break. I find the cafeteria in the Invalides (next to the ticket office by the Dome Church) too canteen-like and malodorous, after the fashion of school dinners, and recommend a stroll across the Place Vauban to Le Vauban. This busy café caters also for the busloads who arrive at the Invalides in those green-windowed, double-decker kerbcrawlers labelled Carlux Paris Vision and suchlike, but never mind, the place is seldom crowded both inside and out. More important are the wonders that a *salade niçoise* and a Kronenbourg, a *croque monsieur*, a cup of tea or an ice cream can do for the fading Slow Walker. Take your break on the terrace and watch the pigeons forage in the square for bread, then suddenly take flight, flapping themselves aloft into the plane trees for digestion and a doze.

Back, then, to the East block, and up to what they call the 2nd floor (1st floor really, or Level 2). These rooms, and others on the 3rd floor, contain a chronological review of army life. It begins with the Rooms of the Ancienne Monarchie (1618–1792), then on to the First Republic (1793–1804), First Empire (1804–14), Restoration (1814–30), July Monarchy and Second Republic (1830–52), Second Empire and War of 1870 (1852–70) and the period up to World War I (1870–1914).

Weapons, uniforms, flags, paintings, models and personal possessions are grouped in a succession of small rooms, the intention being to evoke the particular flavour of each military age. Among the more unexpected treasures is the sedan chair which bore the crippled veteran Comte de Fontaine on to the field of Rocroi (1643), where he was mortally wounded; the cannonball which killed Marshal Turenne at Sasbach (1675), and the backplate of the cuirass he was wearing when struck; Napoleon's battlefield bivouac with his camp bed, table, folding chair and personal effects; the Emperor's white horse, Le Vizir, stuffed for posterity; a reconstruction of the room at Longwood, St Helena, where Napoleon died; nearby, his death mask.

Church of St Louis des Invalides

This is the Soldiers' Church. It shared a single sanctuary with the Dome Church until, in 1842, Visconti rearranged the central altar of the latter and built the crypt to receive Napoleon's tomb; in 1873 Crépinet's large window was installed behind the high altar of St Louis and the churches were then separated.

The Church of St Louis is another Bruant-Mansart creation. It is bare and severe-looking, decorated with captured enemy colours which hang from the galleries. The flags continue a tradition begun in the vaults of Notre-Dame Cathedral, where at one time three thousand were on view. The church's finest hour came in 1837, when the first performance of Berlioz's *Grande Messe des Morts* welled from the seventeenth-century organ and a full orchestra, the sounds augmented by the crash of artillery on the Esplanade.

To identify the flags, walk up the outer aisles and read the framed lists on the pillars. Although the flags on view date from 1805 and so are fairly 'modern', you may be surprised to find that the three most recent are German, from the Second World War, the very last that of an SS 'Strasbourg' detachment captured in February 1945 by Algerian troops operating near Paris.

The World War rooms

By comparison with the rooms in the East block, which deal in a spacious, rather leisurely way with the period up to 1914, the World War rooms are crammed with specimen cases of military and civilian bric-à-brac: weapons and uniforms, as before, now joined by a surplus-store wealth of badges, bugles, field telephones, ammunition boxes, scale models and dioramas, and, in the Second World War room, masses of personal documents and ephemera which convey a very different atmosphere from that of earlier conflicts. This is total war, and we look at it as through a microscope.

In the First World War room, light-box maps show the fighting in a series of waves, beginning with the campaigns in Belgium and France of August–September 1914, the Allied retreat, Battle of the Marne and the Race to the Sea. The War of Movement came to an end in November 1914 and the rest was a brutal bloody slog which decimated a generation of young European men: a total of 4.9 million Allied military dead (including 50,000 Americans), and 3.1 million among the Central Powers.

The paintings of soldiers are now more intimate and portray living, sweating, pipe-puffing individuals in place of the brilliant regimental clothes-horses of yore. Photographs add their considerable message, and some of the scale models, of tanks, guns and aerial warfare, are strikingly effective. One of these represents 'Ginette', a 370 mm railway gun which was decorated with the Croix de Guerre after its shells destroyed one of the German Paris guns that for several months bombarded the capital.

Many new weapons stand alongside the trusted rifles, swords and bayonets: grenades, trench mortars, gas weapons, and machine guns made by Vickers (GB), St Etienne and Hotchkiss (France), the German Maxim gun and the Austrian Schwarz-Lose. Two large dioramas illustrate the rabbit-warren life of trench warfare and the Siege of Verdun.

The next room, covering 1939–45, sketches a truly *world* war. Emphasis in the presentation is on photographic evidence, items of propaganda and hundreds of small personal documents that in such a small space amount to a slightly dazzling overview. Persevere, though, and every few feet you will find something quite extraordinary. In the seventh window on the left is a strange spherical parcel; in its wrapping it looks like a plum pudding. It contains the helmet of Adjutant-chef Gast, a machine gunner shot down in May 1940; the Red Cross got hold of the helmet and posted it to the man's family. Quite what they thought when this head-shaped package arrived at their door is something we are not told.

The next cabinets portray a life not experienced by the British in their own land. For our much-documented 'Life on the Home

Front', here read 'Life under the Occupation', four years of gruelling oppression. Anti-Jewish propaganda was heavy on the ground – 'Buy Jewish and Ruin French Business' insists one poster. Then the Resistance made itself felt in the undercover war of leafletting, sabotage, supplies by parachute, secret radio transmitters and all the impedimenta of a desperate period.

Move to Europe under German control: the rounding-up and deportation of Jews. So much to show in one room; the biggest risk must be that by brushing so rapidly against such a large subject it will seem trivialised. All the same, when you come upon the photo-boards of life in the concentration camps, the impact is both immediate and lasting. Preserved here are blue-white pyjama uniforms of prisoners in Sachsenhausen and Ravensbrück, letters home from deportees, the clogs they wore – and the key to Buchenwald, a heavy, medieval jailer's implement, gross with oak leaves in the handle, the bit of the key wrought in the shape of a Gothic SS.

On at last to Liberation, prefaced by a gigantic model of the Allied landings in Normandy followed by brief surveys of the Pacific War and Soviet operations in Berlin. It is more than a little cramped, especially towards the end. This museum has special problems. Much as we may enjoy the attics, refectories and courtyards, they were not designed to house museums, and the curators never have space to show more than a small part of their collections.

On the 3rd floor, in studios where the invalids once worked, the Salle des Alliés rounds off the World War coverage with a further display of Allied uniforms, arms and equipment. Also on this floor is the Salle Gribeauval, housing an extraordinary collection of model artillery pieces in scales ranging from 1:4 to 1:10. This is the founding collection of the old Artillery Museum, based on a collection of model guns built up by Marshal d'Humières from about 1685 and now in its expanded form named after Jean-Baptiste de Gribeauval, the inspector-general of artillery who revolutionised French gunnery methods in the late eighteenth century.

Musée des Plans-Reliefs

Up, finally, to the roof where, dimly lit beneath the eaves, is a rare exhibition. In 1668, when France had the most powerful army in Europe, Louis XIV received his war minister, the Marquis de Louvois, and Sébastien de Vauban, France's leading authority on siege warfare. It was Vauban who perfected the design of the star-shaped fort, wrapping whole towns in a hedgehog of precisely gauged bastions, half-moon outworks, ditches, ramparts and sloping glacis. At this meeting they agreed to commission a three-dimensional catalogue of France's frontier and maritime towns. Plans would be made of every street, square and building, and a model of each town constructed on the common scale of 1:600.

The fruits of that survey are what you see today. More models were added in the eighteenth century and for many years the collection was regarded as top-secret material, for the eyes only of specialists and high-ranking military officials.

In a small cinema at the far end you can watch a short loop illustrating how the tiny matchbox houses were made, then coloured and installed, street by street. The film, for all its brevity, is a touch ponderous but worth seeing through for its evocation of a seventeenth-century army on the move.

Before leaving the Musée des Plans-Reliefs, look through the bull's-eye windows and share a soldier's view of barrack life three hundred years ago. In his niche on the south side of the *cour d'honneur*, Napoleon glares towards the banks of the Seine.

Our Slow Walk ends here. Nearest refreshments, as before, are at Le Vauban, in the square facing the Dome Church. Or try for a table at the tiny but delightful Chinese tea room, La Pagode, 57 *bis* Rus de Babylone, attached to a cinema in the old Imperial Chinese Embassy; open 16.00 to 21.45.

Walk 18 ⚲

8ᵉ The Department Stores

A tour of the *Grands Magasins* around the Madeleine and Opéra districts – Aux Trois Quartiers and Madelios, Au Printemps and Brummell, Galeries Lafayette and Galfa Club. Visit the Church of Ste Marie Madeleine, the flower market and some of the finest food shops in Paris.

Allow 4–5 hours.

Best times Not Sunday.

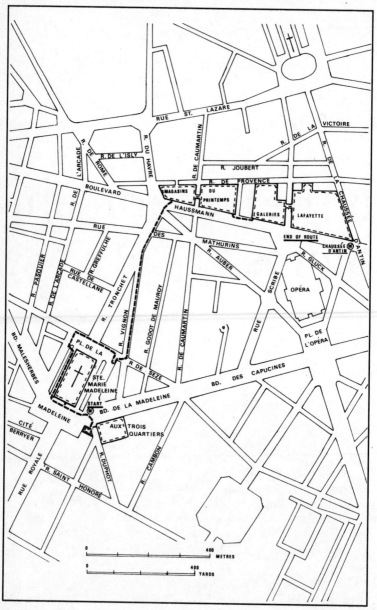

ROUTE

Begin at Ⓜ Madeleine. Nearest buses 24, 42, 52, 84, 94. Exit next to Aux Trois Quartiers (store being virtually remade, ready 1990). Visit Madelios men's shop (No. 10). Cross road to flower market and look in to church. Walk round W side of square to Hédiard (No. 21), then across N side past Marquise de Sévigné (No. 32) to Fauchon (No. 26).

At NE corner of square, turn left into Rue Vignon and walk up via Rue Tronchet to Bd Haussmann. Au Printemps is opposite ☞; open 09.30 to 18.30, closed Sunday. Visit W building (Le Printemps de la Maison) and take escalator to 9th floor terrace café, then work down. At 3rd/2nd floors, take bridge across to Le Printemps de la Mode. Brummell men's store is in block behind (Rue de Provence), also reachable by bridge.

Return to Bd Haussmann and walk E past stalls to Galeries Lafayette ☞; open 09.30 to 18.30, closed Sunday. Work downwards through store, beginning at one of the cafés or terrace on roof and crossing bridge to Galfa Club.

Walk ends here. Nearest Ⓜ Chaussée d'Antin.

𝕂 **Wet Weather Route** Same as ordinary route. If weather totally dreadful, go direct to Ⓜ Havre-Caumartin and join walk at Au Printemps.

Place de la Madeleine

I have always thought of this kind of shopping as a rather private activity: a leisurely browse or stalk, usually carried out solo or with a maximum of one understanding friend, meandering and backtracking until all possibilities have been surrounded and weighed up, followed by a lightning raid on the winning counter to seal the purchase and carry it eagerly home. Faithful to these ideals, I propose here only the roughest of itineraries. In a big store like Galeries Lafayette, the best I can do is to point out where things are and retire. The rest will be up to the reader.

The beginning of this walk is not as marvellous as it should be. Aux Trois Quartiers, hitherto a safe but rather dull institution, is being mightily refurbished both inside and out, and unless it is raining heavily you may not want to venture inside before 1990, when the new store should be ready. Madelios, the ATQ men's shop across the road, was as sleepily old-fashioned as ever on my last visit. Some people find it reassuring, of course, to have a good old steady they can go to when the years have begun to tick away. Thus the section known optimistically as 'Madcorner' is not a place for demented youth to go in search of dashing beachwear. It sells cotton plaid trousers just like the pro golfers have been wearing for a quarter of a century on the US Tour. Regular customers don't seem to mind this. As I have already suggested, they want ze Burlington socks and ze Henry Cotton rainwear. It matters little that Henry's greatest decade was the Thirties.

Mary Magdalen Church

The square, though full of traffic most of the time, is spacious and charming with plane trees along the south side. Step across to the flower market and take a look inside the Church of Ste Marie Madeleine. This is a most cosmopolitan building. It was originally designed as a Greek temple dedicated to the glory of Napoleon's *Grande Armée*, then its function was changed by Louis XVIII who decreed that it should become a church. The architect Vignon deftly adjusted his temple plans and carried on. In 1828 he died and was buried beneath the portico; after further delays the church was consecrated in 1845.

Inside, the atmosphere is brisk and matter-of-fact as representatives of the church attend to the needs of a constant file of visitors. A notice-board lists 'Your Clergy' for the week. A gift and bookshop sells religious texts, crucifixes, guides and souvenirs. In the Reception booth a white-bearded priest listens to the story of an unseen visitor, screened by a curtain. Through the open door in summer the low drum of the boulevard traffic is pierced by the wail of police sirens and, also unusual in a church, your nose must deal with the unmistakable smell of burger cuisine, from a nearby stall.

In the plan of the church all is symmetry: the single nave and semi-circular choir; above, three shallow domes with bas-reliefs of the Apostles. On the high altar two kneeling angels flank the central group by Marochetti: *The Ascension of St Mary Magdalen*. All is very balanced, the statues polite, as though on their best behaviour.

The most distinctive elements of the exterior are the green roof, the all-round colonnade of fifty-two Corinthian columns and the monumental flight of twenty-eight steps leading up from the square. From this vantage point an impressive view extends along the Rue Royale to the Place de la Concorde and the columns fronting the Palais Bourbon (French House of Commons) across the river.

We make our way to the west side of the square, and on the island beside the church come upon the very useful Kiosque Théâtre, which sells half-price theatre tickets on the day of the performance; open Tuesday to Saturday 12.30 to 20.00, Sunday 12.30 to 16.00, closed Monday and July and August..

Further up and across the road is the first of the wonderful food shops on our route: Hédiard (No.21), a grocery shop with a tiled floor and shelves piled to the ceiling with preserves in jars. There are wonderful terrines, pieces of salmon, half lobsters, fine wines, and a luxurious restaurant on the 1st floor.

Then comes the Marquise de Sévigné (No.32), more a way of life than a chocolate shop, then the two shops of Fauchon. At No.26 is a crowded but highly rated cafeteria, and a shop selling confectionery, chocolates and *pâtisseries*. Across the corner of Rue de Sèze are the magical windows and counters of No.24, filled with gourmet delicacies: charcuterie, quiches, *tourtes*, jams, mustards, biscuits, Art Deco bottles of Vittel water, and Fauchon champagne up to the twelve-bottle size.

Around the corner in Rue Vignon the shops may be smaller but the merchandise is no less refined: cheeses at La Ferme St Hubert (No.21); honey from everywhere a bee has flown at La Maison du Miel (No.24). Ahead lies the tougher, bustling world of the Boulevard Haussmann. Prepare to . . . not exactly do battle, but at least be ready to bring a shoulder or an elbow into play as we tackle the first of our Grands Magasins.

The Grands Magasins

Market research at both Au Printemps and the Galeries Lafayette, coupled with long experience reaching back to the Belle Epoque at the turn of the century, has produced store plans that are fairly similar in many respects. Among the common factors, the ground floors are for perfumes, accessories, jewellery and gifts. The 1st and 2nd floors are for women's fashion, shoes and sportswear. Furniture, carpets and lighting are on the quieter upper floors, away from the main surge of shoppers. Cafés are at the top of the building, using the roof for close-up views of the Opera House and panoramas of the whole city. And the men's divisions are kept separate, though they are directly accessible from the main store.

Both stores also lay on a wealth of customer services, enough to detain you for a whole day should you feel like being so pampered. Ask at the Welcome desk (*Accueil*) on the ground floor and multi-lingual hostesses will ply you with maps and brochures, guide you round the store if necessary or just tell you where things are. Provided you spend enough, 'tourist discounts' are simple to arrange (see page 263 for details of *la détaxe*, i.e. VAT rebates on exported goods). Many credit cards are welcome, and both stores have currency exchange desks. For the price of a phone call beforehand you can see a fashion show or visit the hair and beauty salon, and theatre and travel tickets are always on sale. Sometimes the general atmosphere gets a little hectic, particularly on the ground floors and particularly at the peak hours of mid-afternoon when all the world seems to be flooding through the entrance doors, but that is true of famous stores everywhere and the artful shopper takes evasive action.

The principal differences between the two rivals of the Boulevard Haussmann are less easy to define and have more to do with questions of tone and personal preference. Both stores divide themselves into separate buildings, though, and that is a good place to start.

Au Printemps

This is the senior store. It opened in 1865 and was twice rebuilt in the nineteenth century. Its best face looks west across Rue du Havre, decorated with mosaics and crowned by twin domes. This building is Le Printemps de la Maison, a self-contained store devoted to household goods.

If it is now about lunchtime, collect a mini store guide in the language of your choice and take the escalator directly to the 9th floor for a snack or salad lunch at rooftop level with marvellous views all round. To the north, just left of Sacré-Cœur, the sails of the Moulin de la Galette are skylined. On the way down, the layout should be as follows, subject to seasonal changes:

8th floor	Primavera – smart patio life (they call it a gift boutique).
7th	Wallpapers, upholstery, rugs.
6th	Lighting, carpets, 'classic' furniture.
5th	Contemporary furniture.
4th	Linen, lost and found.
3rd	Toys, special exhibitions.
2nd	China, crystal.
1st	Kitchenware, gadgets, electrical appliances.
Ground	Perfumes, accessories, brushes, jewellery, watches, gifts.
Basement	Books, records, hi-fi.

At the rear of Le Printemps de la Maison, a bridge leads to the Brummell men's store. In descending order, they sell:

4th floor	Suits, shoes, made-to-measure.
3rd	Jackets, trousers, raincoats.
2nd	Weekend shop – leisurewear.
1st	Shirts, pyjamas, bathrobes.
Ground	Sweaters, knitwear, accessories.
Basement	Ski and beachwear, underwear, socks.

Big stores do not change all that much from one year to the next, though I distinctly remember buying some brown earthenware plates in the basement of Le Printemps de la Maison while honeymooning in Paris. My wife agrees we bought the plates then, but says firmly that we got them at Prisunic. (Ah, yes. I remember it well.)

Across a bridge, the Pont de Cristal (on 2nd and 3rd floor levels), is the second Printemps shop, Le Printemps de la Mode, which concentrates on fashion and women's wear. Accounts and restaurants are on the top floors, then the pattern is as follows:

5th floor	Children's wear.
4th	Beachwear, furs, hair and beauty salon.
3rd	Classic fashions, sweaters, dresses, coats, raincoats.
2nd	Sports and casual wear.
1st	Designer fashions, junior fashions, shoes.

Ground   Perfumes, accessories, etc (connects with *Maison* shop).
Basement Lingerie, sportswear (general).

Walk along the boulevard past the stalls which form a jolly bazaar
selling anything from cushions to steam irons, belts, balloons,
bathrobes, sweaters, books and guides. Stallholders rent space from
the store, and the keyword for a bargain (*Solde*) is their main selling
line. Before you reach Galeries Lafayette you come to Monoprix –
high value if not much style, and near the doors a relentless hustler in
a bow-tie who keeps crooning into a microphone about how sparky
everything is. Not strongly recommended. Nor, on the grounds that
I did not come to Paris to visit Marks & Spencer, is the M & S shop
across the boulevard. It is, however, increasingly popular with
Parisiennes who like its food department (*alimentation*) and lingerie.

Galeries Lafayette

Galeries Lafayette nowadays seems to have a stylistic edge over its
neighbours. Of all the stores to spend a rainy day in, this would be my
choice. One advantage it makes clever use of is the magnificent Belle
Epoque dome, 30 m (100 ft) in diameter, the centrepiece of the
interior, beneath which are the galleried fashion departments and
the perfume boutiques on the ground floor.

Originally a small boutique on the corner of the Chaussée d'Antin
and the Rue La Fayette, the Galeries opened in 1895 and the present
store, designed by Chanut, dates from 1912. A special feature of the
decorations is the wrought ironwork by Majorelle, forged by hand
and finished with gold leaf.

A new installation, very much of today, is Matsuzakaya, the
Japanese boutique on the ground floor. Japanese visitors closely
follow Americans as the store's biggest overseas spenders, and to help
them through the trials of mega-choice and the Western alphabet
they now have their own boutique, run by Japanese staff and stocked
with goods likely to interest them. The selection is based on their
known preferences, e.g. for Chanel, Céline and clothes by Japanese
designers.

Foreign customers account for 20 per cent of the store's business
and their buying habits are, not surprisingly, different from those of

French shoppers. At Galeries Lafayette the No.1 foreign sellers are perfumes, beauty products, women's wear, tableware and things for children. French shoppers go principally for women's wear.

To promote their fashion sales, Galeries Lafayette hold twice-weekly shows (*défilés de mode*) which change four times a year with the seasons. Staged for the benefit of international visitors, they take place in the Opéra salon on the 7th floor. Light refreshments are served, and shows begin on Wednesday at 11.00 throughout the year and on Friday at 11.00 from March to October. Entrance is free but anyone interested should telephone in advance to reserve places, or risk being turned away; tel. 48.74.02.30.

The *défilés* are for showing off what is currently on sale in the store, unlike fashion-house shows which preview the coming season. Elegant models parade the catwalk in a succession of lingerie, skirts and jackets, dresses, suits and evening wear by designers too numerous to list but here are one or two: Balmain, Rosy, Cina Bis, J.C. de Castelbajac, Dorothée Bis, Thierry Mugler, Montana, Emmanuelle Khanh, Sonia Rykiel, Pisanti, Yves St Laurent, Christian Dior, Guy Laroche, Lolita Lempicka, Courrèges, Dejac, Fred France. It is obviously one of the great strengths of a large department store that it can gather together, present and sell the clothes of some twenty top designers at any one time.

At Au Printemps, by the way, they follow a fairly similar routine. Their *défilé* begins at 10.00 each Tuesday all the year round, and each Friday from 1 March to 31 October there is a second show, also from 10.00. There is no charge; to apply for an invitation ring 42.82.56.47.

The general layout of the Galeries Lafayette is as follows:

7th floor	Terrace on roof with open-air café.
6th	Cafeteria and grill, books and gadgets.
5th	Linens, special boutiques, e.g. Musée du Louvre, Souleiado (country fabrics).
4th	Rugs, lighting, furniture, hi-fi.
3rd	Children's wear, toys, lingerie (on a vast and luxurious marble floor).
2nd	Women's wear (the more dressy dresses and designer fashions, as modelled at the *défilés*), hair and beauty salon (one of the largest in Europe).
1st	Leather goods, furs, shoes, fashion sportswear.

Ground   Perfumes, accessories, luggage, jewellery, gifts.
Basement China, crystal, gadgets, earthenware, lost and found.
A two-decker bridge connects to the men's shop, Galfa Club, which offers the following departments:
2nd floor   Suits, coats, shoes.
1st   Sportswear, co-ordinates.
Ground   Accessories.
In addition, Galeries Lafayette has a third shop, devoted to sports goods, situated next door at the foot of Rue La Fayette.

Our walk ends here. To rest weary feet, and recover from escalator fatigue, step across the Rue La Fayette to Le Canari, a sophisticated and comfortable brasserie. My general verdict at the end of a Department Store trail: Au Printemps wins for household goods, Galeries Lafayette for fashion and general presentation, and Brummell and Galfa Club are about neck-and-neck for menswear. Aux Trois Quartiers has a lot of catching up to do.

Walk 19

8ᵉ The Champs Elysées

France's most famous avenue. A walk from the obelisk in the
Pl. de la Concorde to the Arc de Triomphe, visiting the Petit
Palais and Grand Palais, exclusive window-shopping in Av.
Montaigne, browsing in galleries at the Rond Point.
Allow 3–4 hours.
Best times Not Sunday, when many shops closed, or
Monday and holidays when Petit Palais closed; Grand Palais
closed Tuesday; top of Arc de Triomphe closed 1 January, 1
and 8 May, 1 and 11 November, 25 December.

ROUTE

Begin at Ⓜ Concorde. Nearest buses 24, 42, 52, 72, 73, 84, 94. Cross from E side of square to central island with obelisk and fountains. Cross to W side of square at foot of Champs Elysées, by *Marly Horses*. On S side of Champs Elysées walk through gardens past Restaurant Ledoyen to Pl. Clemenceau. Visit Petit Palais 👁; open 10.00 to 17.45, closed Monday and holidays. *Admission*.

Across road visit Grand Palais for special exhibition(s) 👁; open 10.00 to 20.00, closed Tuesday. *Admission*. Around corner in Av. Franklin D. Roosevelt is entrance to Palais de la Découverte (Planetarium and scientific exhibitions) 👁; open 10.00 to 17.45, closed Monday and holidays. *Admission*.

Cross Av. Franklin D. Roosevelt and go down Rue Goujon to Pl.

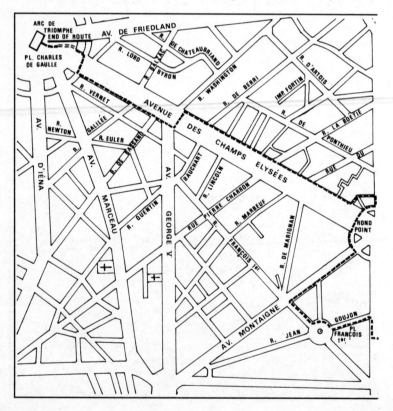

François 1er, then take 2nd right into Rue François 1er and walk to Av. Montaigne. Turn right and walk up to Rond Point des Champs Elysées. Explore shopping galleries and walk up Champs Elysées to Arc de Triomphe (shopping galleries on right-hand side, in sun; most famous café, Fouquet's, on left-hand side, in shade).

To reach foot of Arc de Triomphe, walk through underpass – entrance on N (right-hand) side of Champs Elysées. Take lift to top of Arch ☞; open 10.00 to 17.30, closed on holidays listed above. *Admission*. Walk ends by Tomb of Unknown Soldier at base of Arch. Nearest refreshments Drugstore Publicis at 133 Av. des Champs Elysées. Nearest Ⓜ Ch. de Gaulle-Etoile. Or continue west to La Défense – see essay for details.

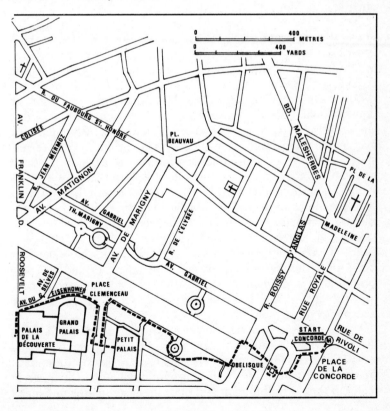

Place de la Concorde

It began as a royal square, laid out in honour of Louis XV. In 1792 the statue of the king was felled and the square became the Place de la Révolution, and for two years Dr Guillotin's razor rose and chopped through more than thirteen hundred necks, among them those of Louis XVI, Marie-Antoinette, Charlotte Corday, Danton and Robespierre. In 1795 the Directory sought to efface the recent past, and with one further blow renamed the square the Place de la Concorde. The change of name was accepted and has not been seriously challenged since. In 1989 the square was the obvious and undisputed venue for the opening ceremony of the *Bicentenaire*, the 200th birthday of the Revolution, or, in the more practical wording used at the time, the '200th anniversary of the French Declaration of the Rights of Man and the Citizen'.

Not every French citizen who passes twice daily through the square thinks automatically of his glorious Republic. He or she is more likely to be glaring out of the window of a bus or car, wondering when on earth the whistling policeman is going to secure their release from it, so they can get to work.

The traffic problems of the Place de la Concorde are so acute, the square would suffocate entirely without the operatic nudges, the deft insertions and the surgical bypasses of that supremely interfering man in the middle with the white gloves and whistle. 'Pee-pee-pee-peee-ouuu!' he goes. This is one of his favourite instructions. Both his arms semaphore crazily, the whistle call is repeated, and at his bidding a northbound No.84 bus which has been in the square for twelve minutes so far, makes a solid gain of three metres. Then the policeman wheels through ninety degrees and attacks the cross-stream. 'Prr-eeeee-ouuu-wee-EE!' he goes – a dramatic change of tune – then he points and prods at individual drivers. Yes, *you*! 'Pee-pee-prrr!' Ushering, pulling forward, thrusting back and sweeping onwards, he again minutely adjusts the sea of foaming motor cars, and the face of the driver of the No.84 bus is a mask of tragic acceptance.

We meanwhile have been luckier. Crossing at the traffic lights halfway along the square we have reached the island and now stand next to one of Hittorf's fountains (1840), modelled on those in St Peter's Square, Rome. Fish-hugging figures stand up to their hips in water in the north fountain, and have survived their damp habitat better than their companions seated round the pedestal, whose layer of bronze has begun to peel nastily.

Gilded pictures carved on the base of the granite Obelisk of Luxor demonstrate how in 1831 the 3,300-year-old monument was dragged to the banks of the Nile, then loaded in the hold of Captain Verninac's purpose-built barge, the *Louqsor,* and towed to France. The Obelisk, 23 m (75 ft) high, was the gift of Pasha Mehemet Ali, and was gladly accepted by King Louis-Philippe who saw in it a most convenient non-political centrepiece for the Place de la Concorde. Models showing the Obelisk's journey to France are on view in the Maritime Museum (see *Walk 15*).

Around the edge of this admirably spacious square – best seen after the early-evening traffic rush or on Sunday morning – are eight pavilions surmounted by statues representing the eight principal towns of France: Lyons, Marseilles, Bordeaux, Nantes, Lille, Brest, Rouen, Strasbourg. On the north side of the square are Jacques-Ange Gabriel's two fine mansions completed in 1770; on the left is the Hôtel Crillon, now shared between the luxury hotel of that name and the Automobile Club de France, and on the right the Hôtel de la Marine, the Navy Ministry.

The Champs Elysées

At the entrance to the 'rural' end of the Elysian Fields stand replicas of Coustou's *Marly Horses,* brought there from the Château de Marly near Versailles. We stroll through quiet gardens originally laid out in 1670 by Le Nôtre and redesigned in 1765 by the Marquis de Marigny. Allied troops camped there in 1814–16 and it took two years to clear up the mess and restore the gardens. Walk past the bandstand and round by the historic Restaurant Ledoyen, an establishment begun in the reign of Louis XVI, to the statue of Clemenceau, France's Prime Minister at the end of the First World War. The bronze muffler of the journalist-turned-statesman flies out stiffly, its two ends crossing behind his neck.

The Petit Palais – built for the World Exhibition of 1900, as was its conservatory twin the Grand Palais – now contains an assortment of art collections presented to the city. It is well worth a visit, especially if you have already made the rounds of the big galleries – the Louvre, d'Orsay and Modern Art. In these spacious rooms, grouped around a large internal courtyard, you find a satisfying *mélange* of paintings, sculpture and art objects which, though not all of the highest quality, make a relaxing change from the all-star galleries and blockbuster special exhibitions.

Across the Avenue Winston Churchill, the Grand Palais is now one of the main venues in Paris for special exhibitions such as the recent, intellectually intriguing though horribly cramped show *Le Japonisme*, tracing the Japanese influence on European art of the late nineteenth century. Joined to the Grand Palais, and entered on the far side, is the Palais de la Découverte, another huge space incorporating the Planetarium and halls for temporary scientific exhibitions. Subjects here range through the sciences: 'Image – Technique or Magic?' was one recent theme, 'Insects – half demons, half marvels' was another, and 'Natural Gas' a third.

We now take to the backwaters at the rear of the Champs Elysées, passing honey-coloured stone apartment blocks where the truly rich must and do live, arriving via the tranquil circus of Place François 1ᵉʳ at the Avenue Montaigne. This is a zone of five-star boutiques: Fouquet's confectionery shop at 22 Rue François 1ᵉʳ, next to Caron's *parfumier*; opposite is Christian Dior, over there is Nina Ricci. Gathered here are the headquarters of those fashion names who unquestionably have made it. At No.49 is Thierry Mugler, at No.51 Jean-Louis Scherrer, and inside No.44 an assistant gently rubs down a couch at Jean-Claude Jitrois, high priest of leatherwear.

If it is now lunchtime, you can avoid the monster prices charged around the flower-bedded Rond Point by crossing to the northern arm of the Avenue Franklin D. Roosevelt. There you will find working Parisians taking a restoring course or two at Le Petit Elysée or Le Ponthieu on the corner of Rue Ponthieu. Opposite, for something bigger, is a Hippopotamus, one of a popular chain offering *formules* with grills, flash cocktails in bucket-sized glasses, pitchers of wine or what you will. (For a fun evening, try the Hippo Citroën just up the Champs Elysées, where you rise in a glass lift to the bar and restaurant on the 1st floor.)

Back at the Rond Point, delve into the gallery behind the St Laurent Rive Gauche boutique, and sample the style of the shopping malls which now run like so many rabbit warrens off the north side of the Champ Elysées. They are today's brassy version of the old Passages, e.g. off the Boulevard Montmartre (see *Walk 20*), with escalators, fountains and jiggy-jig muzak to entertain and keep the crowds on the move. Out in the daylight most people walk on the sunny side of the Avenue des Champs Elysées, stopping at the expensive café terraces, browsing in the galleries or contemplating the fronts of massive cinema complexes and the Lido night club. The rest of the frontages belong to impersonal giants like national airlines and car manufacturers. Among the better watering-holes on the shady south side are La Maison d'Alsace, about as far up-market as a brasserie can go before it becomes something else; and Fouquet's, on the corner of Avenue George V, a famous café loved by journalists and the *glitterati*, which the American columnist Art Buchwald found to be ideally placed for watching street demonstrations and which was the setting for his famous article 'Don't Throw the Tables'. Nearer the top of the avenue, the view of the Arc de Triomphe now waxing mightily, call in at the Office de Tourisme to see what is on offer or have a question answered, and note the position of the Drugstore, which has a pharmacy and bookshop as well as a café and may come in handy for refreshments later.

Art Buchwald's penchant for demonstrations is a reminder that this avenue is indeed a major venue for parades and processions. On election nights, victorious voters bring their cars here to process up and down at a crawl, honking their horns; celebratory and political marches still bring in the crowds, and each year the final leg of the Tour de France cycle race is cheered by thousands along a dumbbell-shaped course between Etoile and Place de la Concorde. In former times too, people gathered here in enormous numbers: in 1840 to see Napoleon's hearse pass through the Arc de Triomphe on its way to the Invalides; in 1919 to mark the end of the First World War and in August 1944 the Liberation of Paris; to demonstrate during the Algerian crisis of 1958 and the student rebellion of 1968, and to march in honour of General de Gaulle after his death in 1970.

Arc de Triomphe
However great their reverence for de Gaulle, Parisians find it difficult to call the Place Charles de Gaulle by anything other than its previous

(and still preserved) name: Etoile, the appropriately star-shaped circus from which twelve broad avenues diverge. It was already a major junction, with a semi-circular lawn in the middle, when in 1806 Napoleon commissioned Chalgrin to build a gigantic triumphal arch in honour of the *Grande Armée*. The work was delayed, then abandoned during the Restoration, and the Arch was not completed until 1836, when King Louis-Philippe dedicated it to the Armies of the French.

Walk round the Arch to see the reliefs carved on all four sides: Rude's *Departure of the Volunteers*, also called *The Marseillaise*, which faces the Champs Elysées, is generally thought the most distinguished. Beneath the Arch is the Tomb of the Unknown Soldier: his body was brought there for burial on Armistice Day 1920, and three years later the Flame of Remembrance was lit for the first time.

Take the lift almost to the top of the 50 m (164 ft) Arch, then go up a few steps to the platform. The views all-round are excellent, following the great avenues which march away in every direction. Those to east and west are most compelling of all: down the Champs Elysées to the Place de la Concorde, then the Carrousel Arch at the Louvre and, just off-centre, the Pyramid (not a mistake, this, the whole of the Louvre Palace is on a different axis, following the line of the river). To the west the Avenue de la Grande Armée sets off towards the towers of La Défense and its new centrepiece, the giant cube known as the Grande Arche.

La Défense

Our walk ends at the Arc de Triomphe, though you may like to keep on going west and have a closer look at La Défense, the new business and residential centre. The 73 bus goes all the way, or take the RER surburban express from Ⓜ Ch. de Gaulle-Etoile (special ticket needed). When you arrive, follow signs to 'La Grande Arche'. This great white structure by J.O. von Spreckelsen is the central orna-ment of the whole scheme and stands in direct alignment with the Arc de Triomphe. From the platform at the top of the broad stone staircase, slender pill-shaped lifts rise alarmingly into the belly of the Arche, ferrying visitors to the 'Belvedere'. *Admission*.

The development of La Défense has received many setbacks in its brief history, thanks to top-level changes of policy about funding. People thought it would become a walk-in version of Godard's *Alphaville*, a science-fiction city, but so far it refuses to take on any precise identity, remaining a dislocated collection of office towers, shops and apartments. The shell-roofed CNIT complex is now open, a palace devoted to information technology with ground-floor shops and cafés. The Cocktail Bar, fronted by a terrace of under-worked umbrellas, is probably the best stopping-place for the casual visitor, an indoor refuge safe from the hostile winds that sweep the Parvis, the central square.

At Le Café de France on the Parvis they have (had?) quite the rudest waiter in Paris. When I last called, he had been agitated into astounding acts of disgruntlement, flinging menus at customers who dared to not automatically know what they wanted, exploding at two old ladies who asked after their long-ordered ice creams, complaining bitterly to other francophone customers about the lack of French spoken by a Japanese family. He climaxed this particular run of atrocious behaviour by nearly hitting a French business man who had been waiting thirty minutes for his *croque monsieur*. 'Of course you've been waiting,' he screamed in a Basil Fawlty climax. 'They had a fire in the kitchen and burnt everything!'

It could only happen at La Défense, I thought at the time, watching balls of litter blow across the windy acres of the pedestrian precinct. But do go and see. It can only get better. And, one day, it will be finished.

Walk 20

10e Shopping in Paradise

Classics of crystal, china and silverware in the Rue de Paradis; a tour of the nearby Poster Museum; down past the Folies Bergère to the Passages, plus the waxworks and other attractions of the eccentric Musée Grévin.

Allow   3½–4 hours.

Best times   Not Sunday; some shops in Rue de Paradis also closed Saturday. Poster Museum open 12.00 to 18.00, closed Tuesday. Musée Grévin open every day 13.00 to 19.00.

ROUTE

Begin at Ⓜ Château d'Eau. Nearest buses 38, 47. Exit on Bd de Strasbourg, turn S and immediately right into Rue du Château d'Eau. Take 1st right into Rue du Faubourg St Denis and 1st left into Rue de Paradis.

Crystal, china and all-purpose tableware shops predominate for 500 metres. Wander at random but do not miss the most glamorous of all: the showroom and crystal museum of the Baccarat company (No. 30 *bis*), set back from the road in a courtyard (sign to it on road) 👁 ; open Monday to Friday 09.00 to 18.00, Saturday 10.00 to 12.00 and 14.00 to 17.30.

Also well worth a visit is the Poster Museum (Musée de la Publicité) at No. 18, housed in the old pottery workshops of Choisy-le-Roi 👁 ; open 12.00 to 18.00, closed Tuesday. *Admission.*

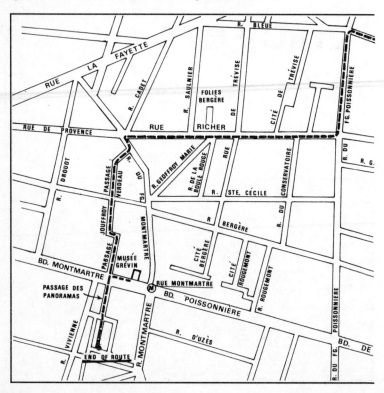

Continue to end of Rue de Paradis and turn left into Rue du Faubourg Poissonnière, then 1st right into Rue Richer. Walk past Folies Bergère and at end of road turn left into Rue du Faubourg Montmartre. Cross road immediately and enter the Passage Verdeau. Stroll through, browsing in the boutiques, and at end of arcade cross road and enter Passage Jouffroy which dog-legs twice before reaching Bd Montmartre.

On left in Boulevard at No.10 is Musée Grévin, offering a strange but friendly mixture of waxworks, distorting mirrors, special effects and magic ☞; open every day 13.00 to 19.00, 10.00 to 19.00 in school holidays. *Admission.* Visit the museum either now or after walking round the Passage des Panoramas and linking galleries, situated at No.11 Bd Montmartre across the boulevard from Passage Jouffroy.

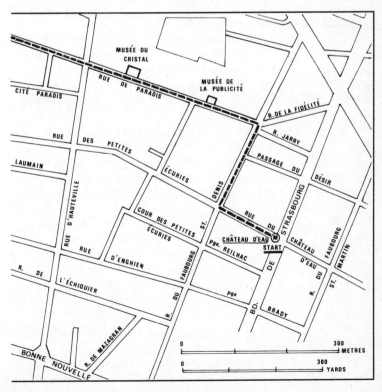

assage des Panoramas. Nearest refreshments in the
tiny Bar des Variétés at No. 12 or, almost opposite,
L'Arbre à ...elle (The Cinnamon Tree) tea-shop and restaurant.
Nearest Ⓜ Rue Montmartre.

Château d'Eau

This walk takes us into a less-than-fashionable commercial quarter,
one that tourists might hardly ever go to were it not the centre of the
tableware trade in Paris, offering magnificently crafted glass, china
and silverware at the most affordable prices you are likely to find
anywhere in the city. Fanciful to pretend that these pieces are *cheap*,
but whether or not you buy even the tiniest porcelain box or crystal
paperweight to mark your visit, lingering for an hour or so amid all
this sparkle and luxury seldom fails to buck the spirits.

At Ⓜ Château d'Eau you reach the pavement via one of Hector
Guimard's sinuous, stalky Métro entrances, designed in 1900 and
now a classic of the Art Nouveau movement, and a listed building as
well; also, alas, in sore need of more green paint – a temporary
oversight, I hope, since not many of these elegant plant-like
structures remain.

The name Château d'Eau (Water Tower) is both interesting and
odd in that there is no sign in the neighbourhood of any watery edifice
to justify it. The name refers to a long-gone fountain with three basins
and eight spouting lions which, more than a hundred years ago, stood
at the far, eastern end of the Rue du Château d'Eau, on the site of the
present Place de la République. This was formerly called the Place du
Château d'Eau and was a very different square from the vast hole-in-
the-houses that you find there today.

We turn along the Rue du Château d'Eau – African hairdressing a
speciality here – and into the Rue du Faubourg St Denis where more
of the same is offered, spectacularly at Beauté des Tropiques, the
windows piled to the top with jars of Cocoa Butter Lotion, etc.

Note for jazz fans

If, at the end of the Rue du Château d'Eau, you keep straight on into
the Rue des Petites Ecuries, you come to the New Morning Club

(No.57-9) where big names appear (recently Chico Hamilton, Art Blakey, Lou Donaldson on separate nights in the same week) provided, of course, they turn up.

Rue de Paradis

As you enter the Rue de Paradis, you may wonder for the first few yards if you are in the right place, but soon the first of several acres of porcelain and pottery, and crystal in every shape from goblets to candelabra or a chunky mustang's head, crowds in to enclose you. Limoges and Meissen, Baccarat and St Louis, Daum and Lalique, Christofle and Tétard – all are here, and many more besides.

Limoges Unic (Nos 8 and 12) and Porcelaine Savary (No.9) offer place settings and table accessories; lots of silverware at the latter, and coffee sets, jugs, mugs and bowls; sumptuous dinner services along the road at Villeroy & Boch (No.17) in delicate patterns and soft pastel colours. Nearly all shops serve both trade and public: signs confirm this with the words *Gros et Détail* (wholesale and retail). Look out for *Soldes* (reductions).

The tableware business settled in this north-eastern quarter because it was conveniently close to the Gare de l'Est. This is the arrival point for glass from the Vosges, a region rich in timber and silicate sand where the great glassmaking houses of St Louis and Baccarat began. It is also the terminus for porcelain and faience from Nancy, Lunéville and Strasbourg.

Poster Museum

Somewhere along the way, take a break from crystal gazing and at No.18 Rue de Paradis enter the covered courtyard leading to the Poster Museum (Musée de la Publicité). Part of the Union des Arts Décoratifs, and housing about 50,000 posters, this quietly charming, ever-so-slightly musty institution retains a visible link with the pottery trade.

Although the museum dates only from 1978, its premises are much older. Built in about 1900, they originally contained the pottery workshops (*faïenceries*) of the house of Choisy-le-Roi. An old railway line curves through the courtyard and the walls are decorated with large tableaux made of ceramic tiles painted in appropriately flattish, poster-like colours.

The museum has posters of all periods from their beginning around 1750 up to the present day, including several from the Revolution of May 1968, though the period of, roughly, 1870 to 1914 provides the core of the collection, a time when Art Nouveau and commercial enterprise made a brilliant fusion. The collection is continually updated with gifts from the Union de la Publicité Extérieure, from artists and collectors. In its cinema the museum shows TV and cinema advertisements and films on graphics and the world of advertising, and there are facilities for researchers which include a specialist library and more than 20,000 posters on transparency.

Lack of space prevents more than a selection of posters being on public view at any one time, so the museum rotates the collection about every three months, grouping exhibits by theme. Recent shows were 'The French Circus', 'Postermania' and 'The English Poster in the Nineties'. I saw 'Rare Posters of the 1900s' which was, I gathered, typical enough to justify a brief trailer.

There were three sections. The first was an international (non-French) assembly, the posters appearing by country of origin. Perhaps the Belgians were the strongest group, with works by Jaspar, Mignot, and Toussaint outstanding; the British had Beggarstaff, Beardsley, Hardy and Mackintosh. In the central alley of the museum, tall like the nave of a church, a group of large posters and a few gigantic ones included three of Manuel Orazi's 1900 series on the American dancer Loïe Fuller, and others by Chéret featuring showgirls. Best of all, in a low-ceilinged, curtained-off room, were showbiz posters from the Gay Paree of legend: brash, black and red, curvaceously lettered street messages in praise of the Moulin Rouge, the Moulin de la Galette, the Cabaret du Néant, Les Noctambules, and various shows starring Aristide Bruant, the foul-tongued but fashionable cabaret singer, defying you not to admire him in the red muffler which Toulouse-Lautrec made famous. For Steinlen fans, and cat lovers too, a diabolical black moggy promotes the Tournée du Chat Noir, enormous whiskers prickling like the antennae of a praying mantis.

Before leaving the Poster Museum, wander round the bookshop

near the exit. They have a large selection of postcards, books and magazines on graphic art, catalogues of previous exhibitions and, naturally, posters, posters and posters.

Back on the Rue de Paradis, turn right and adjust your eyes to the dazzling window at Lumicristal. The best is yet to come. At No. 30, follow signs to the right into a courtyard where, at the end, past the trade-only International Tableware Center, is the headquarters of Les Cristalleries de Baccarat, which along with St Louis, Lalique and Daum is one of the most illustrious of the French crystal houses.

The less said about their modern glazed façade the better – square grey panels fitted round the original Directory-period staircase and doorway, all that survives of the old building. Once through the main door, however, almost everything improves. You are now in the oak-panelled hallway of a distinguished trading house, a discreet chandelier or two hinting at more opulent treasures upstairs in the company's showroom and museum.

I said 'almost everything' improves. At the stairhead there is one more setback. Flanked by two huge and admirable 'Abyssinian' vases, made in 1909 for an international exhibition, is a sorry piece of 1964 kitsch known loftily in these parts as 'Lady Baccarat'. She is a waxwork mannequin wrapped in a chandelier frock who greets new arrivals with arms held stiffly wide, a brandy snifter fitted into one hand and, laid across the other, a crystal version of a glass-maker's blowpipe. Her dress, the *Visitor's Guide* tells us, is 'made up of 3,200 lighting pendants, octagonals, palm leaves and cut crystal pendants'. I wished the *Guide* had also said '. . . which she sewed on herself', and so completed the *Come Dancing* image.

Step, however, a few paces into the showroom and the scene is transformed. Thousands of pieces of crystal (at Baccarat this means glass containing 30 per cent lead oxide) – decanters, fruit bowls, table ornaments, vases, goblets, ashtrays, dishes, menageries of tiny animals sparkle and wink at you from long tables which stretch into the distance. Vast chandeliers dominate the room; bearing up to four or five tiers of candles and weighing in at 75 kg (1½ cwt) apiece and more, they hang in butcher's hook style from a series of iron rails which are themselves suspended from the rafters and bolted to them.

It takes a moment to realise that you are in a gigantic shop, then you notice the prices on the items, then the sales assistants, seldom more than a whisper away. Discretion and calm prevail, and there is no pressure to buy, so feel free to roam up and down at will. For some minutes I greatly fancied, and seriously considered buying, a great crystal ice bucket with walls more than half an inch thick and really big gold handles, but then the sensible voice from within which sometimes says no said No! and I walked on.

After the showroom, be sure to see the company's excellent museum in the adjoining room. The Compagnie des Cristalleries de Baccarat, founded in 1764 in the village of Baccarat in Lorraine, has occupied this building since 1857. Here you will see crystal objects from tiny perfume bottles to massive wheel-engraved vases and table services supplied to presidents and royalty all over the world: the Maharajah of Baroda has some special Baccarat goblets, so do the King of Morocco, President Houphouet-Boigny of the Ivory Coast, the Saudi Royal Family, Prince Rainier III of Monaco, and many more. The oldest piece of crystal in the museum is a duplicate of the ewer presented in 1828 by the company to Charles X of France: a regally solid jug this, intricately banded and decorated with a gold and enamel cameo of the arms of France.

Look out, also, for crystal paperweights, and opalines and other decorative pieces – decanters, vases, cigarette holders – made of coloured agate or alabaster glass, originally intended to imitate precious stones. And if you should think that your dining table at home has everything, consider whether you have any table napkin holders, by which I mean not a silver or porcelain ring but a set of lidded pots in opaque crystal, each with a base and stem painted in gold enamel, the stem moulded with four lions' heads. It is the sort of thing they do very well at Baccarat.

We march on. Out through the courtyard, a former post house for coaches from eastern France, and into the Rue de Paradis where the displays of crystal and porcelain continue to the end of the road and the Cristalleries de St Louis, La Tisanière Paradis, Benardaud, Godin, Daum and others compete for our attention – and will be very pleased to handle anyone's *liste de mariage*.

Turning down the Rue du Faubourg Poissonnière, the old route of the fishmongers travelling to market at Les Halles, we come soon to the Rue Richer and its most glamorous resident, the Folies Bergère. By 8.30 each evening (except on Mondays when they put their feet up for a well-earned *relâche*), all roads in the neighbourhood will be blocked by a trail of cars, coaches and taxis crawling towards the white lights of this revered and ageless symbol of Paris night life. The marvel of it is, they get a virtually full house every night watching a menu of acts which has hardly changed in 120 years.

For all its fame and fondness for tradition, however, the *idea* of the Folies Bergère excites wildly differing responses among people who have never been there. Not everyone realises that it is a review and takes place in a theatre, nor that it is one of the mildest, jolliest shows in town.

The Passages

At the end of the Rue Richer, we turn into the Rue du Faubourg Montmartre and cross the road immediately, entering a rather unclean-looking tunnel which bears the words 'PASSAGE VERDEAU'.

Of the three *passages* in this loose network, the Verdeau is visually the least attractive, and not all the shops are currently let, but do not miss it for the inviting jumble of bric-à-brac on display: cheap jewellery; second-hand books at Librairie Farfouille (No.29); old postcards, paintings, sculptures, ornaments, gems; old and historic cameras at Photo Verdeau (Nos.14–16).

Across the road at the far end is the Passage Jouffroy. Best of all in this first or northern leg of the Passage is Cinédoc (Nos.43–53), a dream in several shopwidths for the movie lover or student of the cinema. Inside, low lights and dark wood cabinets crammed with books impose an air of learning but do not be put off from going in; think of it more as a movie set for a cinema bookshop. The French as a nation have adopted movies as a quasi-religion, and here you can stock up with all the books, posters, postcards and stills you will need until the next time.

Around the double bend in the Passage, the shops grow more like each other, selling unremarkable clothes, etc, though Abel and its neighbour, Galerie 34, are great for walking sticks, maple canes with carved and decorated heads and (Abel only) dozens of brightly coloured parasols and umbrellas. Some coquettish numbers here, with frilled edges, just the thing for an old-fashioned wiggle down the boulevard. Le Bonheur des Dames (No.39) offers gifts for mothers and brides, and Pain d'Epices (No.29) has very pretty toys and puppets. Senanques (No.14) is a ritzy pen shop with broad-barrelled fountain pens in either a plain, Moroccan leather or wood-grain finish. They also sell the smartest dip-pens I have ever seen.

Approaching the Boulevard Montmartre we pass an exit from the weird but always entertaining Musée Grévin, to which we will return in a moment. For now, we cross the boulevard into the Passage des Panoramas. As before, much on offer is modish frippery, but at least you (and I) need never go home without a present. Stamps at Hédrouy and Panoramas Philatélie. A highlight of this arcade is Stern the engraver (No.47): a superbly dignified façade, befitting a firm which since 1840 has produced hand-engraved cards, writing paper, invitations and other printed commissions for royalty, the French diplomatic service and a medley of the well-heeled. At the base of the shop windows is a sign-painted catalogue of the engraver's stock-in-trade.

Here at the junction of the Passage des Panoramas and the Galerie des Variétés, near the stage door of the Théâtre des Variétés, a famous home of operetta and boulevard comedy, look around and contemplate the origins of these glass-roofed Passages. They were built to offer shoppers a covered, gas-lit alternative to the rain, dust, mud and worse flung at them on the roaring boulevard in days when the traffic was horse-drawn. The Passage des Panoramas dates from 1799 and takes its name from two great painted panoramas of capital cities which were installed there in rotundas by the American Henry Fulton, a painter-turned-engineer who is usually associated with early steamships and the submersible *Nautilus*, of 1801, which he tried in vain to sell to Napoleon's ministers. They viewed the design for this ancestor of the submarine with grave distaste and rejected it, saying it was a disgraceful way to fight a war.

Now, as then, the Passages offer a quiet refuge in which to wander, shopping and window-shopping. Around 5.30pm, towards the end of a warm afternoon in autumn, few people are about and a well-fed tabby and white cat sits calmly outside the engraver's shop, asserting its claim to a piece of this agreeable tranquillity. No doubt wary, too, of straying out on the boulevard, where a wilder, noisier, more dangerous race of humans rush about, the sort who have no time for pussies. At 9 pm, proof that the Passages are another world, the iron gates at each end are closed until morning.

Grévin Museum

In 1882 a caricaturist called Grévin opened his waxworks museum at 10 Boulevard Montmartre. In recent years it has become a kind of superior fun palace, attracting flocks of native as well as overseas visitors to its eccentric halls and corridors. Waxworks, distorting mirrors, a magic show, a *cabinet fantastique*, a *palais des mirages* – prepare to be astounded.

There are those who will flinch at the admission charge, which is on a par with riding about 2½ stages up the Eiffel Tower, but on balance I feel you get your money's worth if you take in all the attractions. Buy a (cheap) programme sheet at the souvenir stall and start spotting the celebrities, sports stars, film stars, TV stars and politicians. Here and there wax 'visitors' are planted in the public areas to fool the unwary. One of these, a middle-aged male dressed as a dusty provincial clerk, sits reading on a bench opposite a wonderfully improbable International Space Summit. Mitterrand, Thatcher, Kohl and Gorbachov loll about in space suits generally solving things while, to one side of them, Reagan, Deng Xiao Ping, their stewardess Raquel Welch and a helmeted dog-in-space share a joke.

Downstairs is history, and less easy for non-French visitors. There are 'Scenes from the Revolution' and a 'Panorama of French History from Charlemagne to Napoleon III'. Lots of people are in prison cells, wax rats clustering at their food bowls. Marat in the bath is there – in *the* bath, rather, for a programme note states it is *'une pièce authentique'*, the very *baignoire* in which Charlotte Corday stabbed him!

Suddenly, a loudspeaker began to address us. It urged all the 'Messieurs et Mesdames' in the museum kindly to go upstairs. No reason given – just go. All of us – French, Italians (lots of Italians), Americans, Spanish, Portuguese, English, Japanese – poured hastily up the marble balustraded staircase, as though at a party in a friend's castle, and crowded chattering into the Palais des Mirages, a smallish polygonal room mirrored from floor to ceiling. Stern Buddhas looked down on us from high plinths set against the walls. We were in a sort of Burmese jungle palace; the air was faintly menacing. The lights went down. Someone shut the door.

It would be churlish to describe what happened next, though it was quite nice really. Well, I thought afterwards, that must be about it. But no. Next we were guided through previously unglimpsed corridors into a theatre, and seated ourselves before a cinema screen. A short film plugged Grévin's other Paris museum at the Forum des Halles. Then – a conjuror!

Up went the screen and on to the stage walked a mature Balinese-looking lady in a saffron dress. She made doves appear from handkerchiefs, and handkerchiefs from handkerchiefs, then doves from a box, and a rabbit from a cage which we all thought had doves in it. She also did amazing things with torn-up newspaper, and much else besides. At the end of her act the audience clapped long and loud. Then they either resumed their visit or left the museum, as I did in a state of mild shock. Did we really see all that? Yes indeed we did. At the Musée Grévin you catch a rare taste of boulevard entertainment from the Good Old Days.

Walk 21

16ᵉ Bon chic, bon genre

Take a stroll through Passy and La Muette, the elegant territory of Paris's Sloane Ranger class, the *BCBG*. Visit Balzac's House, the intriguing Museum of Spectacles and Lorgnettes, walk across the Ranelagh Gardens to the Musée Marmottan, and in the Bois de Boulogne take the ferry to the Châlet des Iles.
Allow   4 hours.
Best times   Not Monday or holidays, when Balzac's House and Musée Marmottan closed. Spectacles Museum also closed Sunday.

ROUTE

Begin at Ⓜ Trocadéro. Nearest buses 22, 30, 32, 63. Walk South past the rear of Palais de Chaillot and at Sq. Yorktown bear left into Rue Franklin. At Pl. de Costa Rica continue straight ahead on Rue Raynouard to Balzac's House (Maison de Balzac) ☞; open 10.00 to 17.40, closed Monday and holidays. *Admission (free Sunday).*

At exit, turn right and cross road into Rue de l'Annonciation, then at junction bear left into Rue de Passy. At next junction (Ⓜ Muette), turn left into Av. Mozart and across road at No.2 visit Spectacles Museum (Musée des Lunettes et Lorgnettes) ☞; open Tuesday to Saturday 09.30 to 19.00, Saturday closes 12.30 to 14.00, closed Sunday, Monday. Return to junction and turn left into Chaussée de la Muette. At Ranelagh Gardens (Jardin du Ranelagh) walk past

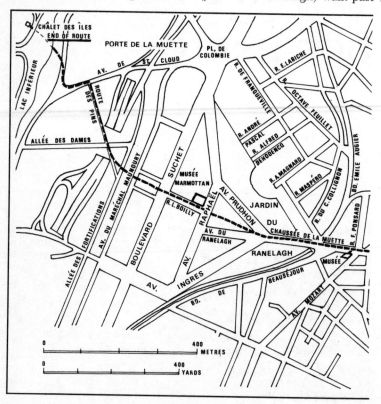

donkey rides and bandstand to Musée Marmottan on far side,
entrance in Rue Louis Boilly 👁; open 10.00 to 17.30, closed Monday.
Admission.

At exit, turn right along Rue Louis Boilly, walk through gardens
and cross Av. du Maréchal Maunoury and Allée des Fortifications.
Two intersecting paths lead into the Bois de Boulogne, crossing a
tunnel section of the Bd Périphérique. Take right-hand path (Route
des Pins) and continue down to lakeside and landing stage for ferry to
Châlet des Iles.

Walk ends at Châlet. Easiest way back is to bear left away from
landing stage, crossing several roads to Porte de la Muette/Place de
Colombie, where No.63 bus goes back to Trocadéro, then on to

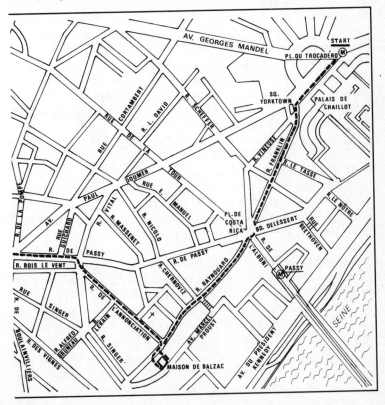

central Paris and Left Bank (Alma Marceau – Quai d'Orsay – Solférino Bellechasse – St Germain des Prés – Pl. Maubert – Gare de Lyon).

On being BCBG

This is the sixteenth *arrondissement* – Passy and La Muette – fashionable and exclusive, the domain of the *Bon Chic, Bon Genre* people, the spiritual cousins of London's Sloane Rangers. Their tribal chronicler, Thierry Mantoux, describes himself as a *BCBG* and it has not done him any harm. The biographical details on the cover of his best-selling book* reveal something of the particularities of a *BCBG*. Thierry Mantoux is president of a large champagne house. He is married to a lady called Marie-Laure, and his sons are called Aymeric, Grégoire and Charles (a good medieval touch there, and perhaps a hint of royalist sympathy, at least with the English Royals). He has a Preppy nephew in New York, and a Sloane Ranger cousin.

I went to look for M. Mantoux's book at Gibert Jeune in Place St Michel. Thinking it must be something like Peter York's *Sloane Ranger Handbook*, I looked for it under Humour, then Gift Books, then Sociology. In vain. I asked an assistant.

'It's over there,' she said, 'in Practical Living (*Vie Pratique*)'.

'Really,' I said, 'Practical Living?'

'It's the bible of the *BCBG*,' she told me gravely.

In the book, the author defines being *BCBG* as adhering to norms of behaviour which set aristocrats and the old bourgeoisie apart from other people, separating the old rich from the new rich. If you are old rich but currently broke, this does not matter since you are *BCBG* anyway.

On a half-day walk we must limit our *BCBG*-spotting to superficial traits. Look out for politely aloof males with neat haircuts wearing a green loden, a blazer or tweed suit with a club tie and well-polished Westons, and naturally restrained females dressed in a Hermès scarf, navy blue twin-set with pearls, perhaps a tartan skirt, navy blue tights and sensible shoes from Gucci, Céline or Carel. Other colours are

*Thierry Mantoux, *BCBG* (Editions Hermé).

possible, but they must be discreet, like beige or khaki. If such rigs do not sound terrifically fashionable, they are not meant to be. A *BCBG* dresses according to standards set by a previous generation; being *à la mode* is very much secondary to being properly turned out.

As we leave the Place du Trocadéro, the first cultural influence is American. After the statue of Benjamin Franklin in the Square Yorktown (commemorating the siege that effectively decided the American Revolutionary War), we continue on Rue Franklin to Place de Costa Rica and shortly come to the former headquarters of the American Field Service, 1914-17. A plaque announces: 'Through the house which formerly stood here passed 2,437 American Volunteers who served under the French flag. Their ambulances carried more than 400,000 wounded *poilus* (soldiers) to safety and 127 gave their lives so that France might live.'

Along the way are some distinguished apartment buildings from the turn of the century. One of the most talked-about is No. 25 *bis* Rue Franklin (1903). Designed by Auguste Perret, it has two side towers and a deeply recessed middle block with huge windows on each storey. This was the first secular building of note to use a framed reinforced concrete construction; the concrete is faced with ceramic slabs, left plain on the essential frame of the building and decorated with a floral Art Nouveau pattern on the non-load-bearing panels.

At No. 8 Rue Franklin is the Musée Clémenceau, where France's war leader lived from 1896 to 1919. His apartment has been kept as it was on the day he died; open 14.00 to 17.00, closed Monday, Wednesday, Friday and August. *Admission.*

Balzac's House

Turn in at the gateway and go down a steep flight of steps to the garden. Honoré de Balzac took this pretty house in October 1840 under the false name of Madame de Brugnol or de Breugnol, went into hiding (not for the first time in his life) and stayed there until April 1847, occasionally rushing abroad to visit his future wife, Madame de Hanska. If bailiffs turned up at the house, he had a choice of exits, on to Rue Raynouard at the front and Rue du Roc (now Rue Berton) at the back. The part of the house he occupied was on the second storey, and he also had the use of the garden and a cellar. Here he pressed on with his Human Comedy cycle, working to a desperately arduous schedule but writing some of his greatest novels: *Une ténébreuse affaire, La Rabouilleuse, Splendeurs et misères des courtisanes, La cousine Bette* and others. Sixty years after his death the house became a private museum, and since 1949 it has been owned by the Ville de Paris.

In these small rooms crowded with portraits, caricatures, books and memorabilia, including his coffee-maker, initialled H.B., there is still a strong sense of the man's bustling creativity. The first object on view near the entrance is a small portrait head by Rodin. The novelist lived until 1850, a decade or so into the first age of photography, and displayed here is a blown-up proof of Nadar's famous portrait. Nearby is a caricature by Jean-Pierre Dantan. Balzac thought the artist had exaggerated his bulk: 'I look like Louis XVIII,' he said.

Throughout his life Balzac amassed huge debts which he worked at a frantic rate to pay off without ever quite catching up. He was a ferocious corrector of proofs, often having a first draft set in type and then rewriting it on the proof. An example in the museum is covered with corrections and includes a note to his printer: 'Charles – quick another proof on the same paper but *double the size . . .*'

Sit for a while in the shady hillside garden. On the north wall is a bas-relief commemorating characters from the Human Comedy.

Passy and La Muette

Passy was once a village inhabited by woodcutters and the Rue de Passy was its main street. Spring waters rich in iron were found there in the eighteenth century and Passy's stock began to rise. Now the tenants of Rue de Passy are distinctly smart – purveyors of the right stuff to the *BCBG* of the *quartier*: steady good taste at Daniel Hechter (No.2 Pl. de Passy), shoes at F. Pinet (No.70 Rue de Passy), then department store fashion at Franck & Fils; opposite, tableware at Christofle (No.95), and around the corner at No.9 Avenue Mozart, classic shoes at Carel.

The optician's shop on the corner of Avenue Mozart is the home of one of Paris's more eccentric museums, the Musée des Lunettes et Lorgnettes. Its subject is the history of eyeglasses revealed in some 2,500 exhibits – binoculars, telescopes and microscopes; spectacles and lorgnettes of the eighteenth and nineteenth centuries, beautifully inlaid and enamelled, and some fascinating celebrity items – the gold monocle worn by Sarah Bernhardt, the spectacles of Sophia Loren, and many more.

Muet, and its feminine version *muette*, means dumb or mute, but the district called La Muette takes its name from another, though disputed, source. Rival claimants both point back to the sixteenth century when Charles IX kept a hunting lodge there. One faction says the name comes from the word *meute*, meaning a pack of hounds, and another says it comes from *mue*, meaning moult and referring to the royal falcons kept there when in moult.

The Chaussée de la Muette runs into the Ranelagh Gardens. The latter was named after the Chelsea pleasure gardens set up in London by Lord Ranelagh. In 1783, Pilâtre de Rozier made the first manned balloon flight from the lawns of the Jardins du Ranelagh. The present gardens, with their donkey rides and bandstand, reflect pleasures of a more tranquil kind and were laid out in 1860 on the site of the earlier, and jollier, establishment.

Marmottan Museum

The largest sign on the front of the building says 'Claude Monet', and his water-lily and rose garden pictures do indeed dominate a strangely mixed collection of paintings, tapestries and furniture of several periods, plus one room crammed with medieval illuminated manuscripts. To add to the confusion, even the Monets are not grouped in one place but are to be found upstairs along with other artists from Delacroix to Sisley, Camille Pissarro and Signac, and also in a new underground gallery along with more by Sisley, Pissarro, Caillebotte, Renoir, etc.

The Marmottan is a major museum for all that, and one should perhaps not mind too much that the whole house could do with a good wash and brush-up. It is run by the Institut de France (Académie des Beaux-Arts) and the patina of academic mustiness seems to be traditional.

The reason the works appear in such a strange order is easily explained, though the fractured layout is not above criticism. The museum in fact houses not one, but five separate collections. In 1882

Jules Marmottan bought the house and installed his collection of paintings, Renaissance tapestries and medieval stained glass. Most of these paintings are by early Flemish, German and Italian masters and include a *Crucifixion* by Albrecht Bouts (*c.* 1500). Jules Marmottan died in 1883 and his collections were taken over by his son Paul, who added works of his own choice, his special passion being for the Napoleonic period. He bought paintings, sculpture, furniture and clocks, travelling throughout Europe to find pieces which had been specially made for the Emperor and members of his family. Paul Marmottan died in 1932 and left the house and all its collections to the Institut de France.

The Musée Marmottan then opened, and in 1950 acquired the Donop de Mouchy collection, originally formed by a Dr de Bellio who had been the doctor and friend of several Impressionist painters. Among these paintings are Monet's *Le Train dans la Neige* (1875), *Les Tuileries* (1876) and *Le Pont de l'Europe Gare St Lazare* (1877), others by Camille Pissarro and Sisley, and Renoir's *Portrait de Mademoiselle Victorine de Bellio* (1892). It was she – de Bellio's daughter and M. Donop de Mouchy's widow – who donated this collection to the museum.

Then in 1971 the Musée Marmottan received Michel Monet's bequest of eighty canvases by his father, Claude, sixteen paintings by Caillebotte, Jongkind, Berthe Morisot and Renoir, and thirty-three pastels, water-colours and drawings by Delacroix, Boudin, Guys, Manet, Renoir and Signac. Outstanding in this group are the water lily (*Nymphéas*), rose garden (*Allées des rosiers*) and Japanese bridge pictures (*Ponts japonais*) which Monet painted in his garden at Giverny between 1883 and 1926.

Finally, in 1980, Daniel Wildenstein donated his father Georges' collection of illuminated manuscripts to the museum. These comprise 228 miniatures gathered over the centuries from prayer books and books of hours, and date from the thirteenth to the sixteenth centuries. Unfortunately they have been thrown on to the walls of a room not nearly large enough for such a number, making it very difficult for the viewer to appreciate their singular qualities.

That, then, is the story of the Marmottan Museum. It is as well to be forewarned, especially if, like me, you prefer seeing things in chronological order: the medieval before the Renaissance, then the

Empire, then the Impressionists together in their own set of rooms. How much more convenient that would be; alas, the powers-that-be at the Marmottan are unwilling to bend, so it seems, and that is that for the time being.

A final note. The museum was hit by a most unfortunate disaster in October 1985, when nine paintings worth incalculable millions were stolen. Among the five missing Monets is the 'founder' painting of the Impressionist movement – *Impression, Soleil Levant* (1872), the sunrise painting which critics seized on to deride the new school, saying they could only paint 'impressionist' pictures.

Châlet des Iles

Out now to the woods. After the Square des Ecrivains Combattants Morts pour la France, our way lies into the Bois de Boulogne across a woodland strip that bridges a tunnel on the Boulevard Périphérique. A few minutes later we reach the bank above the Lac Inférieur and descend to a wooden landing stage. Suddenly we are in a little piece of Switzerland, a lakeside resort remote from the roar of the city. The canopied ferryboat wheels in an arc across the water and deposits us on the terrace of the Châlet des Iles.

The first châlet building to rise on the waterfront here was in fact a real Swiss confection, reassembled from its original site near Berne to satisfy a yearning of the Empress Eugénie, wife of Napoleon III. The Imperial family came here often for parties and to relax, then in 1892 the châlet became a restaurant. It was rebuilt in 1935 and now does a brisk trade in afternoon teas and enormous swirling ice creams. In the restaurant and conference rooms of the main building they can stage anything from a seminar to a wedding reception, and the rural charm of the setting would be difficult to match anywhere else in Paris. Another sight to see before leaving is the domed Emperor's kiosk, built by Davioud in about 1857. Beside the woodland paths, sunbathers sunbathe, and there are peacocks as well as sparrows.

Walk 22

18ᵉ Montmartre

Climb, or funiculate, to the top of the Butte, the hill that dominates northern Paris. Visit the Basilica of Sacré-Cœur and the Church of St Pierre. Stroll in the old Bohemian quarter, down by the vineyard and the Lapin Agile, see the Bateau Lavoir, Moulin de la Galette and Montmartre Cemetery.

Allow   All day.

Best times   Not 1 January, 1 May or 25 December, when Montmartre Museum closed; open 14.30 to 17.30, Sunday opens 11.00.

ROUTE

Begin at Ⓜ Anvers. Nearest buses 30, 54. Walk W along Bd de Rochechouart, past Elysée Montmartre theatre and take next right into Rue Dancourt. At Pl. Charles Dullin, walk round Théâtre de l'Atelier and take next road left into Rue de Steinkerque. Turn right past gardens and at next corner cross road to Museum of Naive Art ☞; open 10.00 to 18.00.

Return past gardens and turn right in Rue Foyatier. Walk up steps or take funicular to Basilica of Sacré-Cœur ☞; buy tickets at souvenir shop by north aisle for access to upper galleries and/or crypt. At exit turn right along Rue Azaïs, past the Reservoir and round corner to front of Church of St Pierre ☞. Visit now or perhaps a refreshment break would be no bad thing.

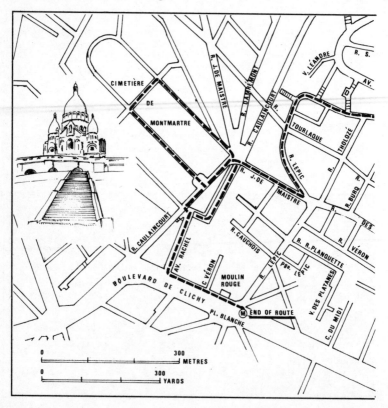

Walk straight ahead to Pl. du Tertre, turn left to Pl. du Calvaire for fine views across Paris. Continue along Rue Poulbot past Historial waxworks (visit optional), go round corner and turn right at 'Utrillo Corner' along Rue Norvins, returing to Pl. du Tertre. Choose lunch-stop.

After lunch, walk north from Pl. du Tertre along Rue du Mont Cenis and take 2nd left into Rue Cortot. At No. 12 visit Montmartre Museum ☞; open as listed above. *Admission.* At exit turn right along Rue Cortot and right into Rue des Saules. Walk down past vineyard to see front of famous cabaret Le Lapin Agile. Return to 'Utrillo Corner' and bear right via Rue Ravignan to Pl. Emile Goudeau for downhill view and look at windows of Bateau Lavoir.

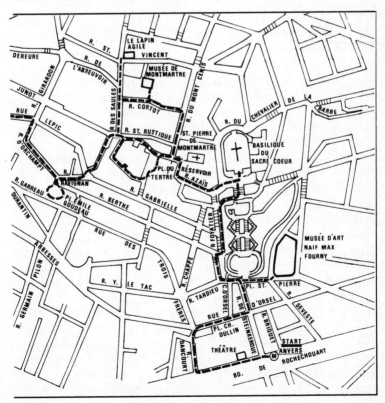

Return to Rue Ravignan and take 1st left into narrow Rue d'Orchampt, then left into Rue Lepic. Walk downhill, round two bends
and turn right into Rue Joseph de Maistre. Turn left at end into Rue
Caulaincourt. Entrance to Montmartre Cemetery is at foot of steps
at left end of bridge, in Av. Rachel 👁. Collect plan at lodge on right
and explore.

At exit walk down Av. Rachel to Bd de Clichy and turn left. Walk
ends in Pl. Blanche, near Bal du Moulin Rouge. Nearest Ⓜ Blanche.
Nearest refreshments not recommended (nor entertainments!).
Suggest take No. 30 bus or Métro to Ch. de Gaulle-Etoile for refresh-
ments in Av. des Champs Elysées at Drugstore (No. 133) on S side or
Fouquet's further along at corner Av. George V.

Beneath the hill

Old Montmartre lost much of its excitement and vigour before the
First World War when the artists and writers – the generation that
spans Van Gogh, Zola, Degas, Picasso and Apollinaire – came down
off the hill (butte) and resettled themselves on the Left Bank. The
district they left behind is still inherently beautiful, though heavily
spoilt in some places.

For an image of the crumbling past, look at the front of the Elysée
Montmartre (No. 74 Boulevard de Rochechouart). The white plaster
decorations seem to be within minutes of falling off the wall – the
floral swags and the Art Nouveau plaque with the theatre's name, and
above them the dancer in her lofty niche, who for the moment
retains her jolly smile. This was a famous music hall in the Belle
Epoque; it struggles on as a Rock venue. A few doors down, at No. 84,
Rodolphe Salis opened his night club Le Chat Noir in 1881; it
survived for about sixteen years, and was at its peak when Aristide
Bruant verbally assaulted the audience with his brutal songs; today it
is a shop, the A Trianon Lingerie Sexy.

Around the next corner and a little way up the hill is a charming
leafy square, the Place Charles Dullin, home of the Théâtre de
l'Atelier, a straight theatre where they may be playing Molière or
Marivaux. The Rue de Steinkerque is filled with shops trading in
violently colourful lengths of cloth; does everyone really want lime
green with black spots this year? At the top of the street is a first view of

the great wedding-cake basilica at the top of the hill, in the
foreground a children's roundabout wrapped in its green overnight
covers.

We divert for a few minutes to the Max Fourny Museum of Naive
Art. In the cool steel pavilion of the Halle St Pierre the museum
shows collections of naive pictures from all over the world, either by'
nation, such as Brazil or Haiti, or by theme, e.g. 'The Dream', to
which artists of all nations contribute. Programmes change every
three or four months. Also under the same roof is the conservation-
minded Musée en Herbe (The Green Museum), with exhibitions
such as 'Australian Aborigines' and 'Portrait of a Forest', an
enterprising evocation of Fontainebleau Forest combined with
paintings from the Barbizon School – men such as Millet, Diaz and
Théodore Rousseau who settled in the village of Barbizon in the
1840s and looked for new ways of portraying landscape.

On the far side of the gardens beneath Sacré-Cœur, take the
funicular to the top of the hill or walk up the steps of Rue Foyatier. If
by any chance the funicular is not working (not unknown) and you
cannot face the climb on foot, continue west from the gardens via
Rue Tardieu and Rue Yvonne le Tac to Place des Abbesses (3
minutes) and catch the Montmartrobus to Sacré-Cœur.

Basilica of Sacré-Cœur

This unmistakable domed white landmark has some way yet to go
before it is even a hundred years old (in 2010). It was brought into
being after the humiliations of the Franco-Prussian War of 1870–71.
A group of Catholics wished to raise a church to the Sacred Heart and
launched a public subscription. In 1873 the State took over the
project; a competition jury chose the design of Paul Abadie and work
began three years later.

Abadie was best known at the time for restoring the Cathedral of St
Front in Périgueux, a twelfth-century building of Byzantine
inspiration which followed almost exactly the floor plan of St Mark's,
Venice (1042–85). For his monumental Paris church the architect
produced his own imitation of the Romanesque-Byzantine style. The
church was completed in 1910 and consecrated in 1919. It is 100 m
(328 ft) long, 75 m (246 ft) wide at the ambulatory and the dome is

83 m (262 ft) high. A principal curiosity of the basilica, the Savoyarde, a huge bell weighing some eighteen tonnes, was cast in Annecy in 1895 and presented by the diocese of Chambéry.

Sacré-Cœur is one of the great landmarks of Paris and receives a constant flow of visitors, including large parties of nuns and schoolchildren. From a distance it impresses and attracts by its bulk and brilliant whiteness . . . after which it is hard to find words of true praise, either about the exterior or the interior. 'Grace without nobility,' 'spacious without being excessive' are typical of the more favourable comments of other writers. Close to, the stone has an almost repellent chalky texture and is surprisingly grubby in parts. Most commentators are agreed that the best thing about the basilica is the view from the upper galleries, from where you can see past the cupolas and gargoyles for up to 50 km (31 miles).

Place du Tertre

The tourist heart of Montmartre is the Place du Tertre, an open-air bazaar of artists hawking kitsch landscapes and instant portraiture. Take in some of this while looking for a café to take a well-earned break. I cannot think of anywhere in the world where the tools of painting are more laughably abused. At least, in the course of many visits, I have never seen anyone buy one of those garish pastels of the square or some other local pretty bit. The artists of the Place du Tertre are licensed, by the way, and anyone consenting to have their portrait drawn should ask to see the artist's card and make sure the price is agreed in advance. Dissatisfied customers should complain to the Mairie, and a notice on the wall by the bus stop gives the address to write to.

Such is the commercial atmosphere around this square, even the café waiters are trying to market the beer they sell. Up here one day I ordered a beer – *un demi*, a half, like an English half-pint.

'What kind of a *demi* would you like?' asked the waiter.

'A *demi* is a *demi*, isn't it?' I said.

'Do you want a twenty-five centilitre, a fifty or a hundred?' he said.

'A twenty-five,' I said.

The waiter went back to the bar and shouted to the bartender: 'Un demi!'

Church of St Pierre

In the dark nave of this church you will find an ancient and mystical atmosphere more profound by far than that of the false-Byzantine basilica around the corner. The Church of St Pierre is the only surviving element of a Benedictine convent, founded by Queen Adelaide of Savoy, and was completed in the twelfth century, making it one of the oldest churches in Paris. Notices point out that it is not a museum and visitors should not walk about during services. In the Chapel of the Holy Sacrament to the left of the altar a boy's clear voice reads from a holy text, a priest follows with a solemn chant, and we are a hundred miles and several centuries removed from the clamour of the Place du Tertre.

Two pairs of ancient columns – one at the west end and one by the choir – are said to be from a Roman temple that once stood on the Mount of Mercury, *mons mercurii*, from which the name of Montmartre derives. From the original church are pointed arches in the choir which date from 1147; the vaulting of the nave was replaced in the fifteenth century but the walls look extraordinarily wonky and seem to lean outwards, close to collapse. The west façade is from the seventeenth century; the bronze doors are by the Italian sculptor Gismondi (1980) who also designed the door to the cemetery in the north wall of the courtyard.

In the Revolution the church became the Temple of Reason and was used as a station for Chappe's new aerial telegraph link between Paris and Lille. The station was not finally removed until about 1850.

Utrillo's Paris

The next part of our walk is a stroll through the winding streets on top of the hill, followed by lunch and a visit to the Montmartre Museum which opens at 14.30 (11.00 on Sunday). At the bottom end of the Place du Tertre the views across Paris are particularly fine from the Place du Calvaire. Further along the Rue Poulbot is the Historial waxworks; open daily 1 April to 30 November, 10.00 to 12.00, 14.30 to 17.30; 1 December to 31 March open only on Wednesday, Saturday, Sunday and holidays. *Admission*. Visitors descend a steep staircase past a framer's workshop to cellars lined with tableaux of local history: the Bateau Lavoir; Gambetta's balloon flight from the Butte in 1870, when he escaped from Prussian troops to form the Loire Army;

Berlioz and friends (Liszt, Delacroix, Chopin, George Sand, etc); Toulouse-Lautrec in his studio with Jane Avril, La Goulue, Aristide Bruant; the Lapin Agile cabaret (still going) and the Chat Noir (vanished, as we saw).

Around the corner is a charming combination of shops and houses, at the junction of Rue Norvins and the Rue des Saules, which in our Route section is referred to as 'Utrillo Corner' – one of the most picturesque spots in the whole of the *quartier* and certainly very familiar to the prolific Maurice Utrillo (1883–1955).

For the most part the poster and souvenir shops sell such trash you almost despair of finding a decent postcard. On the other hand, collectors of kitsch will not want to miss Gault's architectural model shop at No. 5 *bis* Rue Norvins, where you can buy tiny houses and shops and make a street, then a town. It's train-set furniture without the trains. In the window is a slice of old Montmartre, an Alsatian village, a Provençal town; and at their Rue de Rivoli shop (No. 208), I happen to know you can even buy the east or west side of the Place Vendôme; a snip at F17,000. '*Oh, que c'est mignon,*' cooed some ladies, arriving in a cloud just as I was wondering who these toys could actually be for. Their husbands, obviously.

A recommendation about lunch is difficult, since I have no real preferences, and probably not necessary as there are so many adequate-looking places to choose from. For a good vantage point, try the Restaurant/Cabaret de la Bohème on the north-east corner of the Place du Tertre (Rue du Mont Cenis). A plaque on the wall says that the painter Suzanne Valadon dined there regularly from 1919 to 1935, often accompanied by her son Maurice Utrillo.

Montmartre Museum

The Utrillo connection reappears at this charming museum. In a small side room is the old zinc bar from M. Baillot's café in the Rue de l'Abreuvoir, given to the museum after the owner died and the café was demolished. One of M. Baillot's most determined regulars was, of course, young Maurice, who also lived in this house for a while with his mother. Here too is Marcel Leprin's wonderful portrait of *La Belle Cabaretière*, standing behind a bar with a cloth in one hand. Her smile, someone said, is the smile of a woman who is secretly loved.

The guidebooks tend to be unkind or dismissive of this museum, but I like it. Admittedly, some of the paintings are pretty average, though they would find space in most local history collections. Meanwhile, there is so much else that is either aesthetically good or full of interest: portraits, letters, objects, photographs. The original sign of the Lapin Agile cabaret, for instance, and porcelain from the Clignancourt factory, founded in 1770 by the Comte de Provence, brother of Louis XVI, which stood only a few streets away on the corner of Rue du Mont Cenis and Rue Marcadet. From the Chat Noir night club are examples of shadow theatre (*théâtre des ombres*); cat posters by Steinlen; a portrait of the artist Emile Bernard who lived at this address in 1906–8.

The funniest exhibits are the cartoons by Poulbot, featuring his urchin characters. In one cartoon, two of them are on a roof and the leader is lying down and peering through a skylight. 'Quick,' he hisses to his friend, 'he's putting a pillow under her thighs.'

Bateau Lavoir

It may be possible to leave the museum by the rear entrance and walk down the steps next to the vineyard, or you may have to go round via Rue Cortot and Rue des Saules. Try, anyway, to have a look at this semi-rural corner on the northern slope of the hill. The festival that goes with the autumn grape harvest is said to be a most jolly event. Just across the road is the Lapin Agile, a famous hang-out for artists and writers of the *Belle Epoque* before the First World War – and still in business today, each evening from 21.00 (closed Monday) with a trusted menu of *chansons, humour, poésie.*

Returning to 'Utrillo Corner', we begin our final descent through the Place Jean-Baptiste Clément, past the railed garden by the old water tower, to the Place Emile Goudeau, a tiny sloping square with no cars, seventeen chestnut trees, the *pavé* and the park benches rich in bird droppings. It is a peaceful place with downhill views into the avaricious heart of Pigalle, though up here the only commercial activity is an American guest emerging from the Tim Hotel. Next to the hotel are the Bateau Lavoir studios, where many famous paint-ers lived at the turn of the century – Picasso, Braque, Gris (the pioneers of Cubism), also Modigliani and Van Dongen – and the poets Apollinaire and Max Jacob. The studios were destroyed by a fire in 1970 but have been rebuilt to the old plan. Today twenty-five painters and sculptors work there. The shop front at 11 *bis* offers a quick illustrated history of the Bateau Lavoir (the 'floating laundry', as the artists called it); the centrepiece of the window is a version of Picasso's *Demoiselles d'Avignon*, the painting which became the visual manifesto of the Cubist movement.

We squeeze through the Rue d'Orchampt to the Rue Lepic and set off down the long hill. Up on the right is the Moulin de la Galette, its sails just about intact. Some thirty windmills stood on the hill in the eighteenth century, milling corn, pressing grapes and crushing stone. When the quarries shut down, the mills were turned into cabarets and the Galette was one of the most famous and most painted in the *quartier*.

Driving on the Butte is a nightmare. The ninety-degree bend in the Rue Lepic is a famous trap for trucks and coaches, which swivel desperately in the narrow channel left to them. Motorists jam rocks and bricks behind the rear wheels of their cars to compensate for a slipping hand-brake. Competition for parking space is fierce, and meter maids in their Gitanes-blue uniforms are seldom seen without a pen in their hand.

Montmartre Cemetery

This is the only cemetery of any size we enter in the course of these Slow Walks, and though its 10 hectares (25 acres) do not put it in the same league as Père Lachaise, it is an important cemetery where many famous Parisians are buried. A long tour would certainly be tiring at this stage of the day, so I suggest a limited stroll out to Division 22 and back (see plan).

Collect your plan at the lodge and walk under the blue iron road bridge to the circus at the end of the Avenue Principale. On the far side, reached by steps, is the distinctive brown tomb of the Zola family. In the 20th Division the composer Hector Berlioz (1803–69) has a large winged tomb in black marble. The film director François Truffaut (1932–84) is nearby in the 21st Division, as is the writer Alexandre Dumas the Younger (1824–95). In the neighbouring 22nd Division are the dancer Vaslav Nijinsky (1890–1950) and the historian and philosopher Ernest Renan (1823–92). Near to the main gate is the Guitry family tomb (Lucien, Sacha, Jean).

Moulin Rouge

Down on the Boulevard de Clichy it is a mercifully short walk past the old cabaret Théâtre des Deux Anes to the Moulin Rouge. In the 1890s this was *the* night spot, to which people flooded to see the can-can and the rubber woman, La Gommeuse, Yvette Guilbert and Jane Avril. Toulouse-Lautrec brilliantly chronicled the performers of his day – a time that now seems long-gone as we look across the road to the Pornossimo Ciné Sex and step round the hustlers on the pavement. Unfortunately, when the artists left Montmartre at the turn of the century all that remained in some places was the night life. Here now, in the strip between the Place de Clichy and the Place Pigalle, you see the night life of Paris at its worst and seediest, rivalled only by the Rue St Denis. Once seen, best left far behind (see Route section for escape details).

PARIS FROM A WALKER'S EYE-VIEW

WHAT TO WEAR AND CARRY WITH YOU

Much of this is common sense, though in the year and a half I have been street-testing these Slow Walks I have added one or two useful refinements to my baggage train and these I now pass on.

The walks, with one or two exceptions, are fairly short, usually between two and three miles from start to finish, plus the distances walked at places like museums and shops on the way round. No great advance planning is needed, nor any special equipment. We are not ramblers, in need of long socks and woolly hats. All the same, you will probably enjoy yourself that much more if you are comfortable and well supplied in the hours away from your hotel or apartment.

Footwear is important. I wear strong leather shoes with rubber 'Commando' soles. They are probably too heavy for extensive use on city pavements but I feel they make up for this by never pinching and being, in general, the most comfortable shoes I have ever worn.

I have yet to find a pair of trainers with much staying-power, though you may have been more fortunate. Mine tend to disintegrate on the inside at the heel or where the toecap joins the rest of the superstructure. I am still working on this. Whatever you choose to wear on your feet, make day-long comfort your priority.

Cotton socks are best for keeping the feet cool. Wear two pairs if your shoes tend to rub after a lot of walking.

Accept, too, that in your choice of footwear and street clothes you will probably look like a tourist, so never mind what those chic and suave Parisians may think about you, especially shop assistants. Save dressing up for the evening.

Some kind of bag is more or less essential, preferably one you can hang on yourself rather than one you have to carry, and preferably with two or more zip-fastening compartments. Useful items to keep in it are: a camera; extra films; folding umbrella; sunglasses; small two-way dictionary, e.g. Larousse *Dictionnaire Europa*; notebook; folding map of Paris or, better still, an indexed book of maps. And, of course, a copy of *Slow Walks in Paris*.

THE GEOGRAPHY OF PARIS

The city boundary runs for most of its way just outside the ring road (Boulevard Périphérique) and also encloses the Bois de Boulogne in the west. Within that area, Paris is divided into twenty districts or *arrondissements*.

The *arrondissement* system works in a clockwise spiral, beginning with the 1st *arrondissement* (*le premier*, written 1er or 1), and working outwards. Each *arrondissement* is governed by a mayor whose headquarters are the local *mairie* or town hall. The Mayor of Paris occupies the Hôtel de Ville in the 4th *arrondissement* (*le quatrième*, written 4e or 4ème or 4).

The River Seine divides the city into the Rive Droite (Right Bank) and Rive Gauche (Left Bank). As you face downstream towards the west, the Right Bank is on your right. This is the commercial side of the river, and here are most of the 'major' sights, museums and monuments, and big department stores. The Left Bank is quieter and usually associated with the artists' and students' quarters around the Boulevards St Michel and St Germain. Just to prove that there are always exceptions, the Left Bank also contains the Eiffel Tower, Hôtel des Invalides and Musée d'Orsay (Impressionists, etc).

The two islands, Ile de la Cité and Ile St Louis, are strapped to either bank by so many bridges that it is sometimes difficult to think of them as islands, though the Ile St Louis does its best to seem remote.

Streets are numbered according to a system it is worth knowing about, particularly when you are looking for an address in a long street such as the Rue de Rivoli. North-south streets are numbered away from the river, and east-west streets from east to west. Thus, the low numbers of the Rue de Rivoli are in the St Paul district to the east; at the other end, No. 258 is six Métro stops away near the Place de la Concorde.

For the visitor, it is a good idea to concentrate on one side of the river at a time. The twenty-two Slow Walks in this book visit all the more central *arrondissements* and some of the outer ones. If you look at the overall plan of the walks on page 8/9, you will see that many walks end close to where another begins.

Landmarks For instant orientation, when ever-so-slightly lost, imagine Paris as a compass face with the Louvre at the centre. The Eiffel Tower lies to the west, Sacré-Cœur to the north and the Montparnasse Tower to the south.

If more than just slightly lost, look for a street name or Métro station and check its position on your map. This is where a set of indexed maps should prove its worth. If still in doubt, ask a passer-by. If you ask at a café or shop, people are a lot more solicitous if you spend money at their establishment. Whoever you ask, try to hold the conversation in French. Don't worry about making mistakes. A lot of French people nowadays are really pleased to meet a foreigner – especially an English-speaking foreigner – who is interested enough to try to communicate in their language.

Maps The Route map for each Slow Walk should be a sufficient guide for that particular walk, unless you go seriously or wilfully astray. For more detail, folding maps are available free from travel agents and tourist offices. Better still, buy a book of maps. A very reasonable solution is the *Plan de Paris par Arrondissement*, available from news-stands and bookshops; more expensive but very clear are the colour maps in the Michelin *Paris Atlas* (blue cover).

SITU Yellow boxes about 1.5 m (5 ft) in height have landed near a number of Métro stations. You use the keyboard on the front to tap in the address of the place you want to get to next, and by which combination of bus, Métro or walking; the machine then slips you a print-out of the best route to take. Lots of fun. SITU stands for *Système d'Information de Trajets Urbains*, and is run by the RATP, the Paris transport authority. Soon there will be more than a hundred SITUs in Paris, and there are plans to commercialise them in shops, museums, etc.

TRANSPORT

Métro

Buses are fun, but the Métro is quicker. The Paris Underground system is one of the best in the world: efficient, cleaner than most, cheap, and easy to use once you have mastered its basic workings. All Slow Walks begin at a Métro station; another weighty reason for using the network.

The key to it all is knowing which *Direction*, i.e. terminus, you need to aim for. All Métro stations have large network maps, some with buttons you can push to light up your route. Each of the 13 principal lines is colour-coded, and the first step is to locate the route to your destination. Next, look along to the end of the line and note the name of the terminus, e.g. Balard. Now follow the *Direction Balard* signs to the platform. When you have to transfer to another line, look for the orange and white *Correspondance* sign with the name of your next terminus.

There is a Métro map on the back cover of this book.

The service begins at 05.30, and last trains leave at around 00.30, reaching their terminus by 01.15; reduced services operate in the evening and on Sunday.

Keep your ticket with you until the end of the journey. Inspectors travel the network checking tickets and can fine you on the spot for not having one, also for travelling 1st class (middle carriage) with a 2nd class ticket between 09.00 and 17.00; at other times the whole train is 2nd class.

Tickets Buy a *carnet* (set of 10 tickets) to save both money and time in queues. One ticket is good for any one journey on the Métro system – except on some outlying surburban sections. You can also use a Métro ticket to travel on the urban sections of the RER (suburban express service).

Another ticket bargain is the Paris Sésame, a go-anywhere ticket available in 2, 4 or 7-day versions, good for 1st class travel on the Métro and RER lines A and B south of Gare du Nord, and one-class travel on buses, the Montmartre Funicular and the Montmartrobus; this ticket also gets discounts on other fares, e.g. river and canal trips, and rides up the Montparnasse Tower. The 7-day version is better value than the other two and scores over *carnets* if you make more than seven Métro journeys per day and/or use buses (on longer journeys, buses consume *carnet* tickets at a higher rate than the Métro, see 'Buses' below).

Best value of all, for longer-stay visitors, is the Carte Orange, available with a weekly (*hebdomadaire*) or monthly (*mensuel*) coupon and giving unlimited travel on Métro and bus routes. Push the coupon through the ticket machine at station entrances, retrieve it and re-use it for the whole period of its validity. A weekly coupon is valid Monday a.m. to Sunday p.m. Take a passport-sized photograph and your passport or ID card when applying for a Carte Orange.

You can buy all these tickets at Métro stations. For travel on the RER beyond the city limits, the rate (*tarification*) is different and you will need to buy a special ticket.

Buses

Not only can you see so much more from a bus, on certain routes you can do it with the wind in your hair, standing on the open platform at the back. It's almost like the old days, though in these conductorless times there is no rear entrance, guarded by that flimsy leather strap which Parisians casually flicked aside after a swooping chase down the street crowned by a trouser-splitting leap on to the bus. Open-platform buses run on Routes 20, 29, 75, 83, 93.

The service begins at 06.30, and last buses leave at around 21.00; some routes continue until 00.30. For details, check the information displayed at bus stops and in bus shelters. On Sunday and public holidays the service is reduced. All bus stops are request stops (*arrêt facultatif*), so make sure you or someone else has flagged the approaching bus down or, when on board, rung the bell. Inside the bus a sign goes on: '*Arrêt demandé* ' (stop requested).

At night the Noctambus service offers ten routes to the city limits, all departing from Châtelet Av. Victoria. Departures hourly from 01.30 to 05.30.

Tickets These are the same as for the Métro (see above), but the routes are divided into fare stages (details on route map at bus stop). You need one *carnet* ticket for a journey of one or two fare stages, and two tickets for three or more fare stages. On the bus, cancel *carnet* tickets in the machine but simply show the driver your Paris Sésame card or Carte Orange.

Taxis

Taxis can be hailed in the street or found at ranks marked *Taxi* or *Tête de Station*. They are reasonably priced, with day and night fare tariffs displayed inside each metered cab. Make sure the meter is uncovered at the start of your journey, and have nothing to do with larger unmetered limos which cost as much as the driver thinks he can extract from you. Metered taxis legitimately charge extra for station pick-ups and luggage. Three passengers is the usual limit, and for security reasons drivers do not like passengers to sit up front.

TELEPHONES

You can, of course, make calls from your hotel but this is much more expensive than using a public call box in the street or in a post office (look for the PTT sign outside). You can also make local calls from cafés.

There has been a big changeover recently to card-only call boxes, so buy a *télécarte* at a café displaying the red *Tabac* sign. Some cards give details of cheap-rate hours for calls in metropolitan France; calls to the UK are cheapest between 21.30 and 08.00. To dial the UK, dial 19 and wait for a change of tone. Then dial 44 and the STD code and number, deleting the first 0. Thus the code for London is 19-44-1.

MONEY

Banking hours vary quite a lot (see also 'Opening Times' on page 246). Your local bank should be open 09.00 to 16.30, Monday to Friday, though it is worth checking the exchange counter may close for lunch (12.00 to 14.00).

Bureaux de change at the main railway stations are open longer than the banks, and at the time of writing those at the Gare de l'Est, Gare de Lyon and Gare du Nord were open every day of the week until 21.00 or later. For air travellers, the Société Générale runs daily exchange facilities at Orly and Roissy/Charles de Gaulle. Other banks open at the weekend are as follows:

American Express, 11 Rue Scribe, 9ᵉ, 09.00 to 17.00 Monday to Saturday.
CCF, 115 Av. des Champs-Elysées, 8ᵉ, 08.00 to 20.00 Monday to Saturday.
CIC, Gare de Lyon, 07.00 to 23.00, daily.
UBP, 125 Av. des Champs-Elysées, 8ᵉ, open at weekend 09.45 to 13.00 and 14.00 to 18.00.

Travellers' cheques and Eurocheques are the easiest to change. Ask your bank for a list of banks in Paris where it has an agreement. If you have Eurocheques, just look for one of the many banks displaying the

EC sign. Department stores may also be able to help outside banking hours, but you may not relish paying their commission.

Buying some French francs before you leave home has the advantage of getting you straight into the swing of things as soon as you arrive in Paris. If you have a few coins as well as notes, so much the better. You can shop, buy Métro tickets, pay the all-seeing lavatory attendant, etc, as though you had been around for weeks.

Credit cards These are now widely accepted by the larger hotels, shops and restaurants, but many smaller businesses refuse to touch them. Always check before you commit yourself. The best-known cards are: American Express, Diners Club, Access Mastercard/ Eurocard and Barclaycard Visa/Carte Bleue.

Tax-free shopping People living outside France may claim what some shops call an export discount. This is in fact a refund of French VAT, or TVA (*Taxe Valeur Ajoutée*). You need to make a minimum purchase of F1,200 if you live outside the EEC, or F2,400 if you live in the EEC. Some shops limit the purchase to one article; department stores allow totting up. The department store discount on perfumes, furs, jewellery, camera equipment and films is usually 23%; on other articles it is 13%.

Ask for the *détaxe* forms. Good stores have a special department to sort out the details. Take your passport for identification and allow an extra half hour, longer as the afternoon draws on and the store fills up. The discount may be paid then or forwarded to you later. Remember that what you buy under an export discount scheme may attract Customs duty when it arrives in your home country.

To export an antique or work of art you could well need a special permit. Make sure the dealer understands you will be exporting, and provides the correct permit.

Tipping In cafés and restaurants a service charge of 15% is usually added to the bill. After a drink, the usual thing is to leave the centimes from your change on the bar or table; after a meal, leave a little more, say 2 or 3 francs. If the bill states '*Service non compris*' (Service not included), leave 12% to 15% of the bill.

Taxi drivers expect a tip of 10% to 15% of the fare. Most other tips are small but expected: give 1 or 2 francs to cinema usherettes and cloakroom attendants, and up to 5 francs per head to a tour guide. Porters at airports and railway stations have their own fixed rates.

OPENING TIMES

Beware the lunch or afternoon break. Small neighbourhood shops may close for several hours between 12.00 and 17.00. Some museums take a lunch break, perhaps from 12.30 to 14.00, and offices may do the same. The list below is no more than an approximate guide. Opening times for all main places of interest on Slow Walks are listed in the appropriate chapter.

Large shops and department stores Open 09.00–09.30 to 19.00, Monday to Saturday, with a late night once a week.

Small shops and restaurants Food shops open 07.00–07.30. Close for lunch at 12.00–12.30 and re-open at 16.00–17.00. Close at 20.00. May open Sunday until 12.00 or later. Many close on Monday.

Other shops may not open until 10.00 or 10.30 and close at 19.00, Monday to Saturday. Antique shops are usually late openers, e.g. 11.00, and are unpredictable about when they close and on which days.

Most restaurants close one day a week. The annual shutdown (*fermeture annuelle*) is still practised, often in August, by small restaurants and shops.

Banks Generally open 09.00–09.30 to 16.30–17.15, Monday to Friday. They may close for lunch; some close the exchange counter 12.00 to 14.00. All close at 11.30–12.00 for the rest of the day *before* a Bank Holiday.

Museums and churches State museums open 10.00 to 17.00, some with an extra hour in summer, and close on Tuesday; others vary but usually close one or two days a week, often Monday. Admission may be free or reduced on Sunday. Ticket desks (*caisses*) close 30 minutes before closing time.

Churches are open daily; they ask you not to walk round during a service, and some close their doors 12.00 to 14.00–15.00. Admission is usually charged to see treasures, visit crypt, tower, etc.

WATERING-HOLES

If you want a drink and a sit-down, any establishment calling itself a bar, bar-café, brasserie, wine bar or *salon de thé* should answer your needs. It will also have toilets (see below) and most likely a telephone. Let your eyes, ears and nose make the final decision about going in.

In bars and cafés there may be as many as three prices per item –

bar/comptoir, *salle* or *terrasse* – depending on whether you stand at the bar (cheapest), or sit inside or outside. Wherever, in a main street, you come upon a large glossy café with smart waiters (those with short white jackets and coloured epaulettes being the smartest) you can reckon on finding equally good and much cheaper refreshments around the corner in a neighbourhood café. You may, of course, prefer to luxuriate on a glossy terrace and watch the world go by; for a few francs more, it is an excellent pastime.

Small bar-cafés generally serve snacks of the sandwich/hot dog/ *croque-monsieur* (toasted ham and cheese) variety and some offer quite a lot more, including a *plat du jour* (dish of the day). Look for placards and menus to see what is on offer, and for how much.

Brasseries are usually larger than cafés, with a restaurant-sized menu. This tends to be *à la carte*, and quite expensive when all is totted up, but if you are happy, say at lunchtime, with just a *salade niçoise*, a basket of bread and a drink, prices are reasonable and the atmosphere usually warm and bustling.

Wine bars are on the up. Expect to pay quite a bit for good wine, cheese, charcuterie, country bread, etc. Wine bars suit young professional parties.

The *salon de thé* is another category by itself. These genteel purveyors of teas, salads, ice creams and delicious *pâtisseries* flourish in the wealthier *quartiers* at a time when their near-counterpart, the English tea-room, has all but gone under. A shade expensive, though soothing for devotees.

For your evening meal, it is well worth spending some time menu-shopping beforehand. Do this as part of your daily promenading, and make a note of promising places. Bistros and restaurants offer a great and highly competitive range of menus: *à la carte*; *prix fixe* with several choices per course, and *formules* with little or no choice; by UK standards many give tremendous value.

Restaurants fill up according to mysterious laws, and by 20.00 all tables may be occupied, or scarcely any. At the fashionable end of this gastronomic rainbow, some restaurants are booked up for weeks in advance. Newcomers quickly learn the habits of places they like and adjust their timing to fit; if in doubt, reserve. Anything, in my view, is better than queueing.

In the Slow Walks chapters I recommend a number of restaurants we meet as we go round. A more efficient way of lengthening your repertoire is to consult the restaurant pages in a What's On guide (see also below). In *Pariscope*, for example, the 'Restaurants' section is about forty pages long and contains some reviews and copious listings by speciality (fish, grills, regional, etc), places open on Sunday and after midnight, and an alphabetical list.

CLOTHING SIZES
For Women

Dresses, knitwear, blouses, coats (*Robes, tricots, chemisiers, manteaux*)

France	36	38	40	42	44	46	48
GB	10	12	14	16	18	20	22
USA	8	10	12	14	16	18	20

Tights, stockings (*Collants, bas*)

France	0	1	2	3	4	5
GB	8	8½	9	9½	10	10½
USA	8	8½	9	9½	10	10½

Shoes (*Chaussures*)

France	35½	36	36½	37	37½	38	39	40	41
GB	3	3½	4	4½	5	5½	6	7	8
USA	4	4½	5	5½	6	6½	7½	8½	9½

For Men

Shirts (*Chemises*)

France	36	37	38	39	40	41	42
GB	14	14½	15	15½	16	16½	17
USA	14	14½	15	15½	16	16½	17

Sweaters (*Pulls, tricots*)

France	46	48	50	52	54	56
GB	36	38	40	42	44	46
USA	36	38	40	42	44	46

Suits (*Costumes*)

France	36	38	40	42	44	46	48
GB	35	36	37	38	39	40	42
USA	35	36	37	38	39	40	42

Shoes (*Chaussures*)

France	39	40	41	42	43	44	45
GB	5½	6½	7	8	8½	9½	10½
USA	6	7	7½	8½	9	10	11

LIST OF PUBLIC HOLIDAYS

More places stay open than used to on public holidays, but most shops, offices and museums close on these 13 days each year:

1 January: New Year's Day
Easter Sunday
Easter Monday
Ascension Day (40 days after Easter)
Pentecost (seventh Sunday after Easter; and Monday)
1 May
8 May: VE Day
14 July: Bastille Day
15 August: Assumption Day
1 November: All Saints' Day
11 November: Armistice Day
25 December: Christmas Day

TOILETS

An essential function of the watering-hole is, of course, to provide an adequate loo-stop. Facilities, however, vary quite a lot and, while you can rely on being able to go, you may not be able to do so in the comfort you are used to.

Many, but not all, bars and cafés remain faithful to the footplate-and-hole-in-the-ground type of loo, both for *messieurs* and *dames*. Until you are inside the door, you can't really tell what sort it will be. Most larger establishments, e.g. boulevard cafés and brasseries, have conventional toilet bowls with seats; in general, the smarter the café the better your chances of a 'nice' loo.

Some cafés now have the perversity to make a charge, and have installed slot machines requiring 1 or 2 francs. To some extent this is a countermeasure taken to prevent *non-consommateurs* from sneaking in for a free *pipi*. It is nevertheless most unfair on bona-fide customers, and surely outrageous to sell people drinks and then hit them for drainage as well.

Other loos   On grounds of hygiene, one reputable tourist guide warns against loos in museums, Métro stations and underground garages. Railway stations were slightly better. That, unfortunately, doesn't leave a lot: the coin-op self-cleaning street loos are not bad, and those in department stores are generally OK. Hotels are another possibility. I would say that the tourist guide was a little hard on museums, some of which have up-to-date, clean facilities.

WHAT'S ON

Each Wednesday, a new batch of the What's On weeklies arrives on the news-stands. Choose from *Pariscope*, *L'Officiel des Spectacles* and *7 à Paris*. I prefer the first-named and references to it appear from time to time in this book, e.g. 'See *Pariscope* for details'. All give competent listings of current exhibitions, concerts, cinemas, theatres, night life, shows for children, excursions and restaurants.

PARIS BY NIGHT

In Paris it is not necessary to sleep at all, if sleep is what you do when you can't find anywhere else to go. Lots of clubs, discos and bars stay open till 2 am or, less specifically, dawn. The potential for nights on the town is vast, and a whole book could be devoted to the topic, though it would almost certainly be out of date long before it was published. This present book is about daytime excursions, so I don't really feel it is ducking the issue to write only a short piece about *Paris la nuit*.

The Paris night scene is a curiously layered structure of cabarets, *chansonniers*, reviews, dinner-shows, bars, discos, jazz and rock clubs, night clubs, strip clubs and *spectacles érotiques*. At the more fevered end of the range, in particular, it is not uncommon for customers to totter back to their hotels and apartments feeling strangely ridiculous, disappointed and impressively out of pocket. Clubowners would not be able to keep themselves in luxury, alas, without the open-handed assistance of tourists and visiting businessfolk. Parisians seldom go to such entertainments, preferring the customary diet of people in their own city: in Paris this usually consists of apéritifs and dinner, followed or preceded by a visit to the theatre, concert hall or cinema.

Concerts are a strong element of Paris night life, made even more attractive by venues such as the Sainte Chapelle, various churches, and an orangery in the Bois de Boulogne. The cinema, too, is not to be ignored. Paris has about 130 cinemas with, between them, some 335 rooms. The taste for films is deeply rooted in this city and there are always plenty of revivals, special seasons, old favourites that never go away and new releases that may reach Paris six months before they open in London.

Let *Pariscope* or one of the other What's On weeklies be your guide. *7 à Paris* is beamed at a young-ish readership and runs illustrated features on Cinema, Live Rock, Jazz, etc, as well as the usual listings.

Finally, let me recommend a Tour of the Illuminations. Various operators run these after-dark coach trips which you can book either direct or through your hotel or travel agent. Routes vary in detail, but a sample circuit, beginning in the Rue de Rivoli, would take in Place de la Concorde – Champs Elysées – Trocadéro and Eiffel Tower – Invalides – Left Bank – Notre-Dame – Louvre – Place de l'Opéra. The best part is at Trocadéro, where you get out by the Palais de Chaillot and stroll through the crowds on the terrace to see the illuminated fountains; across the river, the Eiffel Tower is spectacularly lit with floods pointing up through the ironwork, colouring it a magnificent glowing bronze. On the terrace, musicians play and nine-foot African gentlemen sell paper birds, beads, balloons and fluorescent headbands.

QUICK PARIS

If you have only a weekend or 3–4 days in Paris, choose from this brief selection of Walks. Check opening times are OK *before* setting off.

Day 1	*Walk 16: Eiffel Tower and Champ de Mars*. Follow with a boat trip on the Seine (see walk for details).
Day 2	*Walk 8: The Two Islands*. Follow with alternative boat trip (see walk for details).
Day 3	*Walk 5: Louvre Palace and Tuileries Gardens*. Then go up Rue Royale to Pl. de la Madeleine and take *Walk 18: The Department Stores*.
Day 4	*Walk 7: The Marais*. Follow with a visit to the Pompidou Centre (description in *Walk 4*). If time, walk along Rue Berger to the Forum des Halles (description in *Walk 2*).
Day 5	*Walk 19: The Champs Elysées*. Follow with a visit to La Défense (see walk for details) or a quick visit to the Invalides and Army Museum (*Walk 17*).
Evening	Take a Tour of the Illuminations.

THINGS IN FLUX

All great cities constantly change, and Paris is emerging from one of its most restless phases. The advent in 1989 of the *Bicentenaire*, the 200th anniversary of the French Revolution, inspired a massive clean-up programme. This, coupled with a number of long-term building and renovation projects, has imposed certain restrictions on what a visitor can actually see.

Below I have noted the biggest projects and the Slow Walks in which they occur. Except for the Cognacq-Jay Museum, which is in limbo until it opens at a new address, all the other scenes of long-term works can be visited, though expect some parts of them to be closed or screened off.

Musée Cognacq-Jay (see *Walk 1*)
La Défense, works around Parvis and behind Grande Arche to west (end *Walk 19*)
Musée du Louvre, reorganisation of galleries (*Walk 5*)
Panthéon, nave (*Walk 10*)
Val de Grâce, cloisters and medical museum (*Walk 11*)

INDEX

INDEX